MASTERING
TYPE

MASTERING
TYPE

{ **The Essential Guide to Typography**
FOR PRINT AND WEB DESIGN }

Denise Bosler

HOW
BOOKS

Cincinnati, Ohio
www.howdesign.com

For more excellent books and resources for designers, visit www.how design.com.

16 15 14 13 12   5 4 3 2 1

ISBN-13: 978-1-4403-1369-1

Distributed in Canada by Fraser Direct
100 Armstrong Avenue
Georgetown, Ontario, Canada L7G 5S4
Tel: (905) 877-4411

Distributed in the U.K. and Europe by F&W Media International, LTD
Brunel House, Forde Close, Newton Abbot, TQ12 4PU, UK
Tel: (+44) 1626 323200, Fax: (+44) 1626 323319
Email: enquiries@fwmedia.com

Distributed in Australia by Capricorn Link
P.O. Box 704, Windsor, NSW 2756 Australia
Tel: (02) 4577-3555

EDITED BY Amy Owen and Lauren Mosko Bailey
DESIGNED BY Grace Ring
PRODUCTION COORDINATED BY Greg Nock

TABLE OF CONTENTS

{ INTRODUCTION }

Communications technology permeates our society. Look around. Typography is everywhere. Commuting to work, grocery shopping, surfing the Web or navigating a smartphone, we are bombarded by words of every shape, size and arrangement. It is essential for designers to understand the basics of typography to get an effective message across instantly. The goal of this book is to guide the reader in building a solid foundation of timeless typographic knowledge, for both print and digital media, while transcending transient technologies.

Regardless of the ever-advancing technology at our fingertips, we still rely on the same twenty-six letters. Typographic basics start with the principles we all learned as children: Letters form words, words form sentences, and sentences form paragraphs. The designer's goal of optimizing communication via legibility, connotation and form are as fundamental as the alphabet. Does this mean we can't use technology to enhance our words? Certainly not. Typography is an art and can be treated as such—but only after the basics are thoroughly understood and ingrained in the mind of the designer.

This book breaks down the study of type into a systematic progression of typographic relationships—letters, words, sentences, paragraphs, pages and screen—through content, examples, interviews and real-world inspiration. It illustrates to the beginning designer how professional type treatment looks, feels and reads. Careful study of these step-by-step details provides a virtual apprenticeship in typography, a valuable education for any designer.

chapter one
{ HISTORY }

Confucius said, "Study the past if you would divine the future." The past shows us where we came from and how we got to where we are today. In typography, many modern-day designs show the influence of the past. We must look to original forms of letters, how they were created and how they were used, to understand typography's full potential. This understanding will help guide us in making the best typographic choices for the future.

IN THE BEGINNING
THERE WAS COMMUNICATION

Cave paintings are the first recognized form of human communication (Fig. 1). Found all over the world, symbols painted on walls and carved in rock represent primitive means of recording information. These pictographs—images that represent their literal meanings—were easily comprehended by the non-literate culture that created them. Pictographs work well for materials that need to communicate to speakers of a variety of languages. Contemporary pictographs are most commonly found on directional signage such as traffic indicators and public toilets.

Ancient Egyptians utilized pictographs in their hieroglyphics, although their language took the idea of using pictures one step further (Fig. 2). Phonograms—images that represent sounds—were also incorporated into their writings. This language allowed the Egyptians to communicate both concrete things and abstract concepts. Because the Egyptian language used both pictographs and phonograms, though, it was undecipherable to early discoverers of the beautiful murals and carvings depicting Egyptian history. It wasn't until 1799 that Pierre-François-Xavier Bouchard, a French captain, discovered the Rosetta Stone. This stone was the key to unlocking the until-then uninterpretable languages of the Egyptians. The Rosetta Stone had the exact same text carved in hieroglyphics, plus the demotic and Greek alphabets. This allowed scholars familiar with the Greek alphabet to decipher Egypt's past.

Around the same time ancient Egyptians were creating hieroglyphics on walls and in stone, the Sumerians in Mesopotamia were writing on clay tablets. The Sumerians' written language was called *cuneiform*, symbols that were pressed into clay with a wedge-shaped stylus (Fig. 3). Cuneiform used both phonograms and ideograms, sometimes using the same symbols for both. Ideograms are symbols or a combination of symbols that represent a concept. A modern-day example of this would be an image of a man holding a broom to represent the verb *sweep*, instead of meaning literally a man holding a broom. Reading cuneiform was not easy, as it required knowledge of both ideograms and phonograms, plus the ability to differentiate when a symbol was part of an ideogram and when it represented a sound.

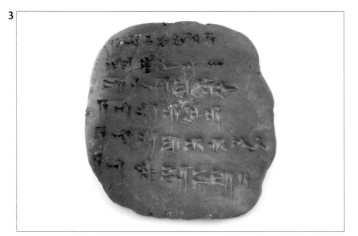

BIRTH OF THE MODERN WRITTEN LANGUAGE

During the fifteenth century B.C.E., the Phoenicians developed an alphabet that consisted of twenty-two characters, all consonants (Fig. 4). The Phoenicians were the first to combine these characters to spell words, writing right to left. This alphabet spread throughout the Mediterranean region because of extensive trading. This writing system became the precursor to the Greek, Latin, Arabic and Hebrew alphabets.

Around the eighth century B.C.E., the Greeks incorporated the Phoenician alphabet into their own language by adding vowels, dropping a few consonants and adding others; this brought the total number of letters to twenty-four (Fig. 5). The Greeks also began writing left to right. Spreading quickly, this alphabet became key to recording history. In fact, many texts from the Bible were written in Greek.

The Roman alphabet evolved from the Greek alphabet (Fig. 6). Also called Latin, it is widely recognized as today's modern Western written language. Originally made up of twenty-three letters, the alphabet consisted of square capitals that were the Romans' formal writing system; it had no lowercase letters. Used mainly for carving inscriptions in marble and stone, these letters were the forerunners of modern-day serif typefaces. The Romans also used rustic capitals, a less formal alphabet used primarily for text written with a pen. Both forms are recognizable as letterforms that make up the Western alphabet.

1 1,500-year-old cave painting in the Cederberg region of South Africa. 2 Egyptian hieroglyphics. 3 Cuneiform on a baked clay tablet.

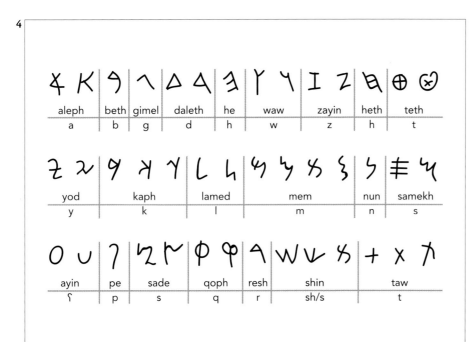

aleph	beth	gimel	daleth	he	waw	zayin	heth	teth
a	b	g	d	h	w	z	h	t

yod	kaph	lamed	mem	nun	samekh
y	k	l	m	n	s

ayin	pe	sade	qoph	resh	shin	taw
ʿ	p	s	q	r	sh/s	t

4 Phoenician alphabet. **5** Greek text in the Celcus Library, Ephesus, Izmir. **6** Roman text engraved in marble of the Santa Cecilia church, Rome. **7** A sheet of papyrus.
8 A tenth-century manuscript written on parchment.

The spread of the modern alphabets accelerated with the invention of papyrus and parchment. They provided a more portable way to transmit text, as carrying clay or stone around was unwieldy. Papyrus, a paper-like material made from the papyrus plant, was invented in Egypt (Fig. 7). This material was cheap, easy to produce and quite portable. It had disadvantages, though: It was fragile, it couldn't be folded, and only one side could be written on. It was also prone to deterioration depending on storage conditions. Parchment, a thin material made from animal skin, was invented as an alternative to papyrus (Fig. 8). Parchment accepted ink well and became quite popular. People could fold it and write on both sides of it; it was also very durable over time. Until the Middle Ages, when what we think of as paper came into use, parchment was the predominant writing media for the Western world.

USES OF TYPE

One notable use of the Roman alphabet was illuminated manuscripts (Fig. 9). These were texts created as early as 600 C.E., decorated or illustrated with gold and silver leaf. Created by hand and incredibly laborious to produce, these books were owned mainly by religious entities and the very wealthy. The images filling these books illustrated the text for the benefit of those who could not read. Highly decorated letters called initials were incorporated into the text. The idea of combining text and imagery has continued

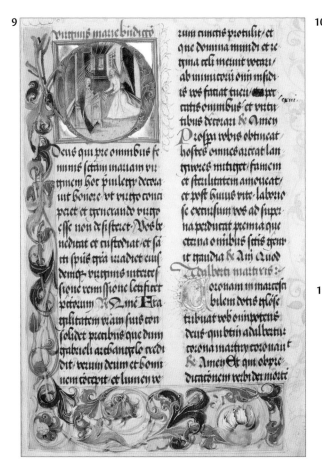

9 The Annunciation from the "Pontifical of Bishop Erasmus Ciolek," c.1510 (tempera and gold on parchment) by Polish School (sixteenth century). **10** Illustration of Johannes Gutenberg and his press. **11** An assortment of metal type.

through history and is most commonly found today in children's books and graphic novels.

Manuscripts and documents continued to be written by hand in the Western world until the 1400s, which was when the invention of the printing press suddenly made the written word much more readily available to the public. Printing itself was not a new invention, as the Chinese had already been using woodblock printing for centuries. The revolution was the invention of movable metal type. Johannes Gutenberg developed this new printing method, called the letterpress, in 1452 (Fig. 10). He used a retrofitted wine press combined with oil-based inks to print books. Moveable type used a punch and mold system for each letter. Multiple copies of each letter were then used to assemble an entire manuscript page for printing—a process called typesetting (Fig. 11). After the desired number of pages was printed, the letters were reassembled to create the next page. Gutenberg still needed large numbers of letters in different typefaces and sizes, but storage of these libraries was a small inconvenience in exchange for the vastly increased speed with which books could be produced. The first

complete book printed using this method was Gutenberg's forty-two-line Bible, so named because each page had forty-two lines of type per column (Fig. 12). This invention marked the beginning of mass production.

For the next 400 years, printing changed very little. It wasn't until the dawn of the Industrial Revolution that significant improvements were made to the printing press. The invention of the steam press and subsequent rotary press replaced the hand-operated press and made publications affordable to the masses. Typesetting also saw an improvement in 1889, when Otto Mergenthaler developed a technique that allowed him to produce an entire line of type at once. Called the Linotype machine, it used a keyboard to compose a line of type with letter molds (Fig. 13). Molten lead was then used to fill molds and create the line of type as one solid piece. This machine eliminated the need to set one letter at a time, speeding up the printing process ten-fold. Later, after the line of type was used for printing, the metal could be melted down and re-used for another line.

12
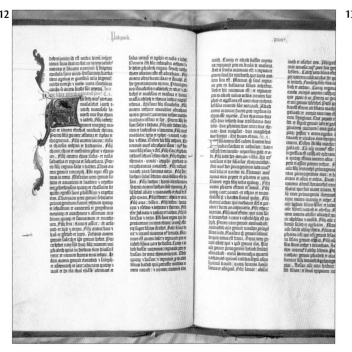

13

12 Two folios from a Gutenberg Bible, printed in the workshop of Johannes Gutenberg in 1455 (vellum) by German School (fifteenth century). **13** Otto Mergenthaler's Linotype machine.

TYPE AND ART

Several artistic movements occurring at the same time as these advances in printing also influenced typography. The first of these was the Arts & Crafts movement in the late-nineteenth-century United Kingdom, which involved William Morris and the Kelmscott Press. With the advent of the Industrial Revolution, a small group of artists and designers were dismayed as the production of previously hand-created items became coldly mechanized. Their movement encouraging traditional craftsmanship was a pushback against industrial technology. The Kelmscott Press, founded in

1890, printed classic titles in addition to original works. Ornate, decorative designs were used for the type, ornamental letters and illustrations (Fig. 14). These elaborate typographic works were in direct contrast to the generic, albeit affordable, pages being produced by mechanized printing presses. This was how William Morris kept artistic typographic design alive.

During the same time period, 1890–1914, Art Nouveau was France's answer to the Industrial Revolution. The goal was to create an international style based on decorative elements. Unlike the Arts & Crafts movement, Art Nouveau tried to integrate the decorative style into everything from visual arts to applied arts and

14 The "Kelmscott Chaucer," published 1896 by the Kelmscott Press by William Morris (1834–96). **15** Poster advertising "L. Marquet Ink, the Best of All Inks," 1892 (color litho) by Franz Grassel (1861–c.1921).

architecture. Lavish flowers, abstract lines and intricate borders were a few of the elements worked into the art (Fig. 15). Type, too, was highly decorated, as artists strove to create new typefaces that contrasted with the utilitarian feel of metal type. Type took on an organic look that was often integrated with art inspired by nature.

A movement arose in Switzerland from 1916 to 1930 that was a direct contrast to the decorative and pleasant nature of Arts & Crafts and Art Nouveau. Dada, an anti-art movement, used type to make a statement about the horrific nature of World War I. It produced purposely incomprehensible pieces that were both abstract and expressionistic. The artists reveled in confusion, eliminating any meaning from the text or typographic elements employed in the images (Fig. 16). Type was set on the page forward, backward, upside down, angled, in a spiral and every which way, with no concern for flow or continuity. Dada was an introduction to the idea that type could be art.

The Bauhaus was a revolutionary art school in Germany from 1919 to 1933. The school's two mantras were "Form follows function" and "Less is more." These two principles were applied to all aspects of art, including design, furniture and architecture. Its adherents

were firm in their belief that the purpose of an item came first and its aesthetics were secondary. Bauhaus embraced modern technologies and production advances, striving to reduce everything down to its barest essential form. Type was unadorned and simple, with clean, clear, concise execution in the design layout (Fig. 17). Color was kept to a minimum and, if needed for emphasis, was limited to primary colors.

In the 1920s, Russia found itself in a civil war after Czar Nicholas II was assassinated. A Soviet youth movement, Constructivism, threw its efforts behind the revolution, showing its support by creating graphic design and photomontage pieces with very distinctive typography. Diagonal and perpendicular lines of heavy, bold type played off each other, framed by heavy shapes or rules (Fig. 18). Primary colors, particularly red and black, were used extensively. The designs were striking, bold and authoritative when combined with photomontage and collage.

Constructivism's heavy, bold and daring designs were a world apart from the classic and stylish look of France's Art Deco movement of the 1920s and 1930s. Art Deco epitomized elegance and sophistication. Although Art Deco is more known for its influ-

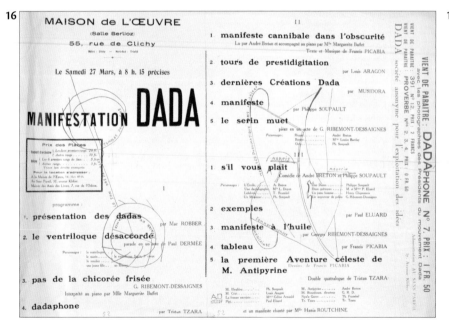

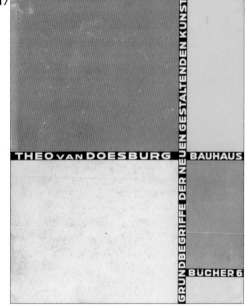

16 Dada Manifestation, c.1921 (litho) by French School (twentieth century). **17** Book cover, from the "Grundbegriffe der Neuen Gestaltenden Kunst," sixth in a series of Bauhaus books, published 1925–30 (color litho) by Theo van Doesburg (1883–1931).

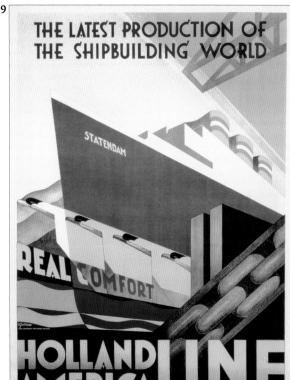

Helvetica

ence in fashion and architecture, it made a significant impact on the typographic world as well. Featuring sharp lines married to graceful curves, the typography was popular in the ever-growing world of advertising. Poster advertisements are the most recognizable remnant of the Art Deco era (Fig. 19). The streamlined and geometric style looked to the leisurely future, to a life not bogged down by the heavy realities of the day.

The International Typographic Style from Switzerland in the 1950s showed an evolving trend of functional typography and minimalist graphics combined into simple geometric designs. The movement presented typography as the focus by using primarily sans-serif typefaces and grid-heavy layouts. If imagery was needed, the precise, mechanical look of photography was preferred over hand-rendered illustrations. Also called the Swiss Style, this movement was responsible for introducing the world to Helvetica, and

the style caught on within the design community (Fig. 20). Many corporations adopted it for its clean, no-nonsense look. Many design schools also adopted the Swiss Style as their primary design theory. It is still taught in many programs today.

TYPE MOVING FORWARD

Type continued to be set by hand up until the middle of the twentieth century. Foundries produced lead type, and printers continued to store large libraries of alphabets containing hundreds of letters. The sheer volume of lead type filled rooms. Then in the 1960s, a light-based photographic system, called phototypesetting, was invented for setting type. Phototypesetting's main feature was a disc with photographic negatives of letters around the edge. This disc was inside a typesetting machine. Simply put, as the technician

18 Illustration from "The Results of the First Five-Year Plan," 1932 (collage) by Varvara Fedorvna Stepanova (1894–1958). **19** Advertisement for the Holland America Line, c.1932 (color litho) by Hoff (fl. 1930s). **20** Helvetica, designed by Max Miedinger as part of the International Typographic Style movement.

typed letters on a keyboard, light would shine through the letters on the disc. The disc would spin to spell out the typed line, burning each letter onto photosensitive paper (Fig. 21). One or more pages could now be typeset with ease. In addition to being faster and less cumbersome than moveable metal type, the letters could be resized without having to change the disc. This was accomplished by changing the distance between the disc and the light source. Prior to phototypesetting, a designer needed to choose a different size type from the cast metal sets of letters. The typesetting machine could also be adjusted to overlap or even distort letters. None of these effects were possible with metal type, without custom molds, which were very expensive. The end result of phototypesetting was a complete page ready to be turned into a negative for printing.

This negative was used with a printing technique called offset lithography. Up until the 1950s, letterpress printing was the most common form of commercial printing. Improvements to inks, paper and technologies helped offset lithography to supplant older techniques for commercial printing (Fig. 22). In offset printing, a photo negative's image is burned onto a metal plate. The plate is then treated with a chemical process to repel ink in some areas and accept it in others, allowing ink to stick to type and imagery and not to the blank areas. The plate is then loaded onto the upper roller of a large press, while a rubber "blanket" is attached to a lower roller. The metal plate is coated with ink and then turns and makes contact with the blanket roller. The ink is transferred to the blanket, which then transfers the image to a piece of paper. This method prevents the sharp edges of the plate from pressing into the paper, dulling the plate and tearing the paper. The rubber blanket helps the plate last much longer before replacement. The process is called "offset lithography" because the plate offsets the image to the blanket instead of directly onto the paper.

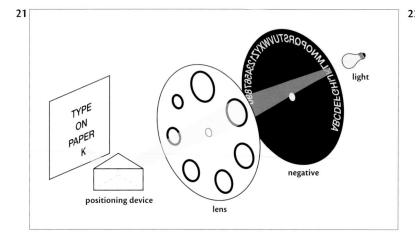

21 Phototypsetting. **22** One-color offset lithography printing press. **23** Very early desktop computer.

By the mid 1980s, computers began replacing typesetting machines, opening up a tremendous range of typographic possibilities (Fig. 23). Designers now had complete control over the design, allowing them to create typefaces for all kinds of uses. The typographic world exploded with new fonts. Type foundries originally established to produce metal type and phototype either closed up shop or converted their business to the development and distribution of digital type. One of the foundries that successfully made this conversion was International Typeface Corporation (ITC). Founded by Aaron Burns, Herb Lubalin and Edward Rondthaler in 1970, ITC made great inroads into the digital type world. Their success arose partially because they were able to convert their collections of metal and phototype into digital files. This meant that the traditional typefaces designers relied upon continued to be available to them as they transitioned into the new digital medium. ITC was also at the forefront of new typeface design.

MODERN TYPE DESIGN

Modern type design is ever evolving. New typefaces and new uses for type are created every day. The short history of modern type design boasts several notable designers in the forefront of innovation and creativity.

Whether he realized it or not, David Carson was the first of many modern-day designers to emulate the Dada movement. He is known for his grunge-inspired work that uses layers of classic and funky fonts to create texture and mood (Fig. 24). Immersed in the Southern California surf and skate culture in the 1980s, he first began his experimental expression with typography working for *Beach Culture* and *Transworld Skateboarding* magazines. He further expanded his experimentation at *Ray Gun*, a rock and roll magazine, as its founding art director. Here, his abstract and often illegible sense of aesthetics became a defining style of the 1990s.

Another groundbreaking and influential magazine that rocked the typographic world was *Emigre*, published from 1984 to 2005. A graphic design magazine written by and for graphic designers, *Emigre* was the brainchild of the husband-and-wife team Rudy VanderLans and Zuzana Licko. VanderLans was responsible for the art direction while Licko created the fonts (Fig. 25). Embracing the then-new Macintosh computer, the magazine broke the boundaries of design. Experimental layouts were used; guest art directors were brought in to design sections and

24 David Carson. **25** Several *Emigre* typefaces designed by Zuzana Licko.

even whole issues. Even today, *Emigre* is considered one of the most progressive endeavors ever. The magazine is defunct, but VanderLans and Licko retained the name. Emigre remains as one of the first independent font houses. Although it began with Licko's font designs, the company has expanded its collection to include other type designers.

Paula Scher is best known for her work with Columbia Records and the Public Theater in New York. Currently a partner with the design firm Pentagram, Paula made her mark in the design world through her bold typographic expressions. Her style of heavy typefaces, interesting juxtapositions, and striking layouts set her work apart from that of other clean, traditional designers (Fig. 26). Some of her most notable work was developed for the Public Theater. Interlocking blocks of text, angular grids and silhouetted images against bright, stark backgrounds gave

theater posters permission to have fun. Reminiscent of the Constructivist movement, Scher's work has influenced many young designers of today.

THE NEXT FRONTIER

The Internet has had an enormous impact on typography in a very short amount of time. The first webpages were designed simply, using few fonts. Coding was simple as well: Basic HTML was used to produce layouts and tables to contain content. Design was limited by the primitive programming language. Over time, programmers developed new ways to code webpages, which brought more flexibility. Cascading style sheets, or CSS, allowed designers to move away from tables and create flexible, customized layouts that resembled printed designs. Adobe Flash was used to create

26 *Some People*, New York, 1994. **27** The official HTML 5.0 logo released by the World Wide Web Consortium (W3C), an international community that develops standards to ensure the long-term growth of the Web.

motion, and direct interactivity was incorporated to give the viewer a more personal experience. Other programming languages created an increasingly personalized web experience. Web 2.0 was developed in 2002, and it quickly became the new standard in web interaction. Users now had a role controlling the Internet as they surfed it. HTML also evolved from HTML 1.0, which could only create the simplest of pages, to HTML 5.0, which will have many new features, including motion graphics and fuller interactivity with the viewer, when fully complete (Fig. 27).

Tens of thousands of fonts are now online and available for download. With the improved user-friendliness of typography creation software, anyone can create a typeface and distribute it online. Additionally, anyone can share a portfolio of designs; many designers attribute their success directly to the Internet. Many design organizations have developed as a result of people's ability to connect to one another around the globe via the Internet. It can only continue to contribute to the future of typography and design. This is why the future of typography and design has never been more exciting.

ABOUT THE IMAGES IN THIS CHAPTER

chapter two

{ LETTER }

A *letter* is defined as a character or symbol that represents sound used in speech. The English alphabet has twenty-six of these characters, from which all of the English language is derived. Twenty-six simple little characters give us the ability to communicate with one another. Each character is unique—it has its own sound, its own shape, its own characteristics and its own rules for use. Understanding these characters individually is necessary to learning how to use typography. Without a proper understanding of the characters that make up a word, sentence or paragraph, a designer cannot properly create good typographic design, which is key to good communication to the intended audience. In order to reach the audience, we need to make sure a design contains appropriate type choices and good use of the characters at our disposal. Our job, as designers, is to give the reader a way to understand the information we're giving them. Packages on the shelves, posters on the wall, brochures in the mail, advertisements in a magazine—all contain information that needs to be communicated. The type needs to be visually interesting, interactive, expressive and captivating. Type cannot merely fall into the background or communication will break down. Each and every letter in the alphabet needs to live and breathe on the page; it must call to the viewer. Each and every letter, therefore, needs to be understood by the designer.

SERIF AND SANS SERIF

The English alphabet is made up of uppercase letters, lowercase letters and a full complement of symbols, including periods, commas, exclamation points, question marks, numbers, hyphens, brackets and many more. The overall look, feel and design of these letters is called a *typeface*. The complete set of letters, numbers and symbols together is referred to as a *font*. It is impossible to say how many fonts exist—the number likely reaches into the hundreds of thousands by now. Most, however, fall into two main categories: serif and sans serif.

A letter in a serif typeface (Fig. 1) has a structural extension that comes off the main body of a letterform. Sometimes it extends in two directions, creating a miniature *T* at the end point of a letter. Other times it extends in only one direction. Serifs also come in many shapes and sizes: fat, thin, tall, short, pointed, curved, squared and cupped. Serifs can be prominent or barely visible, but all extend out from a letter.

A sans serif letter (Fig. 2) has no extensions coming from the letter. *Sans* is a French word meaning "without," hence the phrase *sans serif* means "without serif." These letters are not necessarily plainer than a serif letter; they can be quite interesting. Some are thin and delicate while others are fat and chunky.

Typography

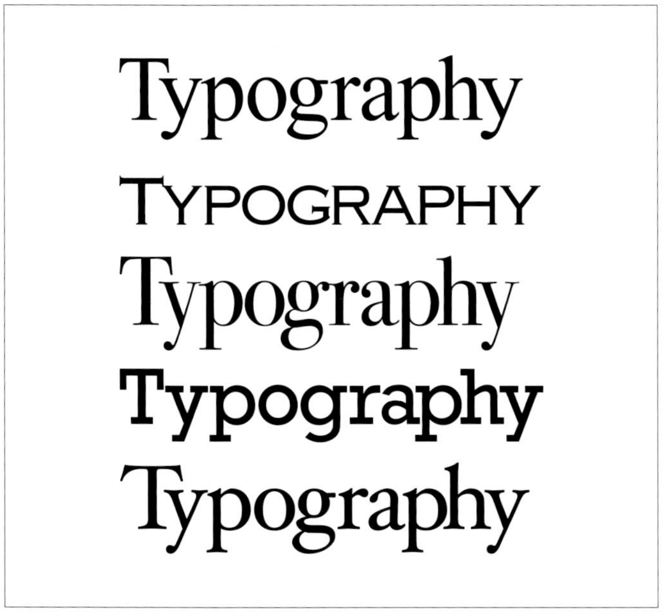

TYPOGRAPHY

Typography

Typography

Typography

Typography

Typography

Typography

Typography

Typography

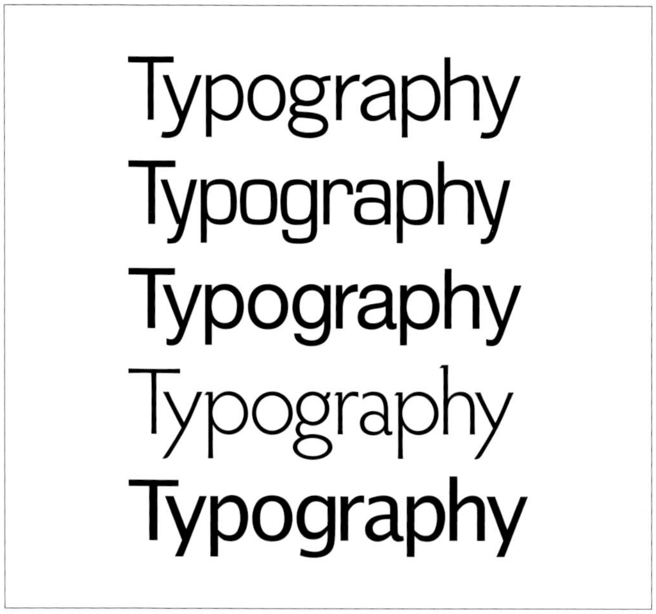

Other than the serifs, the characteristics that make up each letter are the same for both serif and sans serif letters. For instance, the three horizontal prongs of an uppercase E. These individual aspects of a letter are what make each letter distinguishable. By analyzing these parts and understanding what makes typefaces different, the designer can begin making intelligent and appropriate type decisions for the project at hand. Additionally, many characteristics look different when they are different sizes. While one typeface choice may look good as small paragraph text, it may not work as a large headline, or vice versa. Knowing how to distinguish these differences will also help you determine the best choice for your design.

PARTS OF A CHARACTER

STROKE

All characters are made up of one main feature, the *stroke* (Fig. 3). It is a straight or curved line that creates the principal part of a letter. The stroke is the foundation of a letter. In a sans serif typeface, the stroke is the line that creates the whole letterform. In a serif typeface, the stroke makes up the thickest portions of the letter. It is often accompanied by a hairline stroke, thinner than the main stroke, that creates the remainder of the letter. A stroke can end by intersecting with another stroke, with or without a serif.

TERMINAL

An ending without a serif is called a *terminal* (Fig. 4). A terminal can take one of many forms, including blunt, curved, cupped or pointed. A terminal is most common as a stroke ending in sans serif fonts, though it can be found on certain serif letters, such as a lowercase *e* or *t*. Another kind of terminal is called a *ball terminal* (Fig. 5), though it can sometimes be shaped like a teardrop as well (a, c, f, g, j, r, y). A stroke ending in a serif is often "held on" visually by a piece called a *bracket* (Fig. 6). Brackets can be large and graceful, or small to almost invisible (Fig. 7). Sometimes there's no bracket at all. Curved capital serif letters have a terminal ending called a *barb* (C, G, S) (Fig. 8). A barb can be found at both the top and bottom of the letter. Sometimes, however, it is located only at the top. The terminal on straight capital serif letters is called a *beak* (E, F, T, Z) (Fig. 9). A beak is most often on the top of the stroke, but it can also be found on the center and lower strokes of a capital *E, F* or *Z*.

1 Closely examine the above serif typefaces. Take note how they are all different from each other. Understanding the nuances of type design will help a designer choose the best look for a job. **2** Just as serif typefaces have differences among them, sans serif typefaces have an equal amount of subtleties that make them unique.

3

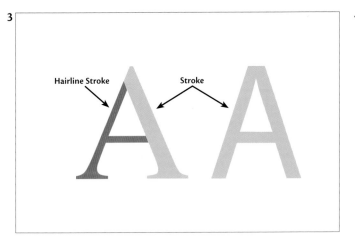

Hairline Stroke   Stroke

4

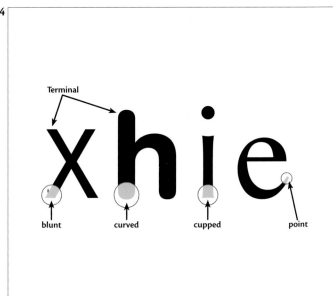

Terminal

blunt   curved   cupped   point

5

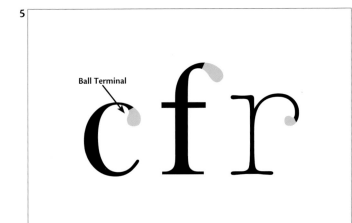

Ball Terminal

6

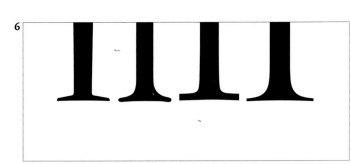

7

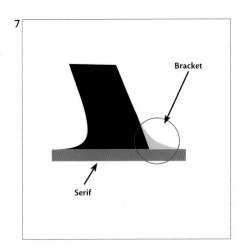

Bracket

Serif

8

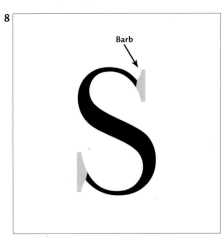

Barb

9

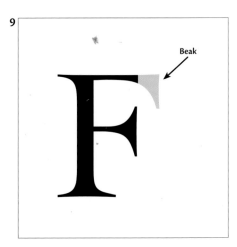

Beak

3 The *stroke* is a straight or curved line that creates the principal part of a letter. **4** An ending without a serif is called a *terminal*. **5** Another kind of terminal is called a *ball terminal*, though it can sometimes be shaped like a teardrop as well. **6** Examples of varying design styles for brackets and serifs. **7** A stroke ending in a serif is often "held on" visually by a piece called a *bracket*. **8** Curved capital serif letters have a terminal ending called a *barb*. **9** The terminal on straight capital serif letters is called a *beak*.

STROKE EXTENSIONS

Strokes that end by touching other strokes can do so in various ways. An *apex* is the top point of a letterform where two angled strokes meet (A, W, M) (Fig. 10). The *vertex* is the opposite of an apex. It is the bottom point of a letterform where two angled strokes meet (M, N, W, V, v, w). These intersections may or may not include a serif. This is dependent on the typeface design. The inside of a vertex is called a *crotch*. This space can have a wide or narrow opening.

A secondary stroke that extends horizontally from a stroke at the top and does not connect to another stroke is an *arm* (E, F) (Fig. 11). One that extends horizontally from the bottom is a *leg* (E, L). A stroke that extends from the center is called an arm or a leg depending on which direction it follows (K, R).

Connections can run horizontally between strokes as well. A *cross stroke* is a stroke that crosses over another stroke but doesn't connect on either side (t, f) (Fig. 12). The cross stroke can end in a variety of terminal styles. A *cross bar* is a stroke that horizontally connects two strokes (A, H) (Fig. 13). It's easy to remember that it's a bar if you think of a barbell. A barbell has a weight on either side just as a cross bar has a stroke on either side. A *shoulder*, another connection stroke, is a short, rounded stroke that connects two

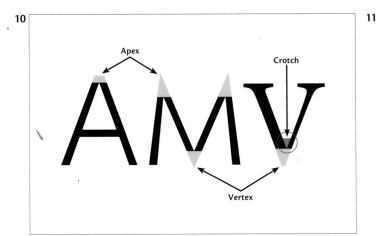

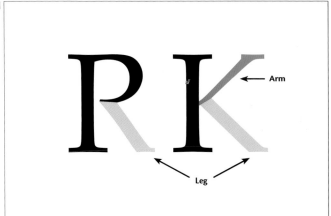

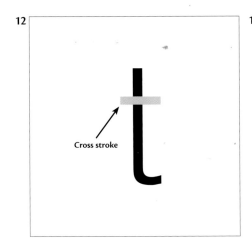

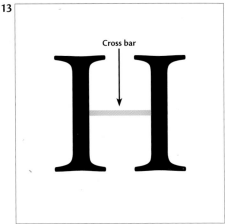

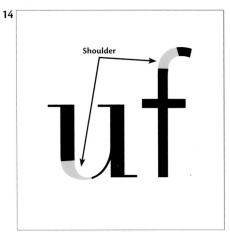

10 An *apex* is the top point of a letterform where two angled strokes meet. The *vertex* is the bottom point of a letterform where two angled strokes meet. The inside of a vertex is called a *crotch*. **11** A secondary stroke that extends horizontally from a stroke at the top and does not connect to another stroke is an *arm*. One that extends horizontally from the bottom is a *leg*. **12** A *cross stroke* is a stroke that crosses over another stroke but doesn't connect on either side. **13** A *cross bar* is a stroke that horizontally connects two strokes. **14** A *shoulder* is a short, rounded stroke that connects two vertical strokes or a vertical stroke and a terminal.

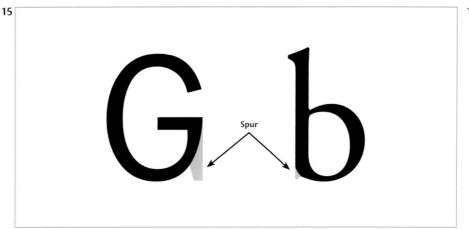

Spur

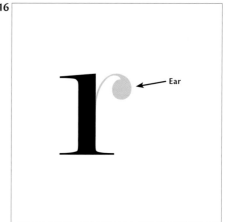

Ear

vertical strokes or a vertical stroke and a terminal (a, f, h, j, m, n, t, u, U) (Fig. 14).

Other pieces can protrude from a stroke. A *spur* is a small pointed extension typically coming off the top or bottom of a vertical stroke that connects to a rounded stroke—often on a serif lowercase letter (b, d, p, q) (Fig. 15). It can also be an extension from the bottom of a capital G. This can make the *G* appear as though it has a goatee. An *ear* is the small extension that protrudes up and out from the top of a stroke or bowl and is often teardrop-shaped or rounded (a, f, g, r) (Fig. 16).

COUNTERS

Any enclosed space is called a *counter* (Fig. 17). A curved stroke that connects to either a vertical stroke or to itself is called a *bowl*. If the space is completely enclosed, it is referred to as a *closed counter* (a, b, d, g, p, q, A, B, D, P, R). An *open counter* occurs when a curved, straight or angled stroke does not connect to another stroke but still creates an enclosed space (c, e, h, k, m, n, s, u, v, w, x, y, z, A, C, E, F, G, H, K, M, N, R, S, U, V, W, X, Y, Z). The letters *e*, *A* and *R* contain both closed and open counters; the letters *o*, *O* and *Q* have main strokes that consist solely of a bowl.

SPECIALTY PARTS

Some letters have specific named components. The curve through the middle of an *S* (s) is a *spine* (Fig. 18). The closed counter of a lowercase *e* is called an *eye* (Fig. 19). In the printing business, pressmen often look at the eye to see if it fills in during printing. This is an indicator that there is too much ink on the press. A traditionally shaped lowercase *g*, also known as *two-story g*, has two specialty parts. The lower bowl is called a *loop*, which can be a closed or open counter, and the small piece that connects the upper bowl with the lower loop is called a *link* (Fig. 20). The stroke that crosses the lower half of an uppercase *Q* is a *tail* (Fig. 21), and the extra flourish that accompanies many script and blackletter style typefaces is a *swash* (Fig. 22). Tails and swashes can be quite simple, with no design at all, or quite fancy, becoming more of a design element than the character itself. Swashes, in particular, are a great way of adding extra personality to a typeface.

STRESS

The stress of a letter also influences the look and feel of the letterform. *Stress* is defined as the axis created by the thick and thin stroke contrast of a letter (Fig. 23). If the axis is straight up and down, the letter is said to have *vertical stress*. If the axis is angled (left or right), the letter has *biased stress*. It is easiest to see the stress in the counters of the letterforms.

CHARACTER ALIGNMENT

All of the letters sit on a horizon called the *baseline* (Fig. 24). The horizon at which all the uppercase letters align at the top is called

15 A *spur* is a small pointed extension typically coming off the top or bottom of a vertical stroke that connects to a rounded stroke. **16** An *ear* is the small extension that protrudes up and out from the top of a stroke or bowl and is often teardrop-shaped or rounded.

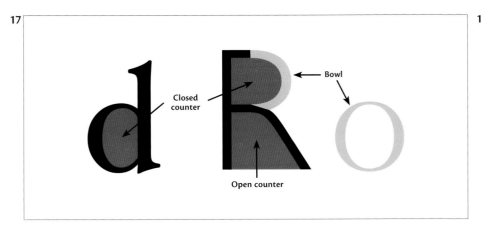

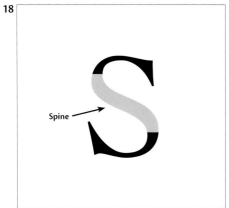

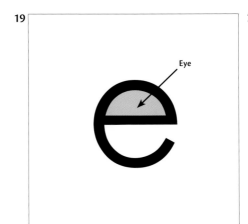

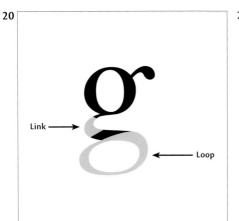

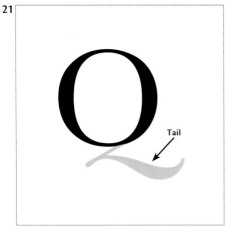

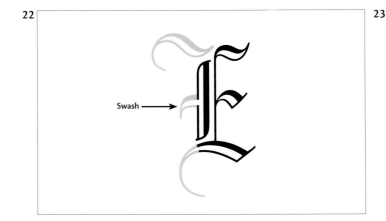

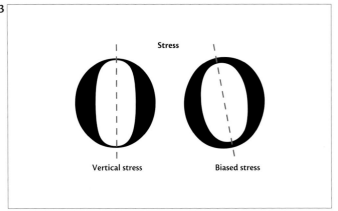

17 Any enclosed space is called a *counter*. A curved stroke that connects to either a vertical stroke or to itself is called a *bowl*. If the space is completely enclosed, it is referred to as a *closed counter*. An open counter occurs when a curved, straight or angled stroke does not connect to another stroke but still creates an enclosed space. **18** The curve through the middle of an S (s) is a spine. **19** The closed counter of a lowercase *e* is called an *eye*. **20** A traditionally shaped lowercase *g*, also known as two-story g, has two specialty parts. The lower bowl is called a *loop*, and the small piece that connects the upper bowl with the lower loop is called a *link*. **21** The stroke that crosses the lower half of an uppercase Q is a *tail*. **22** The extra flourish that accompanies many script and blackletter style typefaces is a *swash*. **23** Stress is defined as the axis created by the thick and thin stroke contrast of a letter. If the axis is straight up and down, the letter is said to have vertical stress. If the axis is angled, the letter has biased stress.

the *cap height*. Letters that are curved or pointed at the top or bottom often extend a tiny bit above the cap height or below the baseline, respectively, to allow them to align optically. If this design adjustment is not made, the letters will appear to be jumping up and down, giving the impression that they are not aligned properly (Fig. 25). Through the center area of the baseline and cap height runs the *x-height* (also called a median or meanline). This line is measured by the height of the lowercase *x*. The line does not necessarily run halfway between the baseline and cap height. It can run higher or lower than halfway. The x-height depends on the design choices made for the letters by the type designer. The part of a low-

ercase letter that extends above the x-height is called an *ascender* (b, d, f, h, k, l, t). In certain typefaces, the ascender extends above the cap height, giving the impression the font is taller than it really is. The part that extends below the baseline is a *descender* (g, j, p, q, y). Descenders typically occur in lowercase letters, but they can occur in the design of the uppercase *Q* and *J* as well.

TYPE MEASUREMENT

Measuring the height of type is done in points. All computer programs utilize this unit; therefore, it is important to understand how much space a point occupies. There are 72 points in an inch (Fig. 26). A font designated as 72 points is therefore 1 inch along the cap height

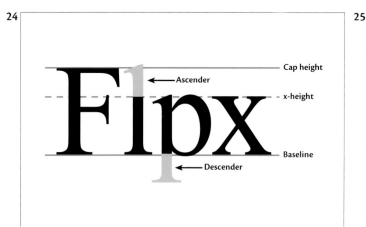

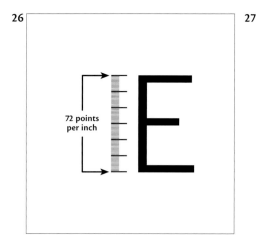

24 The guides for character alignment. **25** Letters that are curved or pointed at the top or bottom often extend a tiny bit above the cap height or below the baseline, respectively, to allow them to align optically. **26** There are 72 points in an inch. **27** Various fonts set as 72-point type. Top row: Hypatia, News Gothic, Haettenschweiler; bottom row: Mona Lisa, Times, Modern No. 20.

line. A font designated as 36 points is one-half inch along the cap height line, 18 points is one-quarter, 9 points is one-eighth, and so on. One important item to note is that it is not uncommon for letterforms to appear as different sizes even when set at the same size by the computer (Fig. 27). This is because variations in the letters' x-height, ascenders and descenders can fool the eye.

CLASSIFICATIONS OF LETTERFORMS

Certain typefaces have historical origins. These origins, along with knowledge of the parts of the characters, can help you determine relationships between typefaces. Understanding how similar letter characteristics go together can help you establish a complete look for your typographic design job. If you can determine the kind of look you want, such as clean, sophisticated, bold, heavy, modern or vintage, it will be easier to home in on the particular typeface you want to use. Sometimes the historical context of the letterforms adds to the effectiveness of a design.

Please note that the classification of letterforms is not an exact science. Early type designers had no classification rules to follow, and type designers of today often follow no rules. As a result, there are many fonts with characteristics of one classification that overlap with the characteristics of another. The classifications discussed here are generally recognized as the most common and widely accepted.

OLD STYLE

Drawn from the Roman lettering found cut into marble and stone, these typefaces were originally created as metal type for early printing processes. Modern-day Old Style versions are based upon the metal type and many still carry the nuances of originally being created and forged by hand. These typefaces are characterized by letters with serifs that run straight or cupped along the edge and that have noticeable brackets. The ends of the serif range from straight to rounded. The letterforms have a biased stress and low contrast between the main strokes and hairline strokes of the letterform. The letters feel somewhat heavy, as the original metal type needed to hold up to the rigors of primitive printing techniques. The x-height tends to be tall in relation to the cap height. The ball terminals are shaped like teardrops, and the ascenders of the lowercase letters tend to be taller than the cap height. Well-known examples of Old Style typefaces are Garamond, Bembo, Janson, Palatino, Sabon, Weiss and Goudy (Fig. 28).

TRANSITIONAL

Transitional typefaces are letterforms from the late eighteenth century that serve as a transition between Old Style and Modern lettering. Printing processes became more refined around this time, allowing the type to move toward more subtle and elegant details. These typefaces have letters with serifs that have a straighter and sharper feel and have fewer or smaller brackets. The letterforms have a slightly biased or vertical stress and medium contrast

28

Garamond
Palatino
Weiss

29

Baskerville
Mrs. Eaves
Times New Roman

28 Old Style typeface examples. **29** Transitional typeface examples.

between the main strokes and hairline strokes of the letterform—more contrast than Old Style. The x-height tends to be tall in relation to the cap height. The ascenders of the lowercase letters can be taller than the cap height. Well-known examples of Transitional typefaces are Times New Roman, Baskerville, Bookman, Corona, Georgia and Mrs. Eaves (Fig. 29).

MODERN

Modern typefaces are products of the late eighteenth and early nineteenth centuries and are the result of further improvements in the printing process. Increased accuracy of presses, more refined inks and better paper allowed for more delicate characteristics. The letterforms of Modern typefaces have serifs that are straight along the edge, with small or no brackets. The letterforms have a vertical stress and high contrast between the main strokes and hairline strokes of the letterform—in some cases to the extreme. The x-height tends to be medium to tall in relation to the cap height. Well-known examples of Modern typefaces are Bodoni, Bernhard Modern, Didot, Walbaum, Modern No. 20, Fenice and Mona Lisa (Fig. 30).

SLAB SERIF

Better presses, inks and paper also allowed for increased ink coverage. Commercial demand for bolder, heavier fonts led to the creation of Slab Serif fonts. Also called Egyptian, these typefaces have thick, heavy serifs (slabs) that are straight across the edge with small or no brackets. In many cases the serif is the same thickness as the main stroke, giving the font a monoline look. The letterforms have a vertical stress and little contrast between the main strokes and hairline strokes of the letterform. The x-height tends to be medium to tall in relation to the cap height. Well-known examples of Egyptian typefaces are Clarendon, Courier, Memphis, Rockwell, Playbill, American Typewriter and Egyptienne (Fig. 31).

SANS SERIF

Sans Serif letterforms are also derived from ancient Roman lettering that was cut into marble and stone. Roman lettering was found in two forms: formal (with serifs) and informal (without them). Typefaces in the Sans Serif category are characterized by the absence of serifs. The strokes end in square, rounded, angled or cupped terminals. The letterforms generally have a vertical stress and no contrast in the strokes of the letterform. The strokes tend to be uniform throughout the entire letter, also giving it a monoline look. The x-height tends to be tall in relation to the cap height. Well-known examples of Sans Serif typefaces are Helvetica, Univers, Eurostile, Gill Sans, Trade Gothic, Futura and Avant Garde (Fig. 32).

Though the classification provides a general overall look, there are exceptions to every rule. One example of a non-typical sans serif is Optima (Fig. 33). Designed in 1958 by Hermann Zapf, this typeface takes the qualities of the main and hairline contrast of

30 Modern typeface examples. **31** Slab Serif typeface examples.

serif stroke weights and combines it with the cupped end terminals of a sans serif. It has become known as a very versatile font, suitable for both headline and paragraph text.

BLACKLETTER

Modern-day Blackletter, also called Gothic, is based upon European script lettering dating back to medieval times. It was used in Germany up through the twentieth century and is most associated with that country. Blackletter brings to mind knights, monks and ancient manuscripts. As a part of history, Blackletter was used in illuminated manuscripts and was the lettering style for the Gutenberg forty-two-line bible. Drawn with a flat pen or nib held at an angle, the typefaces are created using sharp vertical, horizontal and angled strokes. The letterforms have a vertical stress and extreme contrast between the main strokes and hairline strokes of the letterform. The x-height tends to be tall in relation to the cap height. Well-known examples of Blackletter typefaces are Old English, Lucida Blackletter, Fette Fraktur, Blackmoor and Chaucer (Fig. 34).

DISPLAY

Display type covers a wide range of fonts and is generally used for headlines, initials and logos. These typefaces tend to read well at larger sizes but are illegible when smaller or when used in long line lengths of text. Characteristics can include experimental, distressed and handwritten elements. Many budding type designers tackle these kinds of typefaces first because they don't have to

32

Gill Sans
Helvetica
Trade Gothic

33

Optima
AaBbCcDdEeFfGg

34

Blackmoor
Chaucer
Fette Fraktur

35

Addled
Naughties
Ransom

32 Sans Serif typeface examples. 33 Optima is a universally appealing font. Its many uses include the Vietnam War Memorial, John McCain's 2008 presidential campaign materials, Aston Martin and Estée Lauder. 34 Blackletter typeface examples. 35 Display typeface examples.

be as accurate or well formed as the other classifications. Additionally, many budding graphic designers overuse and misuse Display typefaces. It is best to exhibit restraint and use Display typefaces for emphasis only. Some examples of Display typefaces are Addled, Curlz, Neuland, Willow, Naughties, Airstream, Ransom and Skinny (Fig. 35).

SCRIPT

Script typefaces have their origins in handwriting and calligraphy. Found both as formal elegant letterforms and as more casual handwritten-like letterforms, Script typefaces generally have a fluid, cursive feel and can include minimal or elaborate swashes. Scripts can also have extensions that connect letters together, giving them fluidity. These typefaces tend to read better when used sparingly. They work well as headlines or in designs with limited text, such as wedding invitations and posters. They are almost impossible to read when used all in caps. Well-known examples of script typefaces are Snell Roundhand, Edwardian Script, Zapfino, Shelley Script, Black Jack, Mistral and Linoscript (Fig. 36).

DECORATIVE

Decorative typefaces have illustrative and ornamental characteristics that enhance or have been added to an underlying letterform structure. Victorian and Art Deco influences can easily be seen in many Decorative letterforms. Other influences can be found in architecture, nature, human form, fashion and fine arts. As with

Display typefaces, Decorative typefaces work best as headlines, initials or logos. They do not read well at a small size. Many of these fonts are expressive, creative and can be looked upon as art. Examples of Decorative typefaces are Rosewood, Cabaret, Carnavale Delight, Matra, Cottonwood, Critter and Monterrey (Fig. 37).

DINGBATS

Dingbats break away from being a typeface in the traditional sense. Dingbats are strictly illustrative elements that can be typed out on a keyboard. Some Dingbats are fun little illustrations that can be used as clip art elements; others are more decorative and ornate in nature. Originating in wood and metal type, Dingbats serve as enhancements to a typographic design, though they cannot be read as letterforms. Examples of Dingbat typefaces are Big Cheese, Adobe Wood Type, Bodoni Ornaments, Zapf Dingbats, Wingdings, Child's Play, Cheerleaders and Botanicals (Fig. 38).

DOT MATRIX FONTS

Early desktop computers used dot matrix printers for output. Dot matrix printers produced printed text by running a print head over an inked ribbon "punching" out a series of dots to form letters. It worked much like a typewriter. The resolution was quite low but was, at the time, a breakthrough in technology that gave printing capabilities to the home user. The original dot matrix fonts were limited and plain. Apple Computer made great strides in digital type design by creating fonts that worked with the limited dot technology.

36 Script typeface examples.   **37** Decorative typeface examples.

Type designed specifically for Apple by Susan Kare, including Chicago, Geneva, Monaco and New York (Fig. 39), became the new standard of font design for dot matrix printing. Other typefaces included San Francisco, Toronto and Los Angeles—all in keeping with the theme of city-based names. These fonts could also produce solid, rather than dotted, output and held great appeal for graphic designers.

As time went on, laser printers gradually replaced dot matrix printers. Laser printers work with much higher resolution and accuracy for producing type and images. This opened up a whole world of new typeface design since resolution was no longer an issue. The original dot matrix fonts were never eliminated from the Apple font lineup and are still standard fonts found on their machines today. The designs of the dot matrix typefaces were not optimized for laser printing and therefore look "clunky" and out of date. Unless a design job calls for an old-school computer look, a good rule of thumb is to disregard fonts with city names in order to avoid inadvertently using a dot matrix font.

38

Big Cheese

Botanicals

Zapf Dingbats

39

Monaco

Chicago

New York

40

Chophouse

DARWIN

OSPREY

38 Dingbats typeface examples. **39** Dot Matrix typeface examples. **40** Examples of typefaces that don't fit any other category.

EVERYTHING ELSE

There is a whole category of typefaces that resist classification in any one group. This is because they either incorporate multiple distinguishable characteristics or have a complete lack of recognizable parts. Many of these experimental letterforms are deconstructed versions of well-known typefaces, or combinations of two or more fonts. Some don't work well at either a large or small size, deeming them more of graphic elements as opposed to type. There is little doubt that members of the Dada movement would appreciate these fonts. Examples of these typefaces are Blue Eyeshadow, Chophouse, Cretino, Darwin, DIY Foundations, Do Fuse and Osprey (Fig. 40).

TYPE STYLES

If all typefaces had only one look to them, the designs we create would be rather dull. We would have no way of creating emphasis or difference on the page, aside from changing the size. With the introduction of different styles, type can have varying degrees of prominence and differentiation. This is how a word or sentence can stand out from the rest of the page, lending it a louder "voice" or stronger feel. A *type style* is a physical alteration to the original letterform. Thickness around the strokes can be added or taken away; the letters can be angled or straightened, made narrower or wider; or interesting swashes can be added. All of these variations are put together to create a type family within a font.

WEIGHT

Varying the thickness, or *weight*, is one of the most common ways to create visual differentiation within a type family. A bold version of the letter can attract much wanted attention in a design. Many typefaces have increasing degrees of thickness built into the font with a standard range being light, roman (also called *book*), medium, bold, heavy and black (Fig. 41). These varying degrees allow a designer to choose the preferred emphasis needed for a word or body of text. Combining several degrees of weight can also add visual texture to a page.

Be careful, though, because adding extra line weight around the letterform is not the same as making it bold. A *bold* version of a letter is specifically drawn to increase its volume without destroying the essence of the letter. Type designers do this by making subtle shifts in the architecture of the letter itself. Adding a line around the whole letter does not take this subtlety into consideration. Results of adding a line manually include disappearing counters and distorted strokes (Fig. 42).

41

RTF Dokument Light
RTF Dokument Regular
RTF Dokument Medium
RTF Dokument Demi
RTF Dokument Bold

42

Real Futura Bold
Fake Futura Bold

41 RTF Dokument contains sixty type styles. Shown are five extra condensed styles ranging from light to bold. **42** When a stroke is applied to type to make the letters bolder, it destroys the essence of the original font. In Futura, the results make the terminal of the *e* touch the stroke around the eye. In addition, the counters begin to close in and areas in which strokes connect become monoline as opposed to narrowing slightly.

ANGLE

Changing the angle of the letterforms is another way to create emphasis and variation. This angling is called *italic* or *oblique* (Fig. 43). This is different from a biased stress, which is formed by the internal parts of the character and the relationship of the main strokes and hairline strokes. As with weight variations, the italic version of a typeface is redrawn so that the architecture of the letters remains consistent with the essence of the overall look. It is not a simple matter of skewing the letters, as some computer programs allow you to do. Skewing letters alters the architecture of the letters and subtle details can be destroyed (Fig. 44). In many cases, the italic style takes on a completely different look, often verging on a script or handwritten feel. Old Style, Transitional and Modern fonts have this type of change. This variation only adds greater versatility to the type family within the font.

Obliques are letters that angle with little or no change to the letterforms. This style is specifically created to eliminate distortion in the typeface so there is still no reason to use a computer-generated italic. Many Sans Serif and Slab Serif fonts have oblique-style letters within their families.

WIDTH

The width of a letter can also be altered to provide additional variation to a family. Condensing a letter makes the letter narrower, taking up less space along a line and creating a different rhythm within the text. Extending a letter makes the letter wider, taking up more space along a line. Both condensed and extended letters can also have

Garamond Roman
Garamond Italic

Gill Sans Roman
Gill Sans Italic

Trade Gothic Roman
Trade Gothic Oblique

Real Bembo Italic
Fake Bembo Italic

Real News Gothic Cond.
Fake News Gothic Cond.

Real Zurich Ext.
Fake Zurich Ext

43 Garamond's italic can almost be mistaken for a totally different font. Gill Sans's italic is a subtle shift. The lowercase *a* changes from a stacked design to a single bowl design and other letters' shapes slightly alter in form. Trade Gothic's oblique literally looks like someone pushed it over to an angle. **44** Bembo's true italic is reminiscent of a script typeface. Skewing a typeface instead of selecting the italic version results in letters that look "pushed over" as opposed to detailed, and very often, altered letterforms. **45** Horizontally scaling a typeface as opposed to selecting the condensed or extended version results in letters with distorted parts, particularly uneven vertical and horizontal strokes.

Helv Neue 27	Helv Neue 27	Helv Neue 37	Helv Neue 37	Helv Neue 47	Helv Neue 47
Helv Neue 57	Helv Neue 57	Helv Neue 67	Helv Neue 67	Helv Neue 77	Helv Neue 77
Helv Neue 87	Helv Neue 87	Helv Neue 97	Helv Neue 97	Helv Neue 107	Helv Neue 107
Helv Neue 25	Helv Neue 26	Helv Neue 35	Helv Neue 36	Helv Neue 45	Helv Neue 46
Helv Neue 55	Helv Neue 56	Helv Neue 65	Helv Neue 66	Helv Neue 75	Helv Neue 76
Helv Neue 85	Helv Neue 86	Helv Neue 95	Helv Neue 95	Helv Neue 23	Helv Neue 23
Helv Neue 33	Helv Neue 33	Helv Neue 43	Helv Neue 43	Helv Neue 53	Helv Neue 53
Helv Neue 63	Helv Neue 63	Helv Neue 73	Helv Neue 73	Helv Neue 83	Helv Neue 83
Helv Neue 93	Helv Neue 93				

varying weights applied. A word of caution: Never horizontally or vertically scale letterforms manually. Use the condensed or extended version from the type family instead. Just as trying to make a letter bold or italic, manually scaling it horizontally or vertically affects its architecture (Fig. 45). If a font does not have a condensed or extended variation within the family, choose a font that does.

FAMILIES

Sometimes when a type family has many variations in weight, width and angle, there is little reason to look beyond it for a design job. Helvetica, designed by Max Miedinger in 1957, originally had twenty-seven such variations. It was updated in 1983 and renamed Helvetica Neue. The font family now has fifty-one variations (Fig. 46). Other fonts that have large families are: Agilita, with thirty-two style variations, designed by Jürgen Weltin; Mercury, with sixty style variations, designed by Hoefler & Frere-Jones; and Thesis The-Sans, with forty-eight style variations designed by Luc(as) de Groot. De Groot also designed TheSerif and TheMix for Thesis, creating a combined family consisting of 144 style variations.

TYPEFACE DESIGN

There are times when the perfect typeface for a design cannot be found. Or when a designer wants the creative freedom to express herself through typography. Or when a client has dictated a proprietary look for his design. This is when a designer can opt to create an original set of lettering. Be forewarned, however, that taking on the task of creating an entire typeface can be daunting, and it will take a significant amount of time. For a single headline or logo, a designer will often create only the individual letters needed to complete the task. For projects in which the custom type will be used many times for multiple pieces, designing the entire font is the best option.

Before diving into the creation of a new font, first answer a few questions. Why is the font needed? Will the font be used for text, headline or both? Will the font appear on the printed page or on screen? What letters, symbols and numbers will the font need? What feeling does the font need to project? What form does the font need to take—serif, sans serif, script or display? The answers will determine the kind of font to be created.

INSPIRATION

Many beginning type designers start with familiar forms such as their own handwriting, graffiti or doodles. For designs beyond familiar forms, inspiration is key to developing the perfect look. Inspiration is everywhere. A great way to begin is by looking at things that project the same feeling as the intended typeface. For instance, if a classic serif is needed, go to a museum to view ancient Roman statues and other carved stone that contain lettering. If the

46 Helvetica uses a numerical design classification to identify the various styles within the font. For example, a 2 at the beginning of the number signifies that it is Ultra Light. A 6 at the end signals that it is oblique. Therefore, a numerical identity of 26 means the style is Ultra Light Oblique.

typeface needs a structured feel, look to famous architects and the buildings they created. If a decorative look is desired, take a walk through a forest or garden and examine elements found in nature. The trick is to get away from the computer and explore the outside world (Figs. 47, 48, 49).

SKETCHING, SKETCHING, SKETCHING

The next step is to begin sketching with pencil and paper. While many young designers automatically assume they should jump onto the computer, the software used to draw type can be a hindrance rather than a help. Sketching type by hand requires no

specialized skills. This cannot be said for sketching type on the computer. Computer type needs to be drawn using a vector-based program—software that uses mathematical calculations to create images so that it is resolution independent—rather than a raster-based program—software that creates images using pixels and is resolution dependent. Vector-based software is necessary in order to have smooth and accurately rendered letterforms that resize well for both large and small sizes. It also allows for easier editing of the letters once they are drawn. Vector-based programs have a high learning curve and can be cumbersome for someone new to vector-based drawing. Sketching on paper eliminates the need to

47 Letterform inspiration can be found within the architecture of the bridge and its surroundings. *O, r, M, L, I, J* and *D* are a few that can be pulled from this image alone. **48** Trees, flowers, rocks, weeds and other flora and fauna are perfect for inspiring Script, Display and Decorative lettering. Look around the immediate surroundings to find interesting letterform inspiration. **49** This from-below view of Mark di Suvero's Orion sculpture, 2007, in Chicago's Millennium Park, contains a plethora of compelling shapes and forms from which to pull letterform ideas.

master the drawing software so that more time and energy can be focused on the design of the type rather than learning the nuances of a computer program.

Try to capture the essence of the desired type design as you begin sketching. Consider using different writing utensils, such as pens, markers and brushes, to create letters (Fig. 50). It doesn't have to be perfect on the first try. Lay tracing paper over your favorite letters and begin to refine them. As the uppercase and lowercase letters are developed, consider the relationship between them. Decide upon a tall, medium or short x-height and consider whether or not the ascenders should end at the cap height or extend above it. For Display and Decorative letterforms, create the structure of the letters before adding flourishes or illustrative elements. Don't forget about numbers and symbols when creating an entire font. These elements are just as important as the letters, as they are necessary parts for communication in design (Figs. 51, 52, 53, 54).

50
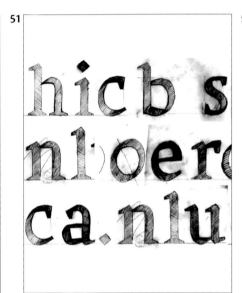

51

52

53

54

50 Pencil, marker and brush renderings of the same letters. These are just a few of the media a designer can use when experimenting with type. Aside from the usual suspects like charcoal, grease pencil or ball-point pen, try using a stick dipped in ink, creating potato stamps or cutting letters out of paper. A creative method used to develop the letters will result in a one-of-a-kind typeface. **51** Grenade serif Beta typeface early sketches. **52** Grenade serif Beta typeface. **53** Millénaire typeface early sketches. **54** Millénaire typeface.

IT'S ALL IN THE DETAILS

A good font designer understands and appreciates every little detail that goes into creating a letter. While inspiration and a good sketch are necessary to begin designing a font, it is equally important to take inventory of the different strokes, terminals, serifs, bowls, counters and other identifying features that will form the new letters, numbers and symbols (Fig. 55). To ensure that the font looks consistent throughout, it is important to follow the Rule of Two: It is crucial for any part of a character to occur at least twice within the font. Failure to do so will result in a disjointed and chaotic font. The only exceptions are letters that contain truly individual parts such as the spine of the S, the tail of the Q, and the loop of the g. Don't be afraid to share parts of one letter with another. Create a library of pieces that can be shared and refer to this library as you complete your type design. You can also mirror whole characters or parts of characters. For example, a lowercase *b* can be mirrored to become a lowercase *d*. Keep a close eye on the baseline, x-height and cap height and allow for optical adjustments as needed.

FINALIZATION

Once your complete font is created on paper, it can be scanned and input into a vector-based software. As with the sketch stage, create a library of parts to ensure a consistent look. The best results will come from tracing each letter manually rather than using an auto-trace command. Auto trace will create more points along a path than necessary, which leads to letterform outlines that are not smooth. Once all characters have been input, take a last look and compare all of the characters. Examine them to see if the collection of characters has a consistent feel. View the characters at a small size. If any characters break down, or have counters that close up or strokes that disappear, then the design needs to be adjusted. View the characters at a large size. Check the edges of the characters to see if they appear smooth and accurately rendered (Fig. 56). If there are any details that need to be fixed, now is the time to make refinements. Lastly, test your characters by creating several long words or sentences. Check for any characters that interfere with others placed next to them and for characters that break the flow of a word. Refine, refine, refine until the characters are perfect.

OUTPUT

If you are using your new characters for just a word or two, the final format can be vector art. If you want to produce a usable font, the next step is to translate your vector art into a font using font creation software. There are several good options available for font creation software. Be sure to review the software manual thoroughly for optimal results. Font software can create Postscript,

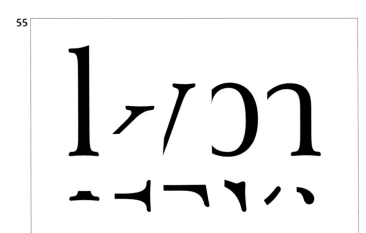

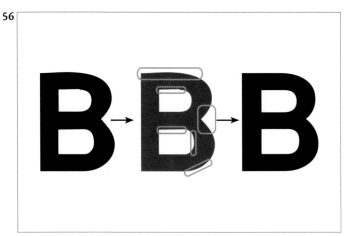

55 Creating a library of letterform parts will not only create better consistency within the new typeface but it will also speed up the design process since these parts can be used repeatedly and do not have to be re-created. **56** When enlarged, the original uppercase *B* had unintended flaws along its strokes. By zooming in and tweaking the lines, the letter was perfected so that it reads well both small and large.

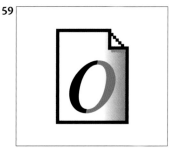

zürich 2014   canela

jörg bäckt quasi zwei haxenfüße vom wildpony   christian groß ♥ interface design

conquistadorz

cada vez que trabajo, félix me paga un whisky

abcdefghijklm
nopqrstuvwxyz
1234567890
àáâãäèéêëìíîïñòóô
õöšúûùýÿž
ct fi fl ff ft st st tt ß
„' ^^~ – – –

the poison ivy

how quickly daft jumping zebras vex

alternative letters

infoarchitecture

abcdefghijklm
nopqrstuvwxyz

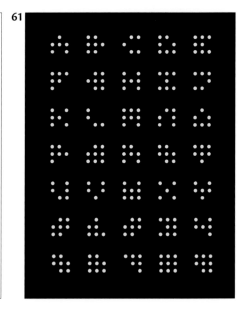

TrueType and OpenType fonts (Figs. 57, 58, 59). Postscript fonts are fonts that have different pieces for the computer's screen display and for printer use. Both pieces must be installed on a computer for the font to work properly. TrueType fonts have the display and printer elements contained all in one. Both Postscript and TrueType fonts are platform dependent, meaning a type designer must create both PC and Mac versions of the font. OpenType fonts are cross-platform fonts, so a single version of the font works on both PC and Mac computers. OpenType fonts also allow for the inclusion of more customized ligatures and symbols, otherwise known as *glyphs*. Unicode, a coding language that uses hexadecimal numbers to represent letters, limits Postscript and TrueType fonts to 256 characters and glyphs. OpenType programming language can have up to 65,000 glyphs. The final font format will depend on the final usage. If the font is solely for your design use, output the font for compatibility with your computer system. If you plan on making the font available commercially, output the font as multiple formats.

DISTRIBUTION

A type designer has several outlets for distributing a new font. The first is through his own promotion and website. Whether for profit or for free, the designer can control who has access to the font. The second option is to offer the font through a website that distributes a collection of fonts for free. Some of these sites take any font offered to them while others have a selection process, so be sure to check their font submission requirements. The third option is

57 Postscript icons. **58** TrueType icon. **59** OpenType icon. **60** Canela typeface. **61** Domino typeface.

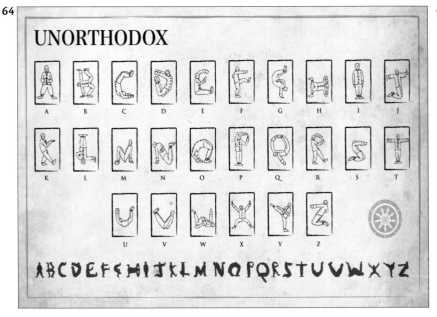

62 Roisin typeface. **63** Rendez Vous typeface. **64** Unorthodox1 typeface. **65** Drone On typeface. Designing fonts to suit a client's needs is very rewarding. Designing a font to satisfy your own need is even better because it allows you the creative freedom to experiment. The only thing limiting you is your imagination.

to offer the font through a commercial font distributor. This is the most difficult to achieve, because font distributors only want the most refined and commercially viable fonts. Still, this option can provide lucrative royalties for the designer if the font is accepted. Whatever option a designer chooses, the satisfaction of creating a font is usually reward enough (Figs. 60, 61, 62, 63, 64, 65).

KALAKARI DISPLAY

66

66 Kalakari Display typeface designed by Beth Shirrell.

Designer Beth Shirrell's experiences and interests in Indian culture led her to create a typeface called Kalakari Display (Fig. 66). She counts the architecture, religion, textiles, animals, landmarks, customs, entertainment and food encountered on her extensive travels in India among the many influences that led to her final design. Her goal was to capture the historical and cultural essence of the country without being cliché.

Shirrell looked for motifs and designs that mimicked contours of letterforms in all kinds of things she observed in her travels. Architecture, henna painting and Hindu iconography ultimately influenced her. In Jali, a perforated stone screen, Shirrell found that the repetition of the design and its shadow created a subtle juxtaposition of geometric and organic shapes (Fig. 67). Kalakari's sinuous line work is pulled from the delicate intricacies of henna patterns (Fig. 68). The male peacock, a prevalent motif in Hindu iconography, inspired the stature of the letterforms. She began the design process by determining that a sans serif capital display typeface would be best to accept the ornate embellishments she envisioned. Using pencil and paper, she traced, rotated, slipped, shuffled, scaled and retraced again and again. Each letter was analyzed in terms of proportion, weight and level of detail. Once all of the letterforms were perfect on paper, she scanned them into the computer and began retracing them as vector art (Figs. 69, 70).

She recognized that motifs needed to be carried throughout the letterforms in order for the typeface to be cohesive and worked to create a library of design variations that she could utilize throughout the process. For Shirrell, a select set of letters was the easiest to create: E, J, B and M. These letter shapes mimicked elements in Indian architecture and henna motifs and, therefore, were easy to translate into letterforms. These letters, in turn, led to design solutions for letters

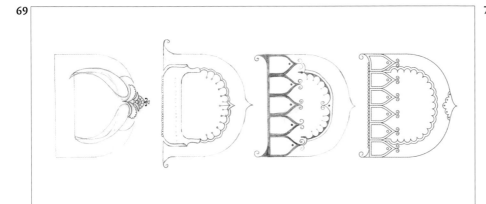

similar in shape, such as *F*, *I*, *R*, *A* and *B*. Some letters were more difficult than others; *G*, *H*, *N* and *Z* proved to be a challenge for her. These letter shapes were completed last, and it was difficult to mesh the letterform characteristics into the design established for the other letters when she really wanted to introduce something new. To do so, however, would have resulted in a disjointed look. Once the letterforms were designed, she chose the name Kalakari to represent the typeface. The word translates from Hindi to mean "ornamentation" and also has a

phonetic connection to the word *calligraphy*, a well-known decorative lettering style.

To showcase the typeface, Shirrell chose to create a series of silk-screened posters. These posters highlight specific cultural influences in Hindi or Sanskrit writing and imagery. Each is accompanied by English explanations. Color, text and design all portray a culture she will forever love. Ultimately, she created a typeface in which the letters are not simply read but experienced.

67 Jali, perforated stone screen, provided Beth Shirrell with the inspiration for interior decorative elements in her letterforms. **68** Shirrell had her own hands decorated with the art of henna, thereby having access to inspiration wherever she went. **69, 70** Sketch after sketch was necessary to develop the finished look of the letterforms. The final *D* took its cue from architectural archways.

DESIGNING WITH LETTERS

Letters are more than just the parts that make up the whole; they are elements that can be just as beautiful when used alone as they are together. Single letters can add visual interest to a page or can be used as a focal point for a logo. Letters can be used as art. They can begin a story or represent a company. They can even symbolize royalty.

ILLUMINATED MANUSCRIPTS

Illuminated manuscripts are an early example of letters as art (Fig. 71). As early as 600 C.E., these books, generally religious in nature, were created to assist in the teaching of manuscripts to the illiterate masses. The books were handwritten and included illustrations, often adorned with gold and silver leaf, which depicted scenes from the stories being told. At the beginning of these stories stood an initial, a letter decorated with an illustration to indicate the beginning of a story or chapter within the story. Some initials were quite detailed and fanciful, while others were simpler and cleaner. Most used vibrant colors and metallic leaf detailing. Due to the meticulous process and materials used, the books were extremely expensive and only the Church and very wealthy individuals could afford them. Monks and other religious craftsmen at monasteries or trained artisans in professional scriptoria created multiple copies of books by hand.

Similar decorative initials can be found throughout history. William Morris of the Kelmscott Press revitalized decorated initials during the Industrial Revolution when people were moving away from the more ornate forms of earlier times. He looked to the fifteenth century's mastery of ornamental typographic style. Artists of the Art Nouveau period created intricate works using letterforms and art influenced by nature. Initials can still be found in use today decorating the pages of children's storybooks. Many designers also use initials in their designs to create emphasis and to separate paragraphs of text (Fig. 72).

CREATING INITIALS

Creating an initial for a design begins much the same way as designing a typeface. Choose a type design that most closely resembles the connotation needed. Place tracing paper on top of a print out of the letter and begin adding decorative elements. Consider all of the little details that can be added to the letter to enhance the

71

72

71 Benedictine from the *Book of Hours*, 1485 **A.D.**, France. **72** Initials can be found in a variety of themes and styles. A designer needs to choose an appropriate look for the job at hand or create his or her own.

final design. Continue working on tracing paper over your letter until you are satisfied with the look of the initial. Scan the sketch and trace it in a vector-based drawing program. Color can be added using either vector or raster-based programs.

MONOGRAMS

Monograms are another great use of individual letters. A *monogram* is a design that contains overlapping letters, usually the first, middle and last initials of a person's name. Monograms originally began as marks on coins to identify Greek and Roman rulers. They came into fashion during Victorian times as personal symbols to represent one's place in society. Over time, the use of monograms became more mainstream. Craftsmen used monograms as marks on goods to identify themselves as the ones who made the product. Monarchs, clubs and organizations all found use for monograms as logos. Modern uses of the monogram are now almost exclusively for marking robes, towels, luggage and other household goods as belonging to a particular person or family. Custom monogram embossers are quite popular as wedding gifts so the newly married couple can personalize their thank-you notes and stationery (Figs. 73, 74, 75).

CREATING MONOGRAMS

To create a custom monogram, begin with the first, middle and last initials of a name in the typeface of your choosing. Move the letters around and see if any combinations of letters create interesting shapes or arrangements. Consider overlapping letters, sharing strokes, sharing counters or sharing and overlapping any other parts of the characters. If the letters are similar, consider mirroring them. Letters can also be broken apart and reassembled. Look to have the letters linked together in such a way that they create a shape, either symmetrical or asymmetrical. If using a swash-laden script, see if the swashes can link together. Be careful not to let the typeface become too decorative, or the letterforms will get lost. Maintain the legibility of your letters throughout this process. The monogram can be applied to any number of items. It can also be made into an embosser or rubber stamp so that stationery and other goods can be personalized.

LETTER-BASED LOGO DESIGN

Some logos utilize single letterforms as a mark or icon for a company. The letters stand for a person's or company's initials, or they can form an acronym. These letters are often very stylized, with significant alterations from their original architecture. Altering the letter makes the mark more distinguishable and, therefore, more amenable to ownership by a company. Using letters is a great way to personalize a company without having to create a symbol. The key to designing logos with individual letters is to customize them so that they are recognizable but also distinct. Strokes, counters, bowls and other parts can be modified to transform the letters. In

73 Monogram by Ken Barber. **74** Personal Monogram by José Domingo Betancur. **75** Look for aspects of letterforms that can be used together, overlapped or shared. For instance, the main bowl of the *G* shares the same stroke as the top swash of the *B*.

addition, letters do not have to stand alone. Letters can be combined with other shapes and icons to create something new. Many famous brands are known for their letter-based logos. Chanel, Gatorade, Armani Exchange, Men's Warehouse, MTV, Sheraton Hotels & Resorts, Texaco and numerous sports teams all utilize stylized letters to represent their company (Figs. 76, 77, 78, 79, 80).

CREATING LETTER-BASED LOGOS

After meeting with a client to explore what they want in a logo, thoroughly review the company's requirements to determine the look you need to create. Begin sketching. If the logo will consist of a single letter, this is the time to begin examining a variety of typefaces. Once several typefaces have been identified, study the letter more closely to determine how it can be modified. It may be as simple as the slightest modification of a stroke, or as complicated as completely redrawing the letter to customize it. Other graphic elements may also enhance a letter. If creating a multiple letter logo, begin the same way with sketches and examining typefaces. As with monograms, look for ways that the letters can overlap or interact with each other. Look closely to see if the letters can share a stroke, a bowl, a counter or other parts. Continue to experiment until you have reached the desired result.

76

77

78
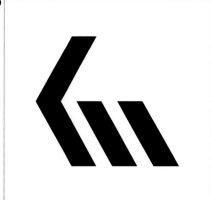

79 **80**
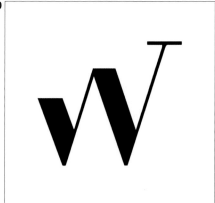

76 The HYP icon was created by overlapping letters in such a way that they formed an abstract plant representational of the budding professionals that form the group. In addition, the lowercase *i* represents the individual within the organization. **77** Utilizing a shared stroke and the negative space of the capital *P*, the combined letterforms do double duty as the two initials of the company's name. **78** The modified *Q* conveys a strong sense of movement, appropriate for an energy drink. **79** Even though the letters have been abstracted, the eye naturally forms the omitted strokes, making these letters easily read as a *K* and *M*. **80** A clever modification of the *W* gives the logo greater meaning.

AN INTERVIEW WITH KEN BARBER

Ken Barber earned his Bachelor of Fine Art degree from Temple University's Tyler School of Art in Philadelphia, where he majored in graphic design. It was there that he met former House Industries partner Allen Mercer and began doing freelance work for the company. After graduating in 1994, Barber worked for several design studios in New York before joining House Industries full time two years later. Presently he is a letterer, type designer and type director at House Industries and a partner of Photo-Lettering, Inc., an online lettering service developed in collaboration between by House Industries, Erik van Blokland of LettError and Christian Schwartz of Commercial Type. Barber teaches at Maryland Institute College of Art and the University of Delaware and regularly lectures and conducts workshops on the topics of lettering and typography. He also manages Type and Lettering (typeandlettering.com), an online showcase for various personal projects.

You've said that Don Martin cartoons from Mad *magazine were an influence for you in the beginning. What are your influences now? Where do you go for inspiration?*

I don't actively look for inspiration, but that doesn't seem to stop me from finding plenty of it, be it an advertisement in a mid-century magazine or antique packaging spied at the local flea market. I try to keep my eyes—and mind—open. Occasionally, I snap a picture of an interesting hand-painted sign or pick up the odd hand-lettering instruction book. I suppose I gravitate towards things that I find unique and well crafted and try to surround myself with them. Though, I suspect this phenomenon is common among designers as a whole.

Whom do you admire among your peers in lettering design? Why?

I wouldn't be so bold as to call myself his peer, but I have always marveled at the work of Doyald Young. His lettering is firmly rooted in history yet manages to be inventive—not to mention, it's executed with a mind-boggling degree of technical precision. Ed Benguiat is another person I greatly respect and with whom I have had the honor and pleasure to collaborate. To be honest, I admire the work of so many talented folks that I run the risk of accidentally omitting some. With that said, Ben Kiel, Tal Leming, Erik van Blokland, Christian Schwartz, John Downer, Alex Trochut, Bruce Willen, Nolen Strals and the guys at Underware are all doing some pretty terrific stuff.

Why create type? Why not be a monster truck stunt driver or professional skier?

I've always been drawn to hand lettering. The simplicity of letterforms allows for a certain amount of latitude in construction and interpretation. At the same time, Latin script letters have been in use for hundreds of years, so one can't stray too far from the model. I enjoy the freedom that lettering allows, coupled with the grounding that history provides. Well-balanced letterforms are engaging and ensure that people won't tire of seeing them expressed in fresh and imaginative ways. Besides, I don't see myself launching a pickup truck over a row of cars or tackling the Alps anytime soon. Drawing a satisfying piece of lettering is enough excitement for me.

Why do you think designers feel so passionate about fonts and typography?

Graphic designers and typographers are passionate about the things that occupy them on a regular basis. Typography is not simply one part of a larger equation that accounts for a designer's livelihood; it is integral to the individual's creative process. Graphic designers express themselves through their work, which would be nearly impossible to do without the use of type. For those that design typefaces, a font is not merely an aspect of one's profession; it is the focus. Why certain people find drawing letters personally satisfying continues to be a mystery to me … and I do it for a living! For some, type design is a curious leisurely pursuit that helps to pay the bills. For others, it borders on an obsession.

Considering the tedium involved, I'm inclined to think that it's a bit masochistic, too.

What do you feel is the most challenging part of being a designer/letterer?

There is never a scarcity of ideas for potential font designs or lettering. However, developing a typeface can take months or even years to complete. Maintaining the necessary level of enthusiasm to push forward with an extensive type design project, while dealing with periodic lettering jobs and other interruptions, can be somewhat challenging. As a perfectionist (read: obsessive-compulsive), I find the factor of time to be the biggest obstacle. There never seems to be enough of that.

What is your process for creating custom lettering or designing a new typeface? What tools do you use?

When designing a new typeface I consider creating something suited for a particular purpose, even if it's simply to get viewers attention or to entertain. I've learned that most things done with intention are better than those that lack it. Do I need a text typeface or display? What aims do I plan to achieve with the design that previous fonts have not already fulfilled? Is a special typeface that works under certain viewing or printing conditions required? Or, do I need a type that has a stylistic flair not addressed by existing retail offerings? If there is a typeface that already answers these questions, then I know that I don't need to design a new one and I've just saved myself a lot of time and trouble.

81

Dollhouse
In Mod We Trust
The Descent of God
Wieñerschmitzël
Suite Andalucía
Extra Large
Gerschtöpenfrümflopen
IS IT MAN OR ASTROMAN?
Chancery titles

82

83

81 Typeface specimens by Ken Barber. 82, 83 Samples of Ken Barber's work.

The research phase during which the direction of a typeface's development is decided is the first and most important stage of the design process. Ideally, the need and purpose of the face drives its development. This will ultimately affect the style, size and scope of the project.

Next, during the sketch phase, general characteristics of a typeface are determined, such as contrast and proportion, among other considerations. Although I tend to make preliminary sketches relatively tight, most often the letters' outlines are altered considerably while digitizing them.

Pencil renderings are then carefully traced in FontLab, the most widely available font editing application currently on the market. It is during this stage that the overall visual color of the forms is balanced, as each letter's contours are finessed and properly spaced. Missing characters, accented letters, ligatures and alternate glyphs are also added. Type Supply's Prepolator and Area51, along with LettError's Superpolator, are other indispensable font production tools. They are especially handy for managing typefaces that contain a large number of fonts.

84

85

86

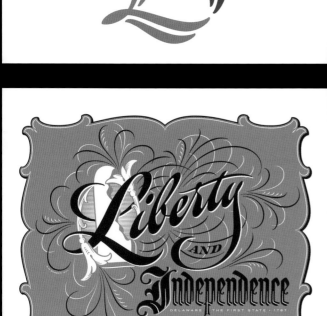

87

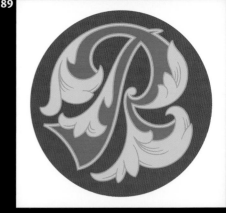

Before a typeface will function ideally it needs to be kerned, a process during which specific letter pairs are individually spaced. I use Type Supply's MetricsMachine to help with this task, which can often be quite daunting. In cases where I want to add unique features or give an additional boost to a font's performance, as I often do with typefaces suggestive of hand-lettering, I utilize OpenType programming. In complex cases, I rely on the help of colleagues such as Ben Kiel and Tal Leming. Finally, the prospective typeface goes through several rounds of thorough proofing.

Sometimes, the final typeface can differ considerably from its starting point; happy accidents and unforeseen obstacles can turn into blessings, shaping the course of a typeface's growth in unexpected ways. Despite working within a relatively strict framework, type design can be a surprisingly organic process.

What advice do you have for young designers who want to break into custom lettering and font design?

Get in touch with type designers and letterers. You'd be surprised; they are usually more than happy to share pointers with those interested in the trades.

Attend workshops and seminars. TypeCon holds an annual conference in the United States, offering a few days of lectures and hands-on workshops. ATypI is great for the more adventure-some type geek, meeting in a different city around the globe each year.

Read up on typographic history and type design basics. There are loads of helpful titles on the subject. Those interested in the nitty-gritty of typeface design should try digging up a copy of Walter Tracy's *Letters of Credit*. It's out of print but worth a read.

What would you consider the number one most important thing to learn about typography? Or, since one thing may be too limiting, how about the top three?

Choosing the right typeface for the job is crucial. Carefully con-sider what the typography needs to accomplish before scrolling through that bloated font menu.

Unless you are designing a Victorian era-style circus poster, less really is more. You would be surprised what a duo of stylisti-cally well-paired typefaces can do. A little goes a long way.

With a few exceptions, free fonts are usually free for a reason. Make your life easy and stick with professionally made typefaces.

With the influx of free fonts being available on the Web, what advice do you have for making sure a designer chooses a "good one"? What characteristics do you look for in a font?

When it comes to free fonts, you get what you pay for. A "good" typeface is not only made well, but it must also be suited to the task at hand. Determining the fitness of a typeface is as much the responsibility of the typeface designer as it is the designer using it. It's a two-way street.

When purchasing fonts, look for ones that are well crafted and designed for particular needs. Generally speaking, good typefaces also exhibit sensitivity to the construction of letterforms and evenness of visual color, even if it's a connecting script or playful display face.

What is one of your biggest type-related pet peeves?

Considering that typesetting tools have practically become part of our daily experience, it irks me that many people think good typography is easy to create. The proliferation of poor typographic practice seen in everything from editorial design to packaging attests to the fact that there is more to good typography than mere typing.

Why is the study of typography so important to the design of typography?

Knowing where you've been is helpful in figuring out where you're going. Western culture has five hundred years of movable type behind it. There is a lot that typographers and type designers can glean from that. Furthermore, there are many mistakes that one could avoid simply by brushing up on typographic history. It might help you to avoid some headaches, too.

What trends do you see emerging for type design in the future? Does the introduction of more and more digital technologies have influence?

The @font-face CSS feature, which allows some fonts to be specified for enhanced viewing on certain web browsers, is beginning to make a significant impact on digital typography and graphic design. More and more foundries, including House Industries, are beginning to convert their libraries to web-friendly fonts. That is just one example of how the shifting digital environment is changing the way that the type design industry must face the future of typography.

Ironically, there has also been increased interest in what I call "naive lettering," which I suppose is "neo-folk" lettering of sorts. When you consider typographic history, anytime technological advancement occurs there is a corresponding return to craft among designers. During the Industrial Revolution of the nineteenth century, the American Arts & Crafts movement flouted the soullessness of machine-made products and championed the warmth and craft of the hand-made. The technological boom that we've been experiencing over the past few decades has prompted a similar parallel movement focusing on artisanship. I, for one, am happy to see it (when it's well done, of course). I appreciate both sides: while I'm not a super tech-geek, digitization figures into much of my work. I like the combination of the two.

Of all the lettering you have created, what is your favorite? Why?

The lettering I'm currently working on is my favorite. My least favorite is the one I just finished.

TYPE TIDBITS

Serif or Sans Serif?
Why not semi-serif? It's the best of both worlds!

Favorite letter?
The space glyph. It's the easiest one to draw.

Favorite symbol?
The ampersand—a letter and word all in one.

Helvetica or Futura?
Futura. Time for another sans serif to have the spotlight.

Favorite complementary font pair?
Paperback and Chalet Book gets the job done for me.

Pen and paper or Wacom tablet?
Neither. Pencil for me, if you please.

Mac or PC?

Mac, of course.

Uppercase or lowercase?

Lowercase. It's more fun to draw.

Design: Lifestyle or just a way to earn a living?

Is "illness" a choice?

Go fishing or draw letters?

My daughter says, "Fishing?! Ewww!" Drawing letters it is.

Disco or heavy metal?

My college band played a mixture of both. You've never heard Barry Manilow's "Copacabana" quite like Bob Morbid and the Impalers' version.

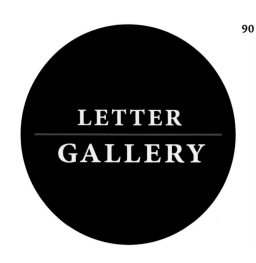

LETTER GALLERY

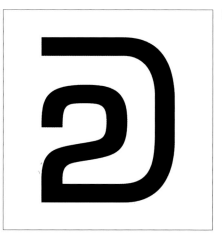

90

91

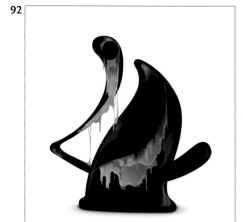

92

93

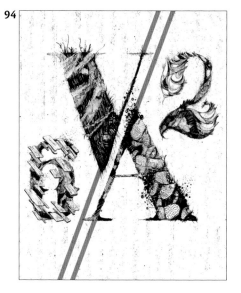

94

95

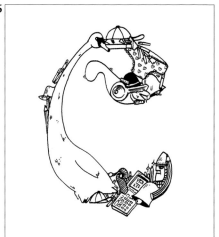

96

97

ALABAMA F1RST
RENEW OUR AIR.

90 2D logo. **91** Christmas card capitular number. **92** Capitular 4 self-promotion. **93** Tehran Urban Bus logo. **94** Studio62 poster. **95** Coredge Software logo. **96** Abécédaire Around Arnold, Letter C. **97** Alabama First logo.

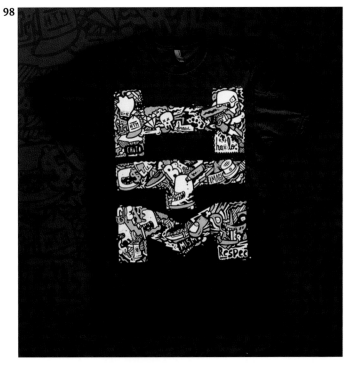

NOTRE DAME **ANNUAL FUND**

HERE SNOWBOARDS™

RIDE HERE. RIDE ANYWHERE.

(is for Bodoni)

98 HTM T-shirt design. **99** Annual Fund logo. **100** HERE Snowboards logo. **101** Guardian Angel. **102** b is for Bodoni. **103** Awakened Wisdom logo.

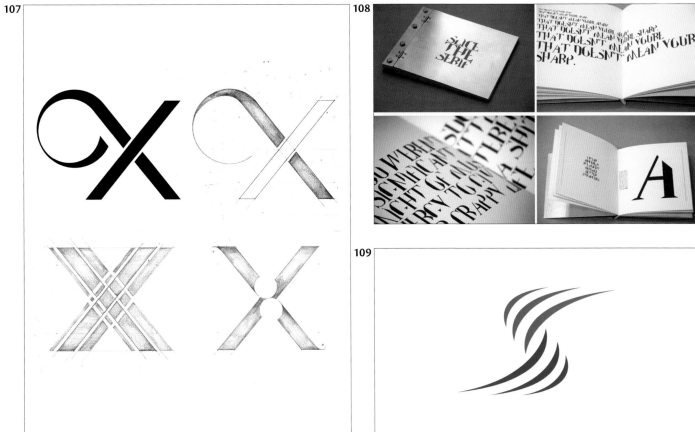

104 Alphabet Design Letter C. **105** T. **106** Number 2. **107** Letterform as Content. **108** Slice the Serif type specimen book. **109** Sky Srpska logo.

110

111

112

113

114

115

116

110 The Graphic Design at Saint Rose Alumni Invitational Exhibit poster.   111 Stream logo.   112 Stereo Wakeski Co. logo.   113 Direct Marketing Company logo.   114 Kahani World logo.   115 Illustype.   116 Stung Media LLC stationery.

ABOUT THE IMAGES IN THIS CHAPTER

Fig. 51
TITLE: Grenade serif Beta typeface early sketches
DESIGN FIRM: Ecole Régionale des Beaux-arts de Valence
ART DIRECTOR: Thomas Huot-Marchand
DESIGNERS: Benjamin Lieb, Valentin Barry, Matthieu Meyer
CLIENT: Ecole Régionale des Beaux-arts de Valence

Fig. 52
TITLE: Grenade serif Beta typeface
DESIGN FIRM: Ecole Régionale des Beaux-arts de Valence
ART DIRECTOR: Thomas Huot-Marchand
DESIGNERS: Benjamin Lieb, Valentin Barry, Matthieu Meyer
CLIENT: Ecole Régionale des Beaux-arts de Valence

Fig. 53
TITLE: Millénaire typeface early sketches
DESIGN FIRM: Kikk
ART DIRECTOR: Anais Krebs
DESIGNER: Benjamin Lieb
CLIENT: Ville de Neuchâtel

Fig. 54
TITLE: Millénaire typeface
DESIGN FIRM: Kikk
ART DIRECTOR: Anais Krebs
DESIGNER: Benjamin Lieb
CLIENT: Ville de Neuchâtel

Fig. 60
TITLE: Canela typeface
DESIGN FIRM: FH Potsdam
ART DIRECTOR: Lucas de Groot
DESIGNER: Christian Groß
CLIENT: Self

Fig. 61
TITLE: Domino typeface
DESIGN FIRM: xpome
DESIGNER: xpome
CLIENT: Self

Fig. 62
TITLE: Roisin typeface
DESIGN FIRM: bombastudio
DESIGNER: Marta Podkowinska
FONT USED: Inspired by ITC Avant Garde
CLIENT: Self

Fig. 63
TITLE: Rendez Vous typeface
DESIGN FIRM: Gwer
DESIGNER: Rutger Paulusse
CLIENT: Self

Fig. 64
TITLE: Unorthodox1 typeface
SCHOOL: Sheridan College
PROFESSOR: Sandra Dionisi
DESIGNER: Andrew West
FONT USED: Unorthodox1

Fig. 65
TITLE: Drone On typeface
SCHOOL: Philadelphia University
PROFESSOR: Maribeth Kradel-Weitzel
DESIGNER: Christina Lanzisero

Fig. 66
TITLE: Kalakari Display typeface
DESIGNER: Beth Shirrell

Fig. 73
TITLE: Monogram
DESIGNER: Ken Barber

Fig. 74
TITLE: Personal Monogram
DESIGNER: José Domingo Betancur
FONT USED: Hand Lettering

Fig. 76
TITLE: Harrisburg Young Professionals logo
ART DIRECTOR: Tracy L. Kretz
DESIGNERS: Tracy L. Kretz, Denise Bosler
FONT USED: Letter Gothic
CLIENT: Harrisburg Young Professionals

Fig. 77
TITLE: Point B Design logo
DESIGN FIRM: Steve DeCusatis Design
DESIGNER: Steve DeCusatis
FONT USED: Custom type
CLIENT: Point B Design

Fig. 78
TITLE: Q Energy Drink logo
DESIGN FIRM: www.kostam.com
DESIGNER: Kosta Mijic
FONT USED: Custom type
CLIENT: Q Energy Drink

Fig. 79
TITLE: Kosta Mijic personal logo
DESIGN FIRM: www.kostam.com
DESIGNER: Kosta Mijic
FONT USED: Custom type
CLIENT: Self

Fig. 80
TITLE: Walk Up Press logo
DESIGN FIRM: Ville
ART DIRECTOR: Joseph Traylor
DESIGNERS: Joseph Traylor, Elizabeth diGiacomantonio

FONT USED: Custom type
CLIENT: Walk Up Press

Figs. 81, 82, 83, 84, 85, 86, 87, 88, 89
Designed by Ken Barber
www.typeandlettering.com

Fig. 90
TITLE: 2D logo
DESIGN FIRM: www.kostam.com
DESIGNER: Kosta Mijic
FONT USED: Eurostile Demi
CLIENT: 2D Solutions

Fig. 91
TITLE: Christmas card capitular number
DESIGN FIRM: MGNTRDR
DESIGNER: José Domingo Betancur
FONT USED: Tiffany Heavy
CLIENT: Self

Fig. 92
TITLE: Capitular 4 self-promotion
DESIGN FIRM: MGNTRDR
DESIGNER: José Domingo Betancur
FONT USED: Inspired in Stylla Caps
CLIENT: Self

Fig. 93
TITLE: Tehran Urban Bus logo
UNIVERSITY: University of Tehran, College of Fine Arts
DESIGNER: Arya Bakhsheshi

Fig. 94
TITLE: Studio62 poster
DESIGN FIRM: MGNTRDR
DESIGNER: José Domingo Betancur
FONTS USED: Bodoni Extra Bold, Tiffany
CLIENT: Studio62

Fig. 95
TITLE: Coredge Software logo
DESIGN FIRM: idApostle
DESIGNER: Steve Zelle
FONT USED: Century Schoolbook Roman
CLIENT: Coredge Software

Fig. 96
TITLE: Abécédaire Around Arnold, Letter C
DESIGN FIRM: Ecole Régionale des Beaux-arts de Valence
DESIGNER: Benjamin Lieb
FONT USED: Inspired by Arnold Boecklin font by the Otto Weiser foundry
CLIENT: Ecole Régionale des Beaux-arts de Valence

Fig. 97
TITLE: Alabama First logo
DESIGN FIRM: Doug Barrett Design
DESIGNER: Douglas Barrett
FONTS USED: Trade Gothic, Century Schoolbook
CLIENT: Alabama First

Fig. 98
TITLE: HTM T-shirt design
DESIGN FIRM: Atelier 33
DESIGNER: chato
FONT USED: Hand lettering
CLIENT: HTM Clothing

Fig. 99
TITLE: Annual Fund logo
DESIGN FIRM: Neha Agarwal Graphic Design
DESIGNER: Neha Agarwal
FONT USED: Baskerville
CLIENT: The Academy of Notre Dame de Namur

Fig. 100
TITLE: HERE Snowboards logo
DESIGN FIRM: Steve DeCusatis Design
DESIGNER: Steve DeCusatis
FONTS USED: Custom lettering, Futura
CLIENT: HERE Snowboards

Fig. 101
TITLE: Guardian Angel
DESIGN FIRM: Steve DeCusatis Design
DESIGNER: Steve DeCusatis
FONT USED: AnnabelleMatinee
CLIENT: JEG

Fig. 102
TITLE: b is for Bodoni
DESIGN FIRM: Patrick Broom Design
DESIGNER: Patrick Broom
FONTS USED: Bodoni Poster Italic, Bodoni Italic
CLIENT: Self

Fig. 103
TITLE: Awakened Wisdom logo
DESIGN FIRM: Steve DeCusatis Design
DESIGNER: Steve DeCusatis
FONT USED: Hand lettering
CLIENT: Flannel

Fig. 104
TITLE: Alphabet Design Letter C
DESIGN FIRM: Tod Seitz
DESIGNER: Tod Seitz
FONT USED: Hand lettering

Fig. 105
TITLE: T
SCHOOL: Miami Ad School Europe

DESIGNER: Matei Curtasu
FONT USED: Hand lettering

Fig. 106
TITLE: Number 2
DESIGN FIRM: TOOCO
DESIGNER: Francisco Miranda
FONT USED: Hand lettering
CLIENT: MTV

Fig. 107
TITLE: Letterform as Content
SCHOOL: Moore College
    of Art & Design
PROFESSORS: Gigi McGee
    and Russell Maret
DESIGNER: Lindsay M Deisher
FONT USED: Hand lettering

Fig. 108
TITLE: Slice the Serif type
    specimen book
SCHOOL: University of the West
    of England (UWE)

PROFESSORS: Gabriel Solomons,
    John-Paul Dowling
DESIGNER: Kathryn Evans-Prosser
FONT USED: Hand lettering

Fig. 109
TITLE: Sky Srpska logo
DESIGN FIRM: www.kostam.com
ART DIRECTOR: Kosta Mijic
DESIGNER: Kosta Mijic
CLIENT: Sky Srpska

Fig. 110
TITLE: The Graphic Design at
    Saint Rose Alumni Invitational
    Exhibit poster
DESIGN FIRM: The College of Saint
    Rose Office of Creative Services
    and Marketing
ART DIRECTOR: Mark Hamilton
DESIGNER: Chris Parody
FONT USED: Franklin Gothic
    Condensed, Bauer Bodoni

CLIENT: The College of Saint Rose
    Center for Art & Design

Fig. 111
TITLE: Stream logo
DESIGN FIRM: Steve DeCusatis Design
DESIGNER: Steve DeCusatis
FONT USED: Hand lettering
CLIENT: Small Planet

Fig. 112
TITLE: Stereo Wakeski Co. logo
DESIGN FIRM: Boris Bonev
DESIGNER: Boris Bonev
FONT USED: M06
CLIENT: Stereo Wakeski Co.

Fig. 113
TITLE: Direct Marketing Company logo
DESIGN FIRM: Bogdan Terente
DESIGNER: Bogdan Terente
FONT USED: Hand lettering
CLIENT: S.C. MD VIKI S.R.L.

Fig. 114
TITLE: Kahani World logo
DESIGN FIRM: www.kostam.com
DESIGNER: Kosta Mijic
CLIENT: Kahani World

Fig. 115
TITLE: Illustype
DESIGNER: Bratislav Milenkovic
FONT USED: Illustrated letter
CLIENT: Self

Fig. 116
TITLE: Stung Media LLC stationery
CLIENT: Stung Media LLC
DESIGN FIRM: Stung Media LLC
DESIGNER: Nandor Tamas
FONT USED: Bitsumishi
CLIENT: Stung Media LLC

chapter three
{ **WORD** }

Letters, like people, form relationships. Some relationships are close; others are looser. In all cases, the best relationships are the ones that make sense and work well together. In terms of type, those relationships are words. Forming words gives letters a sense of purpose.

We use words to communicate many things—emotions, actions, descriptions, places, people and things. Words are essential to our everyday existence. Words convey needs and desires. We need words to function as a society. The English language has an extensive vocabulary; single words can even have multiple meanings. Different people interpret words in different ways. It is the designer's job to communicate a client's words so that they are interpreted correctly. In some cases, words act as a support to the design, while other times words themselves are the whole design.

New, *free*, *sale*, *best*, *better*, *fresh* and *delicious* are words frequently used in advertising. These words are powerful and persuasive. When designed correctly, these words will provoke a person to action. This is important because the goal of advertising is to get someone to buy a product or use a service. In this case, the words support the main advertising message. Companies also need to evoke a sense of trust in their brand. A strong word-based logo will develop that trust by becoming the whole design. Once people become familiar with the look of a company's logo, it will evoke a positive or negative association based upon a user's experience with the company.

EMOTIONAL TYPE

Emotions that spring from seeing words can be quite powerful. Sometimes the emotion moves someone to buy a product. Other times it causes them to feel a personal connection to a brand or to feel confident in a service. When this occurs, it's called utilizing the font's *connotation*. Connotation is the idea or feeling the typography invokes in a person, as opposed to denotation, which is the literal meaning of the word. For example, the denotation of the word *cat* is a small animal with four legs, whiskers and a tail. The connotation of the word varies depending on the font choice (Fig. 1). The words *kitty cat* set in Spookhouse conjure up a vision of a black cat on Halloween, while the same words set in Bellevue give the feeling of a sophisticated Persian. Fontesque conveys a fun-loving alley cat, and Pizzicato reminds a viewer more of whiskers in general than any particular cat.

Conveying the correct connotation for words is just as important as the words themselves. Choosing the wrong font can be disastrous. A bakery would no sooner use a grunge-inspired sans serif than a heavy metal band would use a swash-laden script (Figs. 2, 3). It would convey the wrong meaning. The bakery could be assumed to make cakes that are ugly and tasteless, while the heavy metal band might be seen as a group that plays more ballads than rock.

Connotation, however, is subjective. "Happy" to one person may be best represented by Curlz (Fig. 4), but to another person it may be Baskerville (Fig. 5). You may have a client who wants the design to have a professional feel. In the designer's eyes, professional may mean a sans serif typeface that is very geometric, whereas to the client, professional may mean a serif typeface with

an architectural look. It is important to clearly understand the connotation a client wants to convey before beginning a design to ensure you meet the client's goals.

CHOOSING THE RIGHT TYPEFACE

Choice of typeface can mean the difference between a successful and an unsuccessful design. Within a typeface there are several things that distinguish one word from another. As mentioned in

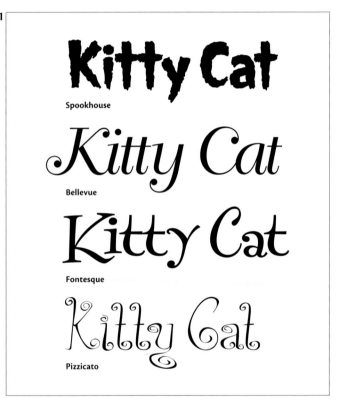

1 Font connotation examples. 2 Poor font connotation. 3 Good font connotation. 4, 5 Views on the right font for the job are subjective. It is very important to discuss these views before showing design options to a client. This communication will spare a designer the trouble of redoing work when a client feels his needs weren't met.

chapter 2, bold, italic, extended and condensed styles of letterforms are ways to create differentiation. They create emphasis by separating the look of a particular word from the surrounding text. Of course, when working with a single word it takes more than that to make the type stand out.

Understanding the design objectives of your client is crucial to your selection of a typeface (Figs. 6, 7). A high-end corporate brochure will require a typeface with good legibility and refinement to convey the company's professionalism. A band's concert flyer should have a typeface with spark and excitement. A logo for a children's clothing company can feature a playful typeface. Always remember that it is the client's objectives and not a designer's personal preferences that should determine the typeface. Too often a young designer will assume that a typeface they love will work with every job. Each project is different; typefaces should be chosen to reflect those differences.

KERNING

When a word is typed on the computer, the letters appear a set distance apart from each other on the screen. These distances are determined by the creator of the font. Consistent spacing between letters is more comfortable for the eye to read. Unfortunately, there are times when two or more letters don't fit together well. They appear either too close together or too far apart. This results in readability issues: A letter appears to combine with the letter next to it or to detach from the word. This is where *kerning*, a manual adjustment of the space between two letters, comes in (Figs. 8, 9). A properly designed font will have kerning pairs incorporated to eliminate suboptimal letter spacing.

Kerning pairs are sets of two letters whose spacing has been modified from the normal pre-set space to reflect a better visual

6 Classic typefaces placed into a modern design keep the poster professional yet still reflect the university's art- and design-based programs. **7** The cute and playful hand-rendered type is perfect for this healthy fast food chain, a frequent respite for families with kids.

8

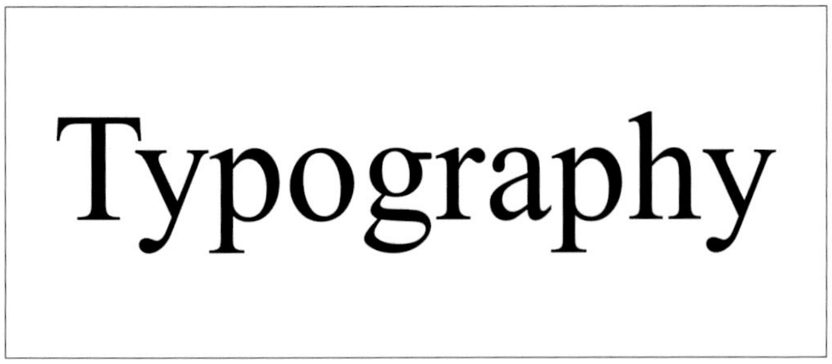

Typography

9

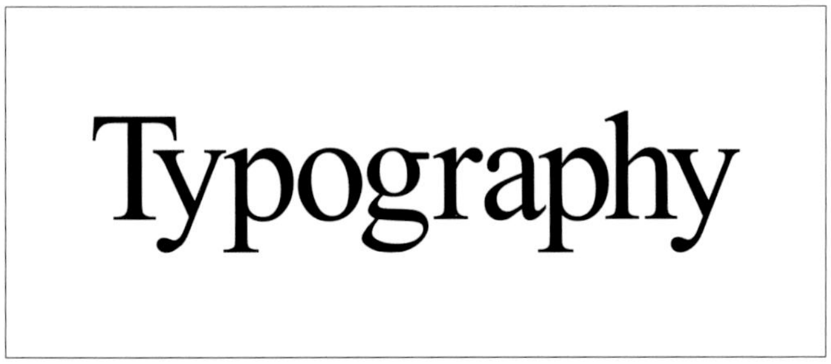

Typography

10

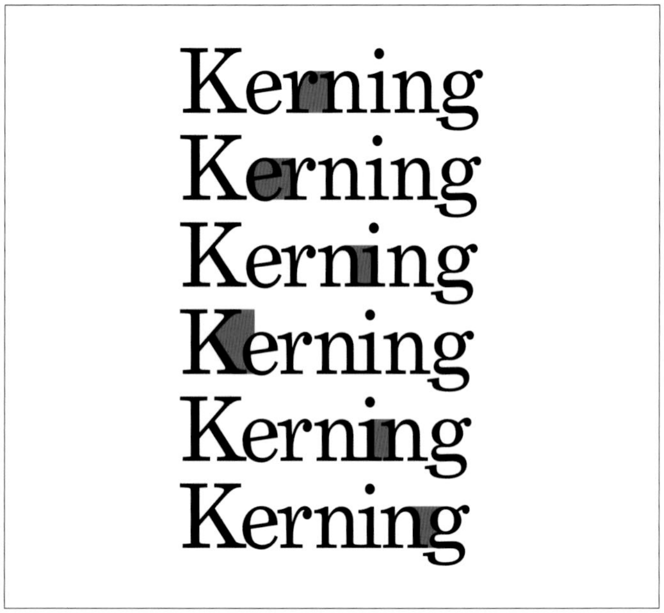

Kerning
Kerning
Kerning
Kerning
Kerning
Kerning

11

Uppercase Pairs	*Lowercase Pairs*	*Upper- and Lowercase Pairs*
AA AC AG AO AQ AT AV AW AY	ac ae ag af at av aw ay	Ac Ad Ae Ag Ao Aq Av Aw Ay
BA BV BW BY	bl by b. b,	Bb Bi By B. B,
CA CO	ca ch	Ca Cr C. C,
DA DO DV DW DY	da dc de dg do dv dw dy d. d,	Da D. D,
EC EO	ea ei em en er et eu ev ew ey e. e,	Ev
FA FC FG FO F. F,	fa fe ff fi fl fo f. f,	Fa Fe Fi Fo Fr Fy F. F, F; F:
GO	ga ge go gg g. g,	Ge Go
HO	hc hd he hg ho hv hw hy	He Ho Hy
IC IG IO	ic id ie ig io it iv	Ic Id Iq Io
JA JO	ja je jo j. j,	Ja Je Jo Ju
KA KO	ka kc kd ke kg ko	Ke Ki Ko
LC LT LV LW LY LG LO LU	la lc ld le lf ll lo lq lv lw ly	Le Lo Ly
MG MO	ma mc md me mg mo mv my	Ma Mc Md Me Mo
NC NG NO	nc nd ne ng no nv nw ny	Nu Na Ne Ni No
OA OB OD OE OF OH OI OK OL OM	ob of oh oj ok om on or ov ow ox oy o. o,	Oa Ob Ol O. O,
ON OP OR OT OU OV OW OX OY	pa pp py p. p,	Pa Pe Po
PA PO PP PY P. P, P; P:	qu	Rd Re Ro Rt Ru
QU	ra rd re rg ro rq rr rv ry r. r,	Sa Se Si So Sp Su S. S,
RC RG RY RT RV RW RY	sh st su s. s,	Ta Tc Te Ti To Tr Tu Tw Ty T. T, T; T:
SI SM ST SU	td ta te to tt t. t,	Ua Ug Us U. U,
TA TC TO	ua uc ud ue ug up uv uw uy	Va Ve Vi Vo Vr Vu V. V, V; V:
UA UC UG UO	va vc vd ve vg vo vv vy v. v,	Wd Wi Wt Wu Wy W. W, W; W:
VA VC VG VO VS	wa wd we wg wh wo w. w,	Xa Xe Xo Xy
WA WC WG WO	xa xe xo	Yd Ye Yi Yu Yv Y. Y, Y; Y:
YA YC YO	ya yc yd ye yo y. y,	Za Ze Zo
ZO	za ze zo	

8 Original unaltered word set in Times New Roman.   **9** Properly kerned word. Note how the spacing between the letters is uniform, thereby increasing the readability.
10 Kerning takes practice to perfect.   **11** Above is a comprehensive, though not all-inclusive, list of kerning pairs for which a font designer should accommodate.

relationship (Fig. 11). Not all fonts are created with kerning pairs, though, and even fonts with kerning pairs can need additional adjustment. Uppercase letters that have a part that hangs over the x-height of the lowercase letters often appear separated from the rest of the word, and so need to be kerned. Two lowercase letters or two uppercase letters may need kerning as well. These gaps between letters break the visual flow. If the font does not have proper kerning pairs, the designer must adjust that space manually.

KERN LIKE A PRO

The goal of manually kerning a word is to make sure the visual space between the letters is uniform. The easiest way to figure out the proper spacing is to first examine the entire word and pick out two letters whose spacing you consider "just right." Look at the letter to the left of the pair. Does it have the same visual spacing? If it does, leave it alone. If it's too close or too far away, adjust the kerning until it looks the same (Fig. 10). Then check the spacing of the letter on the right and adjust this spacing. Keep going back and forth until you have kerned the entire word. Some letters will move dramatically, some may move hardly at all. You will discover that the difference between a properly kerned word and one not kerned at all can be quite dramatic. Please note that when using computer software to kern the letters, your numerical kerning inputs may not be the same exact number. This is okay. You want to judge the spacing by how it looks rather than on the actual numerical input. Also note that this is not an easy skill to acquire, but it can be mastered with practice.

12

kerning
kerning

13

SLICK
SLICK

12 Be careful not to kern too tightly, otherwise you may end up with another word completely. The term *keming* is humorously used to describe this phenomena. The term derives from the word *kerning* being kerned too tightly.   **13** In the comic book world, the word *flick* was banned from use for fear that when set in all uppercase letters, the *L* and *I* would run together and form an unacceptable word. (*Batman Unmasked*, Will Brooker, Continuum International Publishing Group, 2001, p. 63) Take care that any word being kerned does not kern so tightly that it forms another word.

There are a few things to remember about kerning. Sometimes you will be kerning just two letters, while other times you will need to kern a whole word or multiple words. This will be completely dependent upon the kerning pairs built into your chosen font. When using computer programs, kerning a pair of letters only affects the specific appearance of those two letters, and only in that instance of the word. The font itself is not affected. This means you may have to kern the same set of letters multiple times. Particular attention should be paid to kerning in any text sized larger than the paragraph text, because larger type exaggerates poor kerning pairs. The larger the size, the bigger the space. Billboards often have dreadful kerning errors, because they are designed at a small size, on small computer screens, where kerning issues appear insignificant (Figs. 14, 15). Unfortunately, poor kerning becomes truly glaring when enlarged. It is imperative that every design, not just billboards, be enlarged on a computer screen and closely examined before sending it for output. It is also a good idea to print out the design on paper, as it can appear very different than it does on a screen.

Kerning is an often-overlooked detail in today's design world, a disappointment on many levels. Not only does kerning make a word easier to read, but it also shows that the designer cares about doing a good job. It's about making the typography more functional and easier to understand.

TRACKING

Tracking is the spacing between all of the letters in a word or sentence, and it should not be confused with kerning, which is defined as the spatial relationship between two letters. Tracking is just as

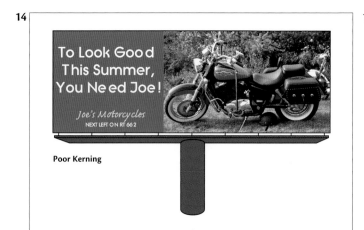

14, 15 Billboards magnify poor kerning. Be sure to examine designs closely to eliminate issues when the file is enlarged.   16 A progression of overly loose to normal to overly tight tracking.   17 Examples of fonts that need tight or loose tracking.

important as kerning and also influences readability, either negatively or positively.

People read by recognizing the shapes of the letters. The correct amount of spacing around each letter helps the brain distinguish one letter from the next. If tight tracking prevents that recognition because the letters are too close together or touching, the design becomes illegible (Fig. 16). Conversely, very loose tracking sets letters so far apart that a viewer cannot distinguish where one word ends and the next begins. Striking the right balance of space in between the letters is key in design communication. This isn't to say a designer can't employ tight or loose tracking; it just needs to be carefully considered.

Open, wide or extended fonts sometimes require tighter tracking to ensure that the letters don't drift too far apart (Fig. 17). Tall, thin or condensed fonts sometimes require looser tracking to ensure the letterforms can be read separately, because they already fit so tightly together. Each font requires different tracking, so it's important to try several different tracking options.

LIGATURES

Simply put, *ligatures* are two or more letters that touch. The most frequently occurring ligature combinations are *fi*, *fl*, *ffi* and *ffl*, though any combination of letters can become a ligature (Figs. 18, 19). Some letters create awkward shapes when appearing next to each other. In the case of *f* and *i*, the dot over the *i* can interfere visually with the ball terminal of the *f*. Many typefaces therefore have special *ligature characters*—single characters that replace the original two letters—built into the font. In the case of *f* and *i* ligature, the dot becomes part of the ball terminal of the *f*, thus increasing the readability of the word in which they appear. It may appear to be a subtle difference from a separated *f* and *i*, but it is an important one, especially in larger type, such as headlines, subheads and logos.

Some fonts have other special ligature characters (Figs. 20, 21). Avant Garde has many different combinations that add great versatility to the font. In logo design, ligatures are essential in creating a proprietary look for a company. They allow the logo to be more than just a series of standard letters. The ligature becomes a design element, every bit as important as an icon or mark. They do need to be carefully considered, though, as specialized letter combinations or too many ligatures can impair readability (Fig. 22). You must also be cautious in a word with loose tracking, as the ligature naturally creates tight letter spacing. A ligature at the beginning of a word looks odd if the tracking of the rest of the word doesn't match (Fig. 23).

18 Adobe Garamond with and without ligatures. **19** Gill Sans with and without ligatures.

20 Æ æ Œ œ iþ ch ct ck tt fj ffi sp st ffl it fu

21 Æ Æ Œ M̄ Ē Ħ M̄ U̶P MB TY V̄H CT TT

22 THE THUMB

23 flower flourish defiantly

20 Alita specialized ligature examples. **21** Mantinia specialized ligature examples. **22** A word of caution: Using too many specialized ligatures will make your type difficult to read. **23** While loose tracking adds an elegant touch to a line of type, ligatures need to be left out so that the letters do not create inconsistent spacing.

SMART FONTS

Some font houses are using custom software to create "smart" fonts. The House Industries font Ed Interlock has the ability to change with words as they are typed to create intricate interlocked characters. The appearance changes automatically as the word is typed. The font boasts over 1,400 different sets of ligatures so that no matter the combination of letters, the words will always fit together like a puzzle.

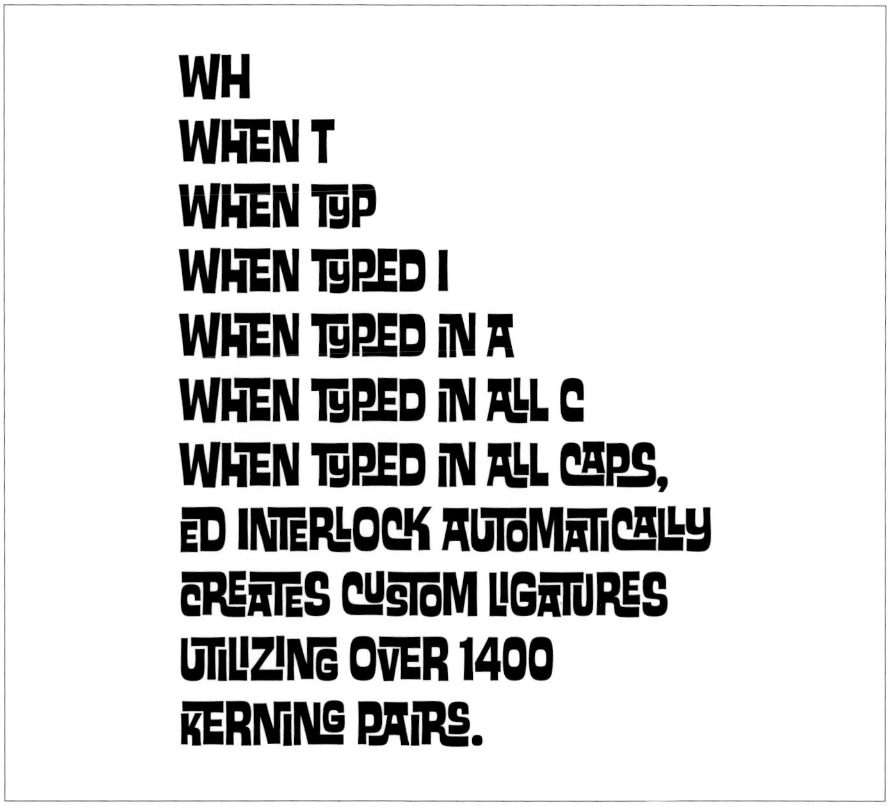

24 Ed Interlock in action.

CASE

The case of a word influences readability. *Uppercase* (all capital letters) reads differently than *lowercase* (all small letters), which in turn reads differently from the combination of uppercase and lowercase letters, known as *title case*. Different cases create a different visual look for a word. Text written in all uppercase letters forms a block of type—the letters all line up along the baseline and cap height. Uppercase can read well or poorly, depending on the font. Most serif and sans serif fonts work very well in all uppercase. Scripts, however, do not read at all (Fig. 25). The swashes run together, creating a jumble of intersecting lines that renders the word unrecognizable.

Uppercase, or caps, can connote many things: importance, confidence, action, risk, jeopardy, urgency or danger. Uppercase should be used sparingly, though, as it does not read as easily as lowercase or title case (Fig. 26). When someone looks at type, the eye moves across the top edge of the letters (Fig. 27). Letters that vary along that top edge, such as lowercase or sentence case, can be distinguished more easily than letters with little variation, such as uppercase. This is why books, magazines and newspapers all utilize title case for their paragraph text (Fig. 28). Small caps can also be used as a variation

MOST PEOPLE WHO BOTHER WITH THE MATTER AT ALL WOULD ADMIT THAT THE ENGLISH LANGUAGE IS IN A BAD WAY, BUT IT IS GENERALLY ASSUMED THAT WE CANNOT BY CONSCIOUS ACTION DO ANYTHING ABOUT IT. OUR CIVILIZATION IS DECADENT, AND OUR LANGUAGE—SO THE ARGUMENT RUNS—MUST INEVITABLY SHARE IN THE GENERAL COLLAPSE. IT FOLLOWS THAT ANY STRUGGLE AGAINST THE ABUSE OF LANGUAGE IS A SENTIMENTAL ARCHAISM, LIKE PREFERRING CANDLES TO ELECTRIC LIGHT OR HANSOM CABS TO AEROPLANES. UNDERNEATH THIS LIES THE HALF-CONSCIOUS BELIEF THAT LANGUAGE IS A NATURAL GROWTH AND NOT AN INSTRUMENT WHICH WE SHAPE FOR OUR OWN PURPOSES.

–GEORGE ORWELL

26

MOST PEOPLE WHO BOTHER WITH THE MATTER AT ALL WOULD ADMIT THAT THE ENGLISH LANGUAGE IS IN A BAD WAY, BUT IT IS GENERALLY ASSUMED THAT WE CANNOT BY CONSCIOUS ACTION DO ANYTHING ABOUT IT. OUR CIVILIZATION IS DECADENT, AND OUR LANGUAGE—SO THE ARGUMENT RUNS—MUST INEVITABLY SHARE IN THE GENERAL COLLAPSE. IT FOLLOWS THAT ANY STRUGGLE AGAINST THE ABUSE OF LANGUAGE IS A SENTIMENTAL ARCHAISM, LIKE PREFERRING CANDLES TO ELECTRIC LIGHT OR HANSOM CABS TO AEROPLANES. UNDERNEATH THIS LIES THE HALF-CONSCIOUS BELIEF THAT LANGUAGE IS A NATURAL GROWTH AND NOT AN INSTRUMENT WHICH WE SHAPE FOR OUR OWN PURPOSES.

–GEORGE ORWELL

27

Our civilization is decadent

60

CHAPTER THREE

28

Most people who bother with the matter at all would admit that the english language is in a bad way, but it is generally assumed that we cannot by conscious action do anything about it. Our civilization is decadent, and our language—so the argument runs—must inevitably share in the general collapse. It follows that any struggle against the abuse of language is a sentimental archaism, like preferring candles to electric light or hansom cabs to aeroplanes. Underneath this lies the half-conscious belief that language is a natural growth and not an instrument which we shape for our own purposes.

–George Orwell

29

MOST PEOPLE WHO BOTHER WITH THE MATTER AT ALL WOULD ADMIT THAT THE ENGLISH LANGUAGE IS IN A BAD WAY, BUT IT IS GENERALLY ASSUMED THAT WE CANNOT BY CONSCIOUS ACTION DO ANYTHING ABOUT IT. OUR CIVILIZATION IS DECADENT, AND OUR LANGUAGE—SO THE ARGUMENT RUNS—MUST INEVITABLY SHARE IN THE GENERAL COLLAPSE. IT FOLLOWS THAT ANY STRUGGLE AGAINST THE ABUSE OF LANGUAGE IS A SENTIMENTAL ARCHAISM, LIKE PREFERRING CANDLES TO ELECTRIC LIGHT OR HANSOM CABS TO AEROPLANES. UNDERNEATH THIS LIES THE HALF-CONSCIOUS BELIEF THAT LANGUAGE IS A NATURAL GROWTH AND NOT AN INSTRUMENT WHICH WE SHAPE FOR OUR OWN PURPOSES.

–GEORGE ORWELL

30

universal case   UNIVERSAL CASE

25 Text set in uppercase script is impossible to read. **26** Uppercase letters are difficult to read in paragraph form. **27** A person's eye distinguishes letters by tracking the tops of letterforms. If type needs maximum readability, set the text as a sentence case. **28** Sentence case creates maximum readability. **29** Small caps can bring elegance to type though it reads poorly if used for more than a few words. **30** Universal Case typeface examples, Unif and Disturbance.

to all caps. It can give the impression of sentence case without using lowercase letters, as the uppercase letters conform to the same x-height as the lowercase letters. As with uppercase letters, small caps can be difficult to read if used in paragraph text (Fig. 29).

Some fonts have a *universal case*, meaning that the font is made up of letters that don't distinguish between upper and lower case, or x-height and cap height (Fig. 30). In 1925, designer Herbert Bayer created a typeface called Universal. The goal was to produce a simple sans-serif typeface that could do it all. While the font never made it to production, it was the inspiration for ITC's Bauhaus, which is still in use today.

NUMBERS

Numbers deserve just as much attention as letters. Numbers come together in groups like letters do in words. A phone number, zip code or statistic forms a unit that needs to read like a word. Numbers need to be kerned and tracked. They need to have the right connotation, and they need to be readable.

There are two kinds of numbers. The first is *old style numbers* (Fig. 31), designed to have varying heights with ascenders and descenders when set along the baseline. These can be likened to lowercase letters because of their variation. Typically the *1*, *2* and *0* align with the x-height, the *6* and *8* have ascenders, and the *3*, *4*, *5* and *7* have descenders. Old style numbers have taken on a more elegant connotation over time and are not as common in contemporary fonts, though they do still occur. Old style numbers have a tendency to read better in a paragraph of text because of their height variation.

The other style of numbers is known as *lining numbers* (Fig. 32). These numbers line up along the cap height. They can be likened to uppercase letters because there is no variation along the top

31 Old style number examples. **32** Lining number examples. **33** By downsizing the numbers, the numbers become part of the type as opposed to standing out from it.

edge. Lining numbers are far more common than old style numbers and are associated more with everyday use because they aren't as "fancy." Designers must use their judgment when using lining numbers within paragraph text, however. If used in combination with lowercase letters, lining numbers can sometimes appear too large, with their "all-caps feel." It is therefore common practice to reduce the size of the numbers by .5 or 1 point in order for them to look comfortable within the text (Fig. 33).

ONE IS THE LONELIEST NUMBER

Because a *1* takes up significantly less space than the other numbers, it usually needs to be kerned. If placed at the beginning of a set of numbers, the *1* often looks completely separate. If placed in the middle of a group of numbers, it sometimes causes the group to seem divided in two. Examine your numbers carefully to optimize readability.

LEGIBILITY VS. READABILITY

Legibility and *readability* are two terms used to describe how easily type can be read. These terms, however, are quite different from each other. Legibility refers to the design of the words, while readability refers to the way a designer arranged the words.

Legibility involves all parts of a character and all the styles within a font family. These elements create the different features that set apart one typeface from another. These qualities also influence the ability of the viewer to discern the letterforms themselves. Communication with wide audiences requires highly legible typefaces (Fig. 34). Counters should be clear and open, stroke weights should be consistent and letterform shapes should be easily distinguishable. This is especially true when words are set in smaller sizes. A designer should never make a reader struggle to interpret words. You can utilize decorative or embellished typefaces when the connotation is more important than reading the words. Sometimes it doesn't even matter if the word cannot be read at all (Fig. 35).

Readability is ensured by arranging letters set in the chosen typeface and adjusting their size, style, kerning, tracking and case. Color is also a factor. The audience must be considered when addressing readability. For children and older adults, words should be larger, kerned and tracked to a comfortable distance, and set in title case. For teenagers and younger adults, type can be smaller and more extreme tracking can be used. Knowing your audience is important to ensure excellent readability. You can even make a poorly legible typeface readable if the right adjustments are applied.

34 A legible typeface. **35** An illegible typeface.

DESIGNING WITH WORDS

There are times when a single word can convey everything about a company. How is it possible for a few simple letters to do this? The answer can be found in the company's logo. When a designer is asked to develop a logo for a company, the designer is challenged with capturing what the company does, its values, the public image it wants to portray and the vision of what the company will become in the future. This is a tall order for any designer. Typography is an intrinsic part of the design itself. The logo becomes the foundation for everything else—the business card, advertising, website, packaging, brochures. Everything begins with the logo. Poor typography can ruin a good company. Good typography can make even a bad company look good.

LOGO DESIGN

What we think of today as a logo had its origin with the ancient Greeks and Romans. Early logos were monograms that represented rulers or towns and were found on coins. Monograms continued to be used as logos throughout the Middle Ages for merchants, tradesmen and royalty. By the eighteenth century, virtually every commercial business had a logo. With the Industrial Revolution and the boom in advertising, logos became an integral part of society. Some of what we consider early recognizable modern-day logos still in use, though with some modification, are Coca-Cola's script, designed in the early 1900s; Volkswagen's VW letter combination, designed in 1939; Prudential's Rock of Gibraltar, designed in 1896; and RCA's dog listening to a phonograph, designed in 1910. Audi's logo dates back to 1932, maintaining the typeface from the original Audi company logo before it became the auto union of Audi, Auto Union, Horch, DKW and Wanderer.

Logos created by hand bring another level of individuality to a company's persona (Fig. 36). By rendering letters from scratch, the designer creates for the company a logo that is truly its own. No

36

37

38

36 The hand-rendered lettering gives the logo a sense of playfulness and fun. **37** Rendered with an eyedropper filled with India ink, the letterforms reflect the play's elderly assassins. **38** The colorful overlapping letters reflect an artistic event in which children were invited to approach colors and shapes in a fun way.

one else in the world will have the same logo because it cannot be typed on a computer. Hand-drawn type can be subtle and elegant, or vibrant and wild (Figs. 37, 38). There are no limitations. Whatever the designer imagines becomes a reality.

DESIGNING LOGOS

Logos generally consist of two main elements, the name and the mark; however, they can also consist of just the name or just the mark. For the name, typography becomes the key component in ensuring the logo communicates its message clearly. The typography must be distinctive, memorable, versatile and appropriate for the target audience; above all, it must stand the test of time. While a

mark will create a visual association more quickly than typography, it is the word's representation through typography that is spoken and referred to in conversation. If a logo looks amateurish, then the audience will perceive the company as being unprofessional and unreliable. If the logo looks professional, then the audience will treat the company as such.

A company measures success by how many customers it has. Customers equal profits. Profits mean a company stays in business. A company also succeeds by proving that it performs its chosen business better than other businesses of a similar nature. The logo is a part of that equation. If the logo is more distinctive than logos

39

40

41

42

39 Replacing letters with window imagery reinforces the neighborhood arts celebration, with artists displaying works in the storefront windows of businesses. **40** Simple alterations to the letterforms create a more cohesive look. **41, 42** These logos are simple yet still have impact. They keep extraneous information to a minimum in order to keep the viewer focused on the main message.

for competing businesses, then it will stand out in the minds of the customers. Simply using a font as it appears when typed does not result in a creative logo. The most distinctive typographic logos contain type that has been modified, manipulated or created by hand. These modifications and manipulations can include interesting or unusual ligatures, letters that interlock or overlap, letters with pieces added or removed, manually distressed letters, substitution of letters with numbers or shapes, flipped or rotated letters, letters created from other objects, or letters that create other objects (Figs. 39, 40). The word can also use a combination of uppercase and lowercase, combine two different typefaces or combine two varying styles such as roman and oblique. The more a typeface is altered, the more proprietary the logo becomes to the company.

The memorability of a logo is directly related to its simplicity (Figs. 41, 42). Think of some modern memorable logos: McDonald's, FedEx, Dairy Queen, Chicago Cubs, Pepsi, Gap and Post Cereal, to name a few. What do they all have in common? Some use cleverly combined typography, some have bold color, some have custom letterforms—and all are simple in form. The simpler the logo, the more memorable it is. Complex details muddy the brain with unnecessary information. Choose a typeface that is easily readable but still has personality within the letterforms. Be careful of using Display or Decorative typefaces for a logo unless the name of the company is very short. The extra flourish and graphic elements of these styles of typefaces can hinder the legibility.

HELVETICA AND LOGOS

Helvetica has been long considered the perfect typeface for logos. It is part of the brand identity for a plethora of top-performing and enduring companies. Take a look around. 3M, BMW, Toyota, Microsoft, Panasonic, American Airlines, Jeep, Lufthansa, Nestle, Post-it, Sears, Panasonic, Tupperware, CVS and Harley Davidson are all successful brands that use Helvetica. Its familiar, highly legible form borders on generic. Many consider its letterforms to be the epitome of political correctness in the offensive world of Display, Decorative or otherwise unreadable fonts. No matter the word, it always looks good set in Helvetica.

The typeface design lends itself well to the corporate world. Strong, clean lines and spacious counters coupled with a tall x-height contribute to a high degree of legibility. Small or large, condensed or extended, italic or roman, this typeface is readable in any situation. Helvetica is also a universal web font, so whatever brand of computer the end-user may have, it will always display correctly. Its generic yet sleek feel is sought-after by companies that want to make their names last. Not limited to older established brands, Helvetica is showing up in modern

companies' logos as well—American Apparel, Crate & Barrel, Staples, Target, Evian, Skype and The North Face.

Beyond branding, Helvetica, or rather a set of Helvetica-molded lead type, has become part of the permanent collection in New York's Museum of Modern Art. It even has its own documentary, *Helvetica* by Gary Hustwit, that both praises and curses this powerful font.

When approaching a logo design, take a cue from powerful, long-established corporations and give Helvetica a try.

43

43 Love at Helvetica.

SOME LEGIBLE AND ILLEGIBLE TYPEFACES

If the perfect typeface seems elusive, try setting the company name in a classic serif, such as Garamond, or sans serif, such as Helvetica, to see which general style you prefer. Once you determine that one style works better than another, you can begin exploring similar typefaces.

Picture this: A designer creates a beautiful logo. He admires it on the screen. The typeface and color are perfect. He took great care to create beautiful ligatures and spent hours picking just the right shade of blue. The stars have aligned to allow him to create the perfect logo. The designer shrinks it down to incorporate it as part of the business card design. He magnifies the work on screen so that no detail goes overlooked. Everything looks perfect until he prints the design. He suddenly realizes that at actual size, his perfect logo isn't so perfect anymore. At the small size of the business card, the counters of the meticulously combined letterforms cannot even be seen, and the once perfect hue now is barely distinguishable from every other corporate blue. The designer just learned a hard lesson. A logo must be versatile in order to be effective (Figs. 44, 45, 46, 47). It must work well when rendered small on a business card, large on a billboard and every size in between—not to mention working across multiple media. The typeface choice must hold up well at all sizes. A serif font with very thin hairlines may visually disappear, and counters may close in if set too small. A display font may show imperfections in the design when enlarged. A sans serif font with thick strokes may look too bulky at any size. Examine a typeface closely before choosing it for a logo.

The logo's job is to communicate to an audience. Connotation plays a large role in appealing to that target. It is important to draw upon the historic, stylistic and visual associations of the typeface. Choose an appropriate typeface that speaks to the audience about the company. Draw upon the goals of the company to determine if a serif, sans serif, script, display or custom typeface is needed. A word of caution: a logo needs to extend beyond appealing only to the aesthetics of the client or designer. A designer can't risk alienating the audience because of a personal preference for a typeface.

A well-designed logo will stand the test of time. It will look as fresh ten years from now as it does today. It will withstand the comings and goings of trends; in fact, it will reject trend altogether. Nothing dates a logo faster than using the "hot new font," the "color of the year" or the "cool technique" recently added to a software package. Timelessness is a result of all the aforementioned qualities coming together in a carefully crafted logo design. Of course, only time can tell if a design is truly timeless, but a logo that works across various media, is simple yet distinctive and stays in the minds of the customers will succeed.

44

45

46

47

44, 45, 46, 47 When designing a logo, all applications must be considered to ensure good versatility of the logo.

AN INTERVIEW WITH HOLLY TIENKEN

Holly received her Bachelor of Fine Art in communication design from Kutztown University of Pennsylvania in 1997, and her Master of Fine Art in design at the School of Visual Arts in New York in 2001. She is a designer; adjunct instructor; salt-air–loving, will-do-anything-to-be-near-the-ocean woman; runner; Pilates enthusiast; business owner and entrepreneur. Holly owns a design firm, Design Grace, and is partners in a reusable bag company called Bag the Habit.

© Sara Wight Photography

Where do you find your inspiration?

Day-to-day inspiration, the thing that keeps me going, I draw from internally. I fell in love with design my sophomore year in college and at this point know no other way of life. I have a plethora of ideas; I just seem to not have the time to realize them all, or the proper outlet for them.

Creative and artistic inspiration comes from so many places. Music, magazines, *The New York Times*, boatloads of books, TED talks, gallery/museum visits and, last but not least, my community. I am in constant awe of all the creating that goes on in this world.

More and more I seem to be looking away from current design trends and sinking more into the history. Items created with a solid concept and a simple, elegant execution. That is inspiring design. Vintage Penguin covers inspire me; new Photoshop filters, not so much. They both have their place in this world! One is just more appealing to me than the other.

Specific project inspiration comes from the client and what it is they are inspired by for their business/project. Kickoff/new project brief meetings are my favorite moments! When possible, I prefer to meet face to face with a client for a kickoff meeting. It is important to establish that eye contact, to get a solid grasp on their intent and emotions behind a campaign, brand or product. Clients come to me to help them graphically interpret their idea. I just try to keep that feeling in the forefront when I'm doing the work. It isn't about me—it is about me helping them realize their vision. I have been so fortunate because the majority of my clients are conscientious, inspiring people and businesses built with good intentions. It is always a more enjoyable project when there is a mutual, genuine respect for one another.

How do you overcome creative blocks?

If I do have the time to step away, that is the best option. Either move onto a different project for a day or I will go for a long run or walk along the waterfront. Fresh air and nature help me center and also invigorate me. Also, just *try* to take my mind off of the problem, do something completely unrelated to design or the project.

If time is not on my side, which it generally isn't, I will pick up a book (one of my favorites is *Robert Rauschenberg: Combines*) or old issue of *Colors* magazine. Fashion magazines are helpful too, even if for color and patterns. Anything that has *nothing* to do with what I am designing. I generally don't look at design books when I am in the middle of a struggle. It makes matters worse and stresses me out even more for not coming up with a solution.

Sometimes these exercises help, and then sometimes they don't. There have been moments when I was metaphorically on my hands and knees praying for genius to strike like lightning. My experience has shown me to just be with it. Deadlines are deadlines. There certainly have been times when I have been up all night and have sent things to a client that I wasn't 100 percent thrilled with or I know was not my best work. But it had to get done; that is just part of the business. You can't always have an "on" day. And well, if creativity strikes at 2 A.M., then I am right there with it.

Who are your influences?

I am more influenced by the early pioneers than current designers … Bradbury Thompson, Charles and Ray Eames, Alvin Lustig, Terence Conran. Designers that were multidisciplinary. The term *multidisciplinary* now seems to equate to designers who are versed in web and print. But I am more interested and intrigued by designers who work in many mediums. Textiles, architecture, furniture, interiors, graphics, product. Designers who work both 2-D and 3-D. I would say modern-day versions of those creators would be Bruce Mau, John Meada, Tibor and Maira Kalman. Not just designers, they are creators.

What advice do you have for a young designer struggling with creating a successful logo design?

Sketch, sketch, sketch with a pencil and paper! Sketching on the computer can be the biggest waste of time. I have done it, and I have regretted it. Even if it is just for shape and balance, scale of your type versus your icon if there is going to be one—paper and pencil will save you hours of time on the computer. Even loose sketches, I know after a few pages what I am trying to achieve. When working on larger branding projects that involve more than designing a logo, I start by creating a mood board—it could be digitally or a board that I am pasting things to or placing in my sketchbook. I pull images from magazines, books, random packaging examples, texture and type I find inspiring for the brand/logo I am working on. It helps to create the story.

My overall advice … design can be a struggle, but it doesn't always have to be. That was a lesson that took a bit to sink in for me. Just because something takes a long time to create and there possibly was blood, sweat and tears involved doesn't mean it is successful. I have tried explaining that to some students. I have heard things such as "I spent ten hours on that." My response is, Well, great! Hard work always pays off! And if the ten hours of work on one not very successful design led you to the next solution, which is better, that took thirty minutes, then just go with it and be happy you finally got there. Enjoy the process of creating. It is a glorious gift to have."

What is your process for creating a new logo? What tools do you use?

After sketching and deciding on concepts and then looking for fonts, I do all of my logo work in Adobe Illustrator. I have never designed a logo in Photoshop, nor in InDesign. That is equivalent to sitting in a chair with wobbly legs—you can do it but it certainly isn't sustainable or efficient use of energy.

After sketching and concepts are done, I will use FontBook or Suitcase and start paging through looking for complementary type. I generally have a good idea what I am looking for (I need tall ascenders or a short x-height or a slab serif). This process is similar to being a curator for a gallery. There are plenty of options that will fit, but the goal is to find the shining star.

Sometimes, it is the study of one specific letter that has importance in the logo design. For instance, I was working on a logo for a hotel project in Philadelphia.. I spent hours just studying *H*s and *F*s. For another hotel I was studying *V*s (Figs. 48, 49, 50). I will get the selected letters, or even words typed out in the selected typeface, all onto one page and then study them again, and narrow down, or begin to make a hybrid of letters.

I am a purist. I believe that if a logo does not work in black and white, it will never be a successful logo. When presenting a new logo design to a client, the first two rounds at the very least are always in black and white. Once we decide upon a more specific direction, then I will show color options. Color enhances a logo design, but it should never define it. Color can define a brand, but not a logo.

What has been your most challenging (or rewarding) logo design to date? Why?

The logo I am most proud of unfortunately has not seen the light of day to the general public. I was working as a consultant with Mark Zeff Design. The project was a property development called Vision City (Figs. 51, 52). The first phase was a complete branding package that would introduce the Vision City concept to prospective investors—from architectural plans and elevations, renderings of interior design for the hotel and restaurants, retail settings, transportation concepts, entertainment venues …

It took a team of about fifteen incredibly talented people in various design disciplines to put this phase of the project together. It was an honor to work with them all.

What strategies do you employ to create a one-of-a-kind logo for a client? What influence does the typography play in the logo creation?

One question I always make sure to ask a client, if they haven't indicated what they are looking for, is to tell me what they are *not* looking for. Often the "not" is considerably more helpful.

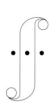

Script and Display Type	San Serif	Classics + Serif

48 Falcon Hotel logo comps. Fonts used: Perla, Bauer Bodoni, Bodoni Poster, Bickham Script. **49, 50** Venn "V" studies.

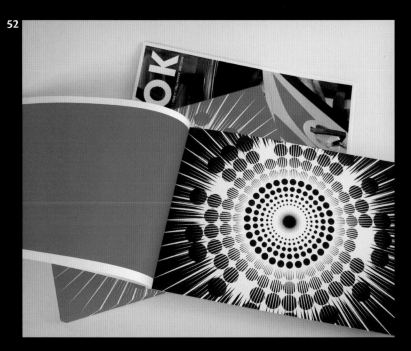

Clients can't always speak in terms of style or aesthetic feel, but they can send me images, websites or logos that they do not find appealing. From this I am able to identify if they are gravitating towards simple or fussy, dimensional or flat …

Typographically speaking, a majority of the time, I redraw letters to fit the design and to make it more original. Things like redrawing a descender to align better with other letters or exaggerating an ascender to balance the look. There is a difference between bastardizing a font and redrawing and refining a letter. You will never see me put a vertical scale on something to make it "condensed," but I may exaggerate a flourish.

How important is typography to logo design?

I think typography is at least 50 percent of the equation and is critical to the successful logo design.

In your opinion, has the plethora of fonts available online in today's digital environment affected logo design?

Yes, and no. In terms of the "free fonts," I do think it has a negative effect on design. Primarily because there is a misconception

floating around out there that if an individual has access to a number of fonts and has some layout software, then they must be a designer!

Additionally, it leads to the thought that all fonts are created equal and designed well. Sadly, free fonts generally are poorly designed and limiting when you get down to serious typesetting. The difference becomes so obvious as designers get more into the finite details of type—and what is a well-designed face and what isn't. They may serve their purpose for small bits of type, but on a large scale I see free fonts as detrimental to our industry. I also feel that when things are free and easy it devalues the art and creation of what we do. What tends to happen now is when I suggest to a client we need to allocate some budget to purchasing fonts, there have been a few cases where they said, "Well, why can't we just get them for free online?" At which point I count to ten and take a deep breath before I respond.

What I do love about the digital environment is, when I do need new fonts, being able to purchase them and download them easily and immediately. I also subscribe to a few typography newsletters and blogs and love when a new face is introduced.

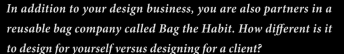

In addition to your design business, you are also partners in a reusable bag company called Bag the Habit. How different is it to design for yourself versus designing for a client?

It is far, far, far more difficult to be the client and the designer than I ever thought it would be! Like many designers, I have a certain aesthetic. The struggle comes in a few forms. Primarily, the ability to step back from it all and make business decisions versus person decisions. Just because I am the designer does not mean I am always going to be the target demographic! The design (whether it be industrial or graphic or informational) is serving a large population, not just what Holly Tienken would like to see out in the world. *But*, that said, Bag the Habit doesn't follow trend

forecasts. We certainly look at them, but they don't dictate what we are creating for our product lines.

The logo development was a bit of a process, to say the least (Figs. 53, 54, 55). When I was sketching and coming up with initial concepts, what kept coming up for me was the link between consumerism and the environment. The first round of designs was extremely fussy—they look more like illustrations instead of icons or logos. The concept was strong but the execution was overdone, more appropriate for a T-shirt graphic. Then, it was like that strike of lightning hit! I was looking at a leaf photograph and somehow made the visual connection of the silhouette of the leaf and the silhouette of a city skyline. And the Bag the Habit logo was born.

Liz Long (my business partner) and I put a lot of love into everything we create. We labor over details, words and colors to the point where others would think we are nuts. But we love it, and we believe this is what sets us apart—our relentless attention to detail. Every little word, typeface selection, color palette, material is a reflection of the company and of us, and we approach all of our communications as if they could possibly be the first introduction a consumer has with our brand, so it is important everything is perfect as it can possibly be.

In your opinion, what separates a good logo designer from a great logo designer?

The ability to create logos in a variety of styles. Not get stuck, locked in or too comfortable in one look. Diversification is important in many areas of life.

What is one of your biggest logo-related pet peeves?

Over-application of filters, shadows, 3-D things, metallic effects …

TYPE TIDBITS

Serif or Sans serif?
Sans … no serif … no sans … OK. Serif—final answer.

Favorite letter?
Lowercase *g*. Lowercase *e* is runner-up.

Guilty pleasure font?
A super duper voluminous script with loads of glyphs and alternates.

Helvetica or Futura?
Helvetica.

Favorite complementary font pair?
Mrs. Eaves and Trade Gothic.

Pen and paper or Wacom tablet?
Pen and paper, then onto Wacom.

Mac or PC?
Mac. I break out in hives when I am on a PC.

Uppercase or lowercase?
Lower.

Design: Lifestyle or just a way to earn a living?
Lifestyle.

Go shopping or create design?
Design. Close second is shopping for books!

Classic rock or modern rock?
Hmm. Neither! Right now I am into Yo-Yo Ma.

WORD GALLERY

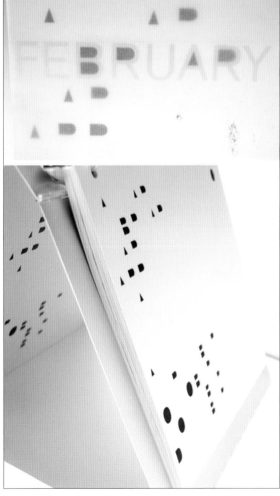

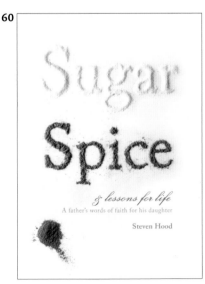

56 2011 Ladies of Letterpress conference logo. **57** Thanks mailer. **58** Counterforms calendar. **59** *KillerBlind*, by Jack Bunds, book cover. **60** *Sugar, Spice & Lessons for Life*, by Steven Hood, book cover.

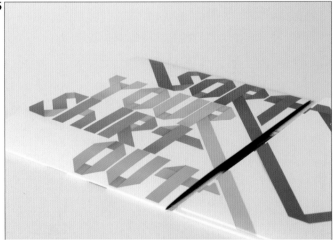

61 FuduMudu logo. **62** Luliboo logo. **63** Albany Center for Art and Design poster. **64** Faerstain logo. **65** End Hunger. **66** AS Colour Catologue and Tee Shirt Folding.

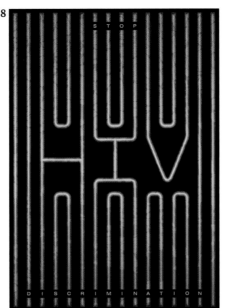

67 Express Yourself With Handwriting poster. **68** HIV Cage poster. **69** Boutique shopping bag design. **70** Don Camaleone logo. **71** Hopewell Valley Bulldogs logo.
72 A&W Sweets & Treats. **73** Audience logo.

74 Dirty Leaves Band logo. **75** Penarious poster. **76** Hate poster. **77** Nice Agency branding. **78** Millian logo. **79** Manuel logo. **80** Tango.

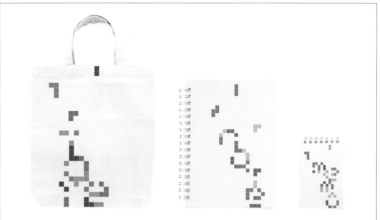

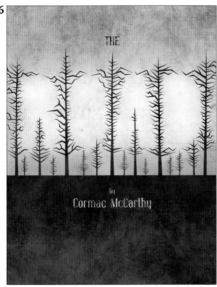

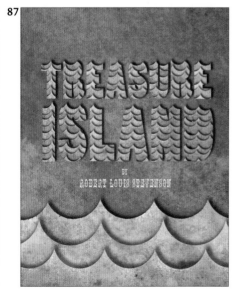

81 Winter Wonderland greeting card. **82** Tetris. **83** Conin identity. **84** Peanut Chews packaging. **85** *Of Mice and Men*, by John Steinbeck, book cover. **86** *The Road*, by Cormac McCarthy, book cover. **87** *Treasure Island*, by Robert Louis Stevenson, book cover.

88 Gangster Clothing 02. **89** Robada EVE Wine brand development. **90** Wordplay. **91** William Fitzsimmons — Tour 2008 poster.

ABOUT THE IMAGES IN THIS CHAPTER

Fig. 6
TITLE: University of Brighton Undergraduate Degree Show 2010
SCHOOL: University of Brighton
DESIGNER: Sara Loiperdinger
FONT USED: Bodoni
CLIENT: University of Brighton

Fig. 7
TITLE: The Nuthouse logo
SCHOOL: Kutztown University
PROFESSOR: Kate Clair
DESIGNER: Jenna Palermo
FONT USED: Hand lettering

Fig. 36
TITLE: Vipiteno Gelato & Caffé
DESIGN FIRM: Morandini Design Ltda
ART DIRECTOR: Adolfo Morandini Neto
DESIGNERS: Adolfo Morandini Neto
FONT USED: Morandini Alegro / Agenda
CLIENT: Vipiteno

Fig. 37
TITLE: *Arsenic & Old Lace*
DESIGN FIRM: Denise Bosler LLC
ART DIRECTOR: Denise Bosler
FONT USED: Hand lettering
CLIENT: Harrisburg Theatre

Fig. 38
TITLE: APOTHEEK Kids
DESIGN FIRM: GVA Studio
DESIGNER: GVA Studio
FONT USED: Hand lettering
CLIENT: Self

Fig. 39
TITLE: St. Johns Window Project identity
DESIGN FIRM: Jeff Fisher LogoMotives
DESIGNER: Jeff Fisher
FONT USED: Circus Dog
CLIENT: St. Johns Window Project

Fig. 40
TITLE: Fresh Cutt logo
DESIGN FIRM: AkarStudios
ART DIRECTOR: Sat Garg
DESIGNERS: Sean W. Morris
FONT USED: Eurostile
CLIENT: Fresh Cutt

Fig. 41
TITLE: AMRES logo
DESIGN FIRM: www.kostam.com
ART DIRECTOR: Kosta Mijic
FONT USED: ZeroThrees
CLIENT: AMRES

Fig. 42
TITLE: Hope logo
DESIGNER: Steven Busuttil

FONT USED: Hand lettering
CLIENT: Hope

Fig. 43
TITLE: Love at Helvetica
SCHOOL: Illinois Institute of Art in Schaumburg
DESIGNERS: Kris Sanchez
FONT USED: Helvetica

Fig. 44
TITLE: Peace, Love + Desserts logo
DESIGN FIRM: Mixon Design
ART DIRECTOR: Jamie Burwell Mixon
FONT USED: Hand lettering
CLIENT: Peace, Love & Desserts

Figs. 48, 49, 50, 51, 52, 53, 54, 55
Designed by Holly Tienken

Fig. 56
TITLE: 2011 Ladies of Letterpress conference logo
DESIGN FIRM: Komprehensive Design
DESIGNER: Jeanne Komp
FONTS USED: Balduina Real OT, Futura Medium Condensed
CLIENT: Ladies of Letterpress

Fig. 57
TITLE: Thanks mailer
DESIGN FIRM: Keystone Resources
ART DIRECTOR: April Guzik
DESIGNER: Judith Uzcategui
TYPE DESIGNER: Judith Uzcategui
FONTS USED: Hand lettering, Nothing You Can Say
CLIENT: Keystone Resources

Fig. 58
TITLE: Counterforms calendar
SCHOOL: Rhode Island School of Design
PROFESSOR: Akefeh Nurosi
DESIGNER: Adam Lucas
FONT USED: Akzidenz-Grotesk

Fig. 59
TITLE: *KillerBlind*, by Jack Bunds, book cover
DESIGN FIRM: Tate Publishing
ART DIRECTOR: Melanie Hughes
DESIGNER: Leah Leflore
FONT USED: Univers 63 Bold Extended
CLIENT: Tate Publishing, Jack Bunds

Fig. 60
TITLE: *Sugar, Spice & Lessons for Life*, by Steven Hood, book cover
DESIGN FIRM: Tate Publishing
ART DIRECTOR: Melanie Hughes
DESIGNER: Leah Leflore

FONTS USED: Adobe Caslon, Exmouth
CLIENT: Tate Publishing, Steven Hood

Fig. 61
TITLE: FuduMudu logo
DESIGNER: Burcu B. Koken
FONT USED: Hand lettering
CLIENT: FuduMudu

Fig. 62
TITLE: Luliboo logo
DESIGN FIRM: Morandini Design Ltda
DESIGNER: Adolfo Morandini Neto
FONT USED: Hand lettering
CLIENT: Luliboo

Fig. 63
TITLE: Albany Center for Art and Design poster
DESIGN FIRM: The College of Saint Rose Office of Creative Services and Marketing
ART DIRECTOR: Mark Hamilton
DESIGNER: Chris Parody
FONTS USED: Battery Park, Bauer Bodoni, Bellevue, Anna, Bauhaus 93, Sketch Block, Americantypewriter Medium, Marcelle Scrip
CLIENT: The College of Saint Rose Center for Art & Design

Fig. 64
TITLE: Faerstain logo
DESIGN FIRM: faerstain.dk
DESIGNER: Simon Faerstain
FONT USED: Hand lettering
CLIENT: Self

Fig. 65
TITLE: End Hunger
DESIGN FIRM: Taber Calderon Graphic Design
DESIGNER: Taber Calderon
FONT USED: Hand lettering
CLIENT: Graphic Responses

Fig. 66
TITLE: AS Colour Catologue and Tee Shirt Folding
DESIGN FIRM: DDB New Zealand LTD
ART DIRECTOR: Dave Brady, James Tucker
DESIGNER: Cliff Li
TYPE DESIGNER: Cliff Li
FONTS USED: Hand lettering, Avenir
CLIENT: AS Colour

Fig. 67
TITLE: Express Yourself With Handwriting poster
SCHOOL: School of the Art Institute of Chicago

PROFESSOR: David Philmlee
DESIGNER: Han Na Jung
FONT USED: Hand lettering

Fig. 68
TITLE: HIV Cage poster
DESIGN FIRM: Zvonimir Cacic
DESIGNER: Zvonimir Cacic
FONTS USED: Hand lettering, Helvetica Neue LT Pro (63 Medium Extended)
CLIENT: Good 50x70

Fig. 69
TITLE: Boutique shopping bag design
DESIGN FIRM: STORYTELLERS
DESIGNER: J.J. Vargas
FONT USED: Pacmania Normal
CLIENT: Boutique Clément

Fig. 70
TITLE: Don Camaleone logo
DESIGN FIRM: Morandini Design Ltda
DESIGNER: Adolfo Morandini Neto
FONT USED: Hand lettering
CLIENT: Don Camaleone

Fig. 71
TITLE: Hopewell Valley Bulldogs logo
DESIGNER: James Lebbad
FONTS USED: Hand lettering, ITC Goudy Sans
CLIENT: Hopewell Valley Central High School

Fig. 72
TITLE: A&W Sweets & Treats
DESIGN FIRM: Sub Zero Design
ART DIRECTOR: Bill Leissring
DESIGNER: James Lebbad
FONT USED: Hand lettering
CLIENT: A&W

Fig. 73
TITLE: Audience logo
DESIGN FIRM: Steve DeCusatis Design
DESIGNER: Steve DeCusatis
FONT USED: Customized
CLIENT: Flannel

Fig. 74
TITLE: Dirty Leaves Band logo
DESIGN FIRM: Studio Harringman
DESIGNER: James Harringman
FONT USED: Hand lettering
CLIENT: Dirty Leaves

Fig. 75
TITLE: Penarious poster
DESIGN FIRM: m2r
DESIGNER: Melanie M. Rodgers

FONTS USED: Helvetica inspired
hand lettering, Clarendon
CLIENT: York College of PA

Fig. 76
TITLE: Hate poster
DESIGN FIRM: Beto Janz
DESIGNER: Beto Janz
FONT USED: Hand lettering

Fig. 77
TITLE: Nice Agency branding
DESIGN FIRM: Socio Design
ART DIRECTOR: Nigel Bates
DESIGNERS: James Cramp,
Nigel Bates
FONT USED: Clarendon
CLIENT: Nice Agency

Fig. 78
TITLE: Millian logo
DESIGN FIRM: Felipe Soares
DESIGNER: Felipe Soares
FONT USED: Hand lettering
CLIENT: Millian Hotel

Fig. 79
TITLE: Manuel logo
DESIGN FIRM: onetreeink
DESIGNER: Marcos Calamato
FONT USED: Hand lettering
CLIENT: Manuel

Fig. 80
TITLE: Tango
DESIGN FIRM: Brand Paradise
DESIGNER: Dennis Silverberger
FONT USED: BodoniXT
CLIENT: Finnish Tango Competion

Fig. 81
TITLE: Winter Wonderland
greeting card
DESIGN FIRM: Fill the Page
DESIGNER: Kate Bosco
FONT USED: Avenir
CLIENT: Self

Fig. 82
TITLE: Tetris
DESIGN FIRM: Fashion Institute
of Technology
PROFESSOR: Haggai Shamir
DESIGNER: Norika Kato
FONT USED: Hand lettering

Fig. 83
TITLE: Conin identity
DESIGN FIRM: TOOCO
DESIGNER: Francisco Miranda
FONT USED: Hand lettering
CLIENT: Conin

Fig. 84
TITLE: Peanut Chews packaging
DESIGN FIRM: The Bailey Group

ART DIRECTORS: Dave Fiedler,
Steve Perry
DESIGNER: Denise Bosler
FONTS USED: Hand lettering, Bell Gothic
CLIENT: Goldenberg Candy Company

Fig. 85
TITLE: *Of Mice and Men*, by John
Steinbeck, book cover
SCHOOL: Art Institute of Pittsburgh
PROFESSOR: Shawn O'Mara
DESIGNER: Mitchell MacNaughton
FONT USED: Lemon Chicken

Fig. 86
TITLE: *The Road*, by Cormac
McCarthy, book cover
SCHOOL: Art Institute of Pittsburgh
PROFESSOR: Shawn O'Mara
DESIGNER: Mitchell MacNaughton
FONT USED: Covington

Fig. 87
TITLE: *Treasure Island*, by Robert
Louis Stevenson, book cover
SCHOOL: Art Institute of Pittsburgh
PROFESSOR: Shawn O'Mara
DESIGNER: Mitchell MacNaughton
FONT USED: Panhead

Fig. 88
TITLE: Gangster Clothing 02
DESIGN FIRM: Art61

DESIGNER: Rubens Ribeiro
FONT USED: LHF Esoteric
CLIENT: Gangster

Fig. 89
TITLE: Robada EVE Wine
brand development
DESIGN FIRM: STORYTELLERS
DESIGNER: J.J. Vargas
FONT USED: Custom Deco Fonts
CLIENT: Robada Winery

Fig. 90
TITLE: Wordplay
DESIGN FIRM: d'Emil
DESIGNER: Emil Holtoug
FONT USED: Hand lettering

Fig. 91
TITLE: William Fitzsimmons —
Tour 2008 poster
DESIGN FIRM: Zwölf, Berlin
DESIGNERS: Stefan Guzy, Björn Wiede
FONT USED: Hand lettering
CLIENT: 2fortheroad Booking Agency

chapter four

{ SENTENCE }

Letters form words and words come together to form sentences, which are the primary means of communication in the modern world. They are how thoughts, ideas and messages are communicated on a daily basis. It is the job of the designer to make sure those messages come through loud and clear. As with letters and words, the right relationship between elements in a sentence is essential to ensuring good communication. Sentences have great impact on our lives. They convince us, inform us, declare to us, question us, exclaim to us and tell us what to do. Sentences can be simple or complex, but in all cases the typography must reflect what is being said.

Say you are called upon to design a billboard demanding that a viewer buy a particular product because it is the *best*. Then the typography needs to have a commanding feel. Soft, sweet scripts do not demand. A bold, powerful typeface is necessary for the connotation to be understood. A Sans Serif or Serif typeface can easily do the job. Certain Display typefaces could also work; however, the one you choose would need to be readable and devoid of excessive swashes and other decoration. At the other extreme, a billboard that informs a viewer about an upcoming bridal expo will insist upon an entirely different connotation and entirely different typeface. Evoking the right reaction is the key for presenting work to the public. Advertising, posters, T-shirts, business cards,

web banners and other persuasion-based forms of communication require excellent legibility and typographic design. From the choice of typeface to the alignment on the page to the space around the letters, every aspect of the sentence must be carefully considered.

WORD SPACING

The spacing between individual words influences the readability of a line of type. When spacing is too tight, the words jumble together, turning the sentence into one long, ongoing word, as opposed to individual words forming a sentence (Fig. 1). When word spacing is too loose, the result is a series of halting, staccato gaps within the sentence, causing the viewer to see fractured words instead of a complete sentence. The proper space between words is generally defined as the space a lowercase *i* would take up in between each word (Fig. 2). This guideline helps to create the right rhythm within the text, allowing the viewer's eye to move smoothly over the sentence and distinguish individual words. Not all fonts are designed with proper word spacing. It is up to the designer to choose a font that spaces well, or to manually adjust the gaps that appear. Use the same methodologies used for kerning to fix these gaps.

If several sentences with loose word spacing occur across multiple lines or a paragraph of text, one may see a phenomenon

BAD

Thisisourhope.ThisisthefaithwithwhichIreturntotheSouth. Withthisfaithwewillbeabletohewoutofthemountainof despairastoneofhope.Withthisfaithwewillbeableto transformthejanglingdiscordsofournationintoabeautiful symphonyofbrotherhood.

–MartinLutherKingJr.

GOOD

This is our hope. This is the faith with which I return to the South. With this faith we will be able to hew out of the mountain of despair a stone of hope. With this faith we will be able to transform the jangling discords of our nation into a beautiful symphony of brotherhood.

–Martin Luther King Jr.

This is our hope. This is the faith with which I return to the South. With this faith we will be able to hew out of the mountain of despair a stone of hope. With this faith we will be able to transform the jangling discords of our nation into a beautiful symphony of brotherhood. With this faith we will be able to work together, to pray together, to struggle together, to go to jail together, to stand up for freedom together, knowing that we will be free one day.

–Martin Luther King Jr.

known as *rivers*. Rivers, white spaces that run vertically through the text, create spaces that distract the viewer and lead the eye down instead of across the text, interfering with readability (Fig. 3). Rivers must always be eliminated to minimize distracting the reader from the message. Factors that increase the occurrence of rivers include narrow columns of type, too-large typeface size and justified alignment. An easy way to check for rivers is to turn the page upside down. This way you can focus more easily on spacing rather than on what the words say.

LEADING

The horizontal white space between lines of text also influences its readability. This space, called *leading* (pronounced *ledding*), changes the texture of sentences on the page. As with tracking,

legibility issues result if the leading is either too tight or close, or too loose or wide.

Visually comfortable leading is key to any design that contains blocks of text. The correct distance between lines helps the reader's eye navigate a sentence from the end of one line to the beginning of the next. If the lines are too close together, a reader may come back to the same line twice. If the lines are too far apart, the reader may lose his place on the page and have to search for the correct line to continue reading.

The length of a font's ascenders, descenders and x-height influence the leading. Fonts with tall ascenders and descenders need more leading to prevent descenders in one line from touching the ascenders of the line below. When characters meet between lines of type, they act as barriers, which prevent the eye from reading across the page. Type is read by following the contour of the tops of the

1, 2 Word spacing is often overlooked when setting type. As with kerning, proper word spacing must be built into a font by the type designer. Word spacing that is too tight or too loose will cause readability issues. **3** Rivers are an eyesore, literally. They distract from the natural flow of a sentence and interfere with readability.

letters. Interfering with this flow hurts readability. Fonts with large x-heights also need additional leading, as the letters create fuller lines of text that need more room to breathe (Fig. 4). Scripts and display fonts also require looser leading because the extra swashes and decorative detail can interfere with letters on lines above and below, making them harder to read (Fig. 5). Some of these fonts require extreme leading, though fonts with smaller x-heights and shorter ascenders and descenders can afford closer leading (Fig. 6).

There is no exact formula for perfect leading. Determining the correct spacing comes with experience. Examine the typeface closely and try a variety of leading distance to see what feels comfortable and maintains maximum readability.

4

This is loose leading. It works best with fonts that have a tall x-height with longer ascenders and descenders. Condensed type also reads better with looser leading.

6

This is tight leading. It works best with fonts that have a smaller x-height with shorter ascenders and descenders.

5

Looser leading also is best for script and display fonts because the extra swashes and type detailing can interfere with letters from one line to the next.

LEADING FORMULA

As a general rule, computer software has a default leading formula for text: the height of the font plus 20 percent. So, if you are using 10-point type, the default leading is 12 points (10-point type × 20% = 2 + 10-point type becomes 12-point leading). Personally, I tend to find the default leading too close for many fonts, and I make it a rule of thumb to add a point or two to the leading. There are always exceptions, however, but for most situations, adding a little extra leading will make the text more readable.

4, 5, 6 Because a computer program can apply default leading is no excuse for ignoring an important type issue. Adjusting the leading to complement the style of font being used shows a good eye for detail and concern for the best possible readability.

ALIGNMENT

Alignment of text on the page is also important for readability. *Alignment* refers to the way rows of text line up on the page. Alignment can be left-aligned, right-aligned, center-aligned and justified. Of these, left-aligned and justified are the most common.

Left-aligned text means that the type lines up along the left-hand side of the block of text, leaving the right edge of the text block with a ragged look (Fig. 7). Because our culture reads left to right, left alignment allows the eye to easily find the beginning of a line. Assuming good leading, word spacing and font choice, left-aligned is the most readable alignment. This makes it a clear

choice when there are large amounts of text on a page. Please note, however, that the amount of raggedness on the right side is also important. Slight to moderate rag allows the text to flow evenly (Fig. 8). Extreme rag can actually break the flow, making it more difficult to read (Fig. 9). Awkward breaks between related words in the sentences also make for halting and choppy readability. Sentences should read as if you are speaking them. This is especially true in headlines. If lines break in the wrong places, the sentence may not read as it was originally intended or it may be more difficult to understand.

Justified text lines up on both the left and right sides (Fig. 10). It gives the type a tidy, crisp, blocky feel and is preferred by many

7

Then all the beasts that walk on the ground
Danced in a circle round and round–
And all the birds that fly in the air
Flew round and round in a circle there,
And all the fish in the Jellybolee
Swum in a circle about the sea,

—Edward Lear

8

GOOD

We shall never surrender, and even if, which I do not for a moment believe, this Island or a large part of it were subjugated and starving, then our Empire beyond the seas, armed and guarded by the British Fleet, would carry on the struggle, until, in God's good time, the New World, with all its power and might, steps forth to the rescue and the liberation of the old.

–Winston Churchill

9

BAD

We shall never surrender, and even if, which I do not for a moment believe, this Island or a large part of it were subjugated and starving, then our Empire beyond the seas, armed and guarded by the British Fleet, would carry on the struggle, until, in God's good time, the New World, with all its power and might, steps forth to the rescue and the liberation of the old.

–Winston Churchill

10

First, he thought how hard the wind was blowing, and how the cold, sharp rain would be at that moment beating in his face, if he were not comfortably housed at home. Then, his mind reverted to his annual Christmas visit to his native place and dearest friends; he thought how glad they would all be to see him, and how happy it would make Rose if he could only tell her that he had found a patient at last, and hoped to have more, and to come down again, in a few months' time, and marry her, and take her home to gladden his lonely fireside, and stimulate him to fresh exertions.

–Charles Dickens, *The Black Veil*

7 Left-aligned text. **8** An example of left-aligned text with slight right rag. **9** An example of left-aligned text with extreme right rag, which needs to be corrected. **10** Justified-aligned text.

First,
he thought how hard
the wind was blowing, and
how the cold, sharp rain would be at
that moment beating in his face, if he
were not comfortably housed at home.
Then, his mind reverted to his annual Christmas visit to his native place and dearest
friends; he thought how glad they would all be
to see him, and how happy it would make Rose
if he could only tell her that he had found a
patient at last, and hoped to have more, and
to come down again, in a few months'
time, and marry her, and take her
home to gladden his lonely
fireside, and stimulate him
to fresh exertions.

–Charles Dickens, *The Black Veil*

12

Once upon a midnight dreary, while I pondered, weak and weary,
Over many a quaint and curious volume of forgotten lore,
While I nodded, nearly napping, suddenly there came a tapping,
As of some one gently rapping, rapping at my chamber door.
"Tis some visitor," I muttered, "tapping at my chamber door-
Only this, and nothing more."

-Edgar Allen Poe, *The Raven*

Once upon a midnight dreary, while I pondered, weak and weary,
Over many a quaint and curious volume of forgotten lore,
While I nodded, nearly napping, suddenly there came a tapping,
As of some one gently rapping, rapping at my chamber door.
"Tis some visitor," I muttered, "tapping at my chamber door-
Only this, and nothing more."

-Edgar Allen Poe, *The Raven*

designers. Despite its neat appearance, justified type has a tendency to form rivers. In order to align both the left and right edges of the text, extra spacing is added between words to tweak each line of type, forcibly filling the line. If several lines in a row have fewer words, the gaps between words can become quite noticeable and run the risk of forming rivers. There are several ways around this problem:

- A small amount of tracking can be added or removed from the individual lines, sentences or paragraphs.

- The width of the text can be widened or narrowed very slightly.

- The size of the type can be made larger or smaller to reflow the text.

- The column of text can be widened or narrowed.

- If possible, the text can also be edited to adjust its flow.

While justified text can cause issues in traditional column form, it works quite well when used to fill an irregular shape (Fig. 11). Because the text is forced to align on both sides, the text can easily take on many shapes, such as circles, triangles and other custom shapes.

Right-aligned and center-aligned text are used less often, but they can be appropriate in certain situations. *Right-aligned* text can be quite difficult to read for readers of Western languages. They have a hard time with text that does not align on the left,

11 Justified-aligned text fitting to a shape. **12** Right-aligned text. **13** Center-aligned text.

BAD

Arthur
Lept
Overboard

GOOD

Arthur
Lept
Overboard

because they read left to right. Right-aligned text rags on the left and aligns on the right, which makes navigating longer sentences and paragraphs from line to line more challenging (Fig. 12). For short paragraphs, poems, captions and the like, right-aligned text can work well and can add variety to a page. Right-aligned text can also allow a design to stand out among other designs, because of the less frequent use of right alignment.

Center-aligned text aligns through the center of the column, causing both the left and the right sides to rag (Fig. 13). It has readability issues similar to right-aligned text. Again, for shorter sentences and paragraphs, or poems, this alignment gives an elegant, formal look. This is why it is commonly found on wedding invitations and business cards.

Sometimes letters don't look right even after you have chosen an alignment. Optical alignment, the visual alignment of letters, can affect readability in left-aligned, right-aligned and justified text. Letters with a curve or angle can appear to be set off from letters with vertical parts (Fig. 14). Just as letters can extend above the cap height to visually appear the same height as other letters, it is sometimes necessary to move letters further left or right to make them align visually (Fig. 15). This requires the application of a negative indent. This process depends on the software program being used. In most cases, though, a negative measurement can be entered into the left indent entry field, which will cause the letters

to move past the alignment axis. In cases of right alignment, the same can be entered into the right indent entry field. Other times the letters just won't align properly no matter what measurements are entered. In this scenario, lines of text need to be separated from each other and moved manually.

LINE LENGTH

It is important to evaluate the length of a line of text when designing a page, as it affects readability. When a line is too long, readers may have trouble finding their way back to the beginning of the next line. If the line is too short, it creates choppy breaks and tires the eyes more quickly. It is important to strike a good balance. Left-aligned and justified text read best when the line length is between sixty to seventy characters (Fig. 16). Physical measurement is hard to determine because type size, kerning, tracking and word spacing all influence how much space sixty to seventy characters take up. If you need to create a longer line length, a larger font (point size, wide or extended) will improve readability. Conversely, though, you need to be careful when shortening lines, maintaining a minimum of twenty characters per line. Fewer than that and eyes need to work too hard (Fig. 17). For short line lengths, a narrow or condensed font, or one that is smaller in point size, would be more appropriate (Fig. 18). However, keep in mind that short line lengths

14 An example of poor optical alignment. The *A* and *O* appear too far in from the *L*, creating an awkward balance along the left side. **15** Good optical alignment. The *A* and *O* have been shifted to the left to visually appear even with the *L*.

We dare not forget today that we are the heirs of that first revolution.
Let the word go forth from this time and place, to friend and foe alike,
that the torch has been passed to a new generation of Americans—born
in this century, tempered by war, disciplined by a hard and bitter peace,
proud of our ancient heritage—and unwilling to witness or permit the
slow undoing of those human rights to which this Nation has always
been committed, and to which we are committed today at home and
around the world.

–John F. Kennedy

BAD

Let every nation
know, whether
it wishes us well
or ill, that we
shall pay any
price, bear any
burden, meet any
hardship, support
any friend,
oppose any foe,
in order to assure
the survival and
the success of
liberty.

–John F. Kennedy

GOOD

Let every nation know,
whether it wishes us
well or ill, that we
shall pay any price,
bear any burden, meet
any hardship, support
any friend, oppose any
foe, in order to assure
the survival and the
success of liberty.

–John F. Kennedy

in justified text can create extreme rivers and word spacing. Also remember that right-aligned and center-aligned text need short line lengths as well, due to the difficulty in reading left-ragged text.

Another method of calculating an appropriate line length is to multiply the point size of the type by two. The resulting number is the ideal length in picas, a traditional measuring system used to measure columns for print publications like newspapers. If the type size of the paragraph text is 12 points, the ideal column width is 24 picas. An inch contains 6 picas—24 picas is 4 inches, thereby making 4 inches the ideal column width for 12-point type. Of course, if the typeface being used is condensed or extended, adjustments may need to be made. This formula is not exact, but it is a good starting point when developing the layout of a design.

PUNCTUATION

Punctuation is an essential element in type. It creates pauses, inflections and separations. It asks questions and screams answers. Without punctuation, written communication would be a jumble of thoughts that all run together. A designer may wonder why he needs to be concerned with punctuation when it's the writer's job to place it in the text. There are several reasons. First, it is critical that a designer read the text that will be used in a design. The text is key to the tone of the design needed to communicate the information being presented. Second, punctuation can be a determining factor in the understanding of a sentence. Proper punctuation can take a sentence that reads, "Did the tiger eat Kate?" to "Did the tiger eat, Kate?" Tuning in to punctuation will help the designer break sentences in the correct place, catch misplaced or misused punctuation, and undo bad habits of non-designers.

SIZE MATTERS

When adding punctuation to a sentence, it's important to look at it as another piece of the puzzle in a well-tuned design. Most of the time, punctuation can be left as is. Large text, however, requires finessing punctuation so that it looks natural and unobtrusive (Fig. 19). Downsizing the punctuation in headlines, subheads and other large type takes attention away from the punctuation and gives

16 An ideal line length is one that makes the sentences comfortable to read and makes it easy to find the beginning of the next sentence. **17, 18** Short line lengths can make readability choppy. Adjust the size of the font or choose a condensed font to allow more words to fit along a short line.

19

BAD

One for the road.

20

GOOD

One for the road.

21

it back to the letters (Fig. 20). The punctuation does not need to be dramatically smaller; a reduction of a few points will do. The kerning between the last letter and the punctuation mark may also need to be adjusted.

AFTER A PERIOD

When using a typewriter, the space before and after every character is exactly the same, whether it is an *M*, *o*, *t* or a period. This is because a small metal plate is needed to hold each letter against the arm—the typewriter component that strikes the key against the ribbon and the paper, very much like the metal type used in a letterpress. This metal plate must be slightly larger and wider than the letter in order to accommodate it. Therefore, spacing around typed letters is always exactly the same, including space around the punctuation marks (Fig. 21). To adjust for the monospacing, the convention arose to add an extra space after a period in order to more easily distinguish sentences from each other. With the invention of the computer, kerning pairs are created in fonts so that the type fits together properly. For example, the space around an *M* on a computer screen is much larger than the space around

a period. Now that type is appropriately and evenly spaced, we no longer need the two spaces after a period (Figs. 22, 23). It is still an ingrained habit taught in many typing and business-based classes, though, so be sure to check the text for double spaces before you finalize any design.

QUOTES: SMART VS. PRIME

It is important to use *smart quotes* (or curly quotes) in your typography. These are quotation marks that curl or angle toward the text. These marks are specifically designed and used for quotations within text. These are often confused with *prime marks* (or dumb quotes), which denote inch and feet. Prime marks look like quotation marks, but instead of angling or curling towards the type, they are straight up and down (Figs. 24, 25). Typing prime marks can easily be avoided since most design and layout software type smart quotes when the quotation mark key is typed on the keyboard. Issues can arise, however, when importing text. Dumb quotes can be found in abundance in word processing documents and on the Web, so be sure to read through text carefully, watching for prime marks where curly quotation marks should appear, especially if

19, 20 Downsizing punctuation is sometimes necessary in headlines and other large type. By downsizing, the reader doesn't get stopped by the punctuation, rather she flows right over it to the remaining text on the page. **21** Typewriter keys.

22

BAD

When I was a child, ladies and gentlemen, I was a dreamer. I read comic books, and I was the hero of the comic book. I saw movies, and I was the hero in the movie. So every dream I ever dreamed has come true a hundred times. I learned very early in life that: 'Without a song, the day would never end; without a song, a man ain't got a friend; without a song, the road would never bend—without a song.' So I keep singing a song. Goodnight. Thank you.

–Elvis Presley

23

GOOD

When I was a child, ladies and gentlemen, I was a dreamer. I read comic books, and I was the hero of the comic book. I saw movies, and I was the hero in the movie. So every dream I ever dreamed has come true a hundred times. I learned very early in life that: 'Without a song, the day would never end; without a song, a man ain't got a friend; without a song, the road would never bend—without a song.' So I keep singing a song. Goodnight. Thank you.

–Elvis Presley

BAD

"I love Typography"

GOOD

"I love Typography"

you receive text from an outside source. If you do need to use a prime mark for an inch or foot measurement, the mark must be inserted manually.

HANGING PUNCTUATION

Optical alignment can apply to more than just letters. In left-aligned text that begins with a quotation mark, the quotation mark causes the first line to appear indented, creating poor optical alignment (Fig. 26). It is necessary to "pull" the line to the left, so that the punctuation "hangs" over the edge of the block of text (Fig. 27). In cases where the text is very large, such as a headline, this is even more important, since alignment issues are magnified with the size of the text. This can be done by inserting a negative left indent or using the automated optical alignment functions found in design software. Hanging punctuation is also necessary for quotation marks, question marks, hyphens, commas, periods

and exclamation points in justified and right-aligned text. There is debate as to whether hanging punctuation is necessary in smaller paragraph text. If the page only has one or two paragraphs, most designers choose to hang the punctuation. If the page or document has multiple paragraphs or pages of paragraphs, then most designers choose to not hang the paragraph punctuation.

SHIFTING UP AND DOWN

Non-letter characters such as @, $, #, & and other symbols are often created in conjunction with uppercase letters within a font. They extend at or below the baseline to the cap height, and when set alongside lowercase letters, appear offset in relation to the baseline (Fig. 28). Therefore, it is necessary to manually shift the characters up or down so they align optically with the lowercase letters. It is best to align them centered along the horizontal axis of the letters (Fig. 29). For instance, parentheses and brackets fall below the baseline, and

22, 23 Two spaces after a period is an old-fashioned concept stemming from the use of manual typewriters. To be current, eliminate all of the double spaces. **24** An example of prime marks. These are not proper quotation marks. They are used to indicate feet and inches. **25** An example of smart quotes. These are proper quotation marks. Smart quotes can be curled or angled but are never straight up and down like prime marks.

26

BAD

"Keep your face
to the sunshine
and you cannot
see the shadows."

–Helen Keller

27

GOOD

"Keep your face
to the sunshine
and you cannot
see the shadows."

–Helen Keller

28

BAD

Billy needed $5.75 for books
(he lost his at school).

29

GOOD

Billy needed $5.75 for books
(he lost his at school).

30

BAD

Vince Lombardi once said:
• Confidence is contagious and so is lack of
confidence, and a customer will recognize both.
• Individual commitment to a group effort—that is
what makes a team work.
• Once you learn to quit, it becomes a habit.

31

GOOD

Vince Lombardi once said:
• Confidence is contagious and so is lack of
confidence, and a customer will recognize both.
• Individual commitment to a group effort—that is
what makes a team work.
• Once you learn to quit, it becomes a habit.

32

Let's jump on the merry-go-round.

33

The play runs August 8–23.

34

Todd created the league—Jami does the marketing.

26, 27 Shifting the punctuation to hang outside of the alignment creates better visual flow through and around the text. **28, 29** Shifting non-letter characters up or down improves readability. **30, 31** Running bullets serve to help highlight the bulleted text by allowing the bullet to separate from the text rather than be hidden within it.
32 Hyphen example. **33** En dash example. **34** Em dash example.

when set beside lowercase letters, they need to shift up to form a relationship with the optical space of the lowercase letters.

BULLETS

Bullets are often used when creating a list within text to call attention to the list and separate its contents. Bullet size varies from font to font, but when used with paragraph-sized text, bullets often appear too large. As with downsizing punctuation when using large type, bullets also need to be downsized. Some designers also choose to hang their bullets outside of paragraph text. Unless other punctuation is being hung outside the text, keep the bullets aligned with the rest of the text.

If your bulleted text sentence flows onto a second line, it is necessary to create a *running bullet*. A properly set running bullet allows the text on a second line to align under the first letter on the first line, not with the bullet. Aligning with the bullet creates an optical alignment issue and causes difficulty reading the bullets as separate points (Figs. 30, 31).

DASHES

It comes as a surprise to many designers that there are three types of dashes in typography. It is very important to learn how to use them correctly. A *hyphen*, the shortest, is used for words that break at the end of a sentence and for compound words such as merry-go-round (Fig. 32) or carry-over. An *en dash* is a medium-length dash indicating a range of items or the passage of time (Fig. 33). Examples include 7–9 P.M., October–December, or listing pages 12–35. An en dash's length is equal to the width of the font's lowercase *n*, hence the name *en* being derived from the sound of the *n*. An *em dash* is the longest dash and indicates either a change of thought or emphasis (Fig. 34). As with the en dash, the em dash's length is equal to the width of the font's lowercase *m* and is named similarly. Utilized in sentences with an independent clause, it can be used in place of two commas, a colon, a semi-colon, or parentheses. Here's an example: "I design the work—he takes all the photos." Just as people use two spaces after a period as a carry-over from typewriters, people will also use two hyphens in a row to indicate an em dash. Make sure to proofread the text thoroughly and fix any misused dashes.

DESIGNING WITH SENTENCES

Sentences are the crux of communication. Sentences are how advertisers direct readers to purchase their products, how corporations communicate their philosophy, how individuals express themselves and how designers interact with clients. Sentences drive our society and the way we interact with each other. They can have one word or many words. The design and interaction of these words determine the success of the communication. As mentioned previously, connotation is extremely important to that success. Arrangement of those words is also important. Poorly arranged words can sometimes completely alter the meaning of a sentence.

HEADLINES

Advertisers rely on designers to present their product in the best possible way. This includes the type that goes along with an image. Headline design is crucial in an advertisement. The headlines are the hook that draws in a reader. Advertisements only have a fleeting moment to grab somebody's attention, whether it is in a magazine or on a billboard. It's true that a picture is worth a thousand words, but a picture in an advertisement with no typographic reference is worthless. A headline gives meaning to the image. A headline can take an uninteresting picture and make it dynamic. Or take an average concept and make it spectacular. Knowing how to design a headline can make all the difference in the success of an advertisement.

DESIGNING HEADLINES

An advertising headline should compel the reader to take action. It may be to buy a product or to request a service. In all cases, the best advice is to keep it simple. Analyze the text to determine which word or words are the most important in the headline. These are the words that require the most focus.

Alignment, size of type, choice of typeface, color and placement on the page will determine the headline's impact. Good headlines speak to the audience. The typeface must be legible and readable in order to speak clearly. Arrange the headline on the page in a way that makes the most impact. Try the headline centered at the top, centered in the middle or right-aligned at the bottom—in every possible place on the page. As you move the headline around on the page, also move the imagery around. The two must play off each other and balance well within the margins of the page. Once the ideal location is settled for the headline and imagery, begin exploring typeface choices. The typeface should connote the right kind of meaning for the advertising campaign. Remember the ad's audience. Make sure the typeface choice is legible, especially at a glance. Also explore varying sizes of type. Headlines don't always have to be large. Small type in a large area of negative space or in a contrasting color can have impact just as well. Headlines do not have to be white or black. Try yellow or red instead.

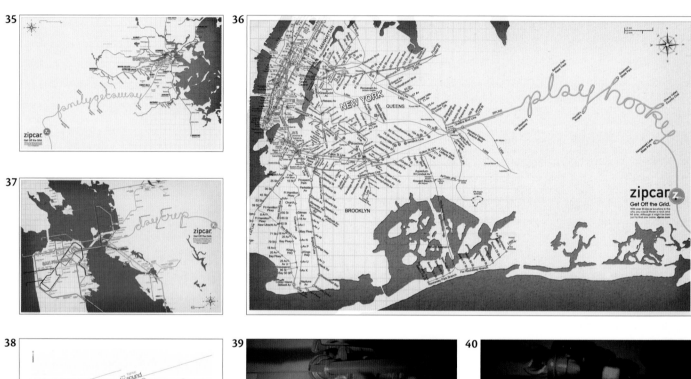

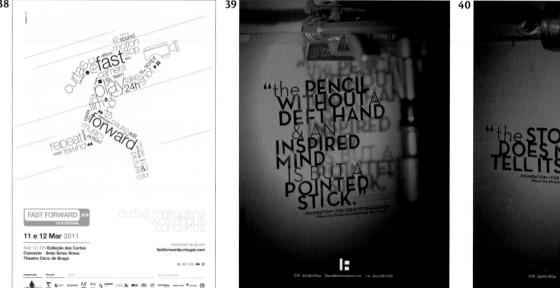

35 Zipcar—Get Off the Grid Boston! 36 Zipcar—Get Off the Grid New York! 37 Zipcar—Get Off the Grid San Francisco! 38 Fast Forward—Film Festival 2011. 39, 40 FOU promotional ads.

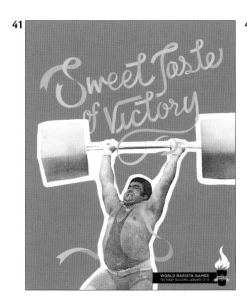

Arrangement of the words within the headline also needs consideration. The way in which a headline breaks affects readability. When setting a headline on more than two lines, read the headline out loud to make sure it makes sense. Break the headline where you would normally take a natural pause when speaking. For instance, consider where to break the headline "Political leaders kill funds for Art League." If the line breaks after "kill" then it gives the initial impression that political leaders are guilty of a capital crime instead of just withholding money. If the headline breaks after "funds" the sentence becomes easier to read and understand at a quick glance.

Punctuation in a headline is up for debate. Some designers will only apply punctuation if absolutely necessary; for example, including a question mark when asking a question. Other designers insist on applying punctuation to every single headline. Unless the headline needs a period to make the statement have more of an impact, or a question mark to indicate to the viewer that it is a question, then leave punctuation out. Punctuation halts the visual flow through the page. The type choice, arrangement and color serve to make a complete statement. If punctuation absolutely needs to be included, just remember to downsize (Figs. 35, 36, 37, 38, 39, 40, 41, 42, 43).

41, 42, 43 World Barista Games flagship poster series.

BUSINESS CARDS

There's no second chance to make a first impression, as the saying goes. In the business world, people meet and greet new potential business associates on a daily basis, and for many a business card acts as the first impression. The way the business card is arranged, how it feels to the touch and how it is typographically designed, all make a statement. Not only does the business card help introduce the business, but it also serves as a reminder for the receiver of the card, so it is important that the card capture the personality and essence of the person and the business. The challenge of designing a business card is similar to that of designing a logo. Much needs to be said in a limited space. A typical business card measures 3×2½ inches, so included text must be carefully considered. Each line of text needs to be cohesive and well balanced. Typical business cards contain the person's name, title, company name, address, phone number, web address and e-mail address. This is a significant amount of information in a very small space (Figs. 44, 45, 46, 47).

DESIGNING BUSINESS CARDS

The key to good business card design is organization. Grouping similar information keeps the card from looking chaotic. One of the most common mistakes is to fill all the open space on the card.

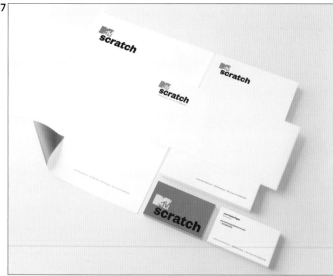

This often takes the form of information placed in each corner as well as in the center of the card. It may seem that spacing the text out around the card would make the information more accessible; in fact, it does the opposite.

Treat each line of text as a sentence. Start the business card design by dividing the text into categories: contact information, name and title, and company-specific information. Keep these categories together in your design. Use similar alignment, text size and color to maintain consistency within each category of information. This helps a viewer recognize related text.

Uniformity throughout the entire card is just as important as uniformity within each category. The best solution is to limit the number of typefaces used on a card. A font family can be used to add variety. The name can be in bold while the title is in regular weight italic. The contact information can be set in regular. This allows for differentiation between text, yet maintains consistency by using the same typeface. Alignment also helps with consistency. If the name and title are left-aligned, then the contact information should be the same.

Play with different arrangements of the text. Try setting the information in a different order. Try the name and title first followed

44 Business by Lily business card. 45 De Keukenkamer business card. 46 Weddings by Lily business card. 47 MTV Scratch Identity.

48

DESIGN COMPANY

1234 Main Street
New York NY, 10012
212.555.1234
fax 212.555.3456
www.designco.com

Carrie Weinmann
President, CEO

Carrie Weinmann
President, CEO

DESIGN COMPANY

1234 Main Street
New York NY, 10012
212.555.1234
fax 212.555.3456
www.designco.com

DESIGN COMPANY

Carrie Weinmann
President, CEO

1234 Main Street, New York NY, 10012
212.555.1234 • fax 212.555.3456
www.designco.com

Carrie Weinmann
President, CEO

DESIGN COMPANY

1234 Main Street
New York NY, 10012
212.555.1234
fax 212.555.3456
www.designco.com

Carrie Weinmann
President, CEO

DESIGN COMPANY

1234 Main Street
New York NY, 10012
212.555.1234
fax 212.555.3456
www.designco.com

Carrie Weinmann
President, CEO

DESIGN COMPANY

1234 Main Street
New York NY, 10012
212.555.1234
fax 212.555.3456
www.designco.com

49

48 The same business card information is presented in multiple layout arrangements. **49** Don't be afraid to take risks when creating business cards.

by the contact information, or the contact information first and the name and title second. Try giving priority to important information such as contact phone or e-mail. Try the web address larger than all the other information. Try holding the card vertically instead of horizontally (Fig. 48). Keep in mind the personality of the person and company when playing with different typefaces and arrangements. If a traditional business card is needed, choose a classic type such as an Old Style or Transitional typeface; arrange the information simply, using left or center alignment. If the company is more willing to take risks, be more daring with the arrangement of the information. Create interesting lockups using justified-aligned text in various sizes. Allow information to run to the edge of the card; use the other side of the card; create a card with a custom fold or die cut; pick an unusual color and reverse information out of the color;

or use a custom or Display typeface (Fig. 49). The greater the card's impact on the receiver, the more memorable the giver.

EXPRESSIVE TYPE

All work and no play makes Janie a dull girl. The same goes for typography. Typography doesn't always have to be about the perfect headline or the best logo. It doesn't always have to be about kerning and tracking and all of the other nuances that go along with using letters. It can be about art and expression. Just like paint, letters can be an artistic medium. The Dadaists of the early 1900s created amazing forms of demonstrative communication using typography. Designers and artists of today also take advantage of this accessible medium. It can be seen on the Web, in museums, worn as jewelry, on park sculptures and in mainstream publications.

50
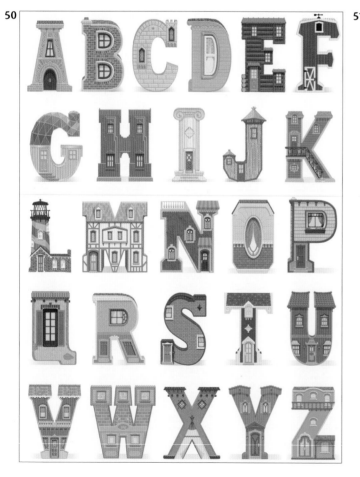

51

50 AbcVille typeface. **51** Knit alphabet.

TYPEFACES AS ART

The most visible form of expressive typography is typeface design. Display and Decorative typefaces are often very imaginative. Custom typography created for logos, book covers, album covers and advertisements also fall within the realm of artistic expression. They can take on an illustrative quality that breaks away from typography in the traditional sense. The process a designer uses to create these pieces is not unlike that of a fine artist. The letters, words and sentences become the form—still life, landscape, etc. Light, shadow, color complements, spatial relations, balance, composition and format are all considered. Fine art media are also used. Many custom typographers still use brushes, ink and other traditional media to create letterforms (Figs. 51, 52, 53, 54).

USING TYPE TO CREATE ART

Designers are immersed in typography every day. Think about how you as a designer use typography. Think about the typefaces you think are beautiful or funky or cool. Bring your thoughts and feelings about typography into an artistic expression. Consider breaking away from the computer and doing something by hand. If the idea of venturing into fine art seems scary, consider that decorative initials, monograms and even Display and Decorative typefaces are all very artistic. Creating hand-drawn type for a design is also art. Book covers and posters are the two most common places to find type like this. Many design firms and font houses market their own art in the form of T-shirts, doorstops, pillows, tote bags, wall décor and various other typography-based projects. Some designers construct typographic self-portraits.

Creating expressive type or type in artistic form doesn't have to make you venture outside your comfort zone. Examine what you enjoy outside of the graphic design world. If you love kitschy T-shirts, then try making one of your own. Come up with a funny quote or create a fun new saying and promote it as a cool catchphrase (Fig. 54). There are many ways to have your own custom designs printed easily. If you like interior design, consider incorporating typography into the look of a room. Embroider letters on pillows; collect vintage advertisements and assemble them into a

52 Construction alphabet. **53** Urban type.

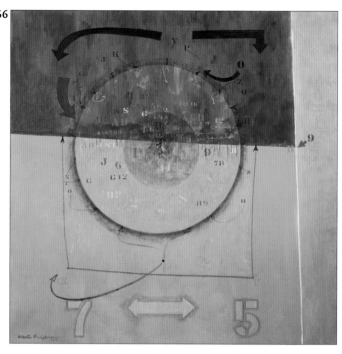

54 Say What You Mean, Mean What You Say. **55** Helvetica Cuff. **56** *Circle Chart*. **57** Don't Go.

collage; cut out letters in a rug and replace the negative space with a contrasting color rug; stencil your favorite quote onto a wall; decorate a lamp base with metal type. If you enjoy jewelry making, get old typewriter keys and make them into earrings, a necklace or a ring. Acid etch letters into a metal cuff (Fig. 55). Find someone to drill holes through metal type for you so they can be strung together into a bracelet. If you dabble with paint, bring words and sayings into your paintings (Figs. 56, 57). If you enjoy photography, create your own typeface by photographing letters found in nature. Use these letters to form inspirational words, then frame and hang them in your office or around your house. The possibilities are endless (Figs. 58, 59, 60, 61, 62).

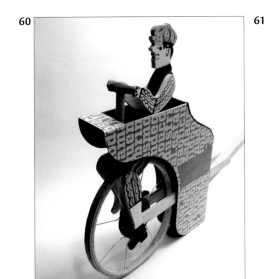

58 Calligraphicow, Harrisburg, PA. **59** Pixel blocks. **60** Ciclista. **61, 62** Letter-Box-Kite.

AN INTERVIEW WITH JESSICA HISCHE

After graduating from Tyler School of Art with a degree in graphic design, Jessica Hische worked for Head-case Design before taking a position as senior designer at Louise Fili Ltd. Spending her days learning about fancy typography with Fili, Hische continued developing her freelance career at night. After two and a half years of little sleep and a lot of lettering, she left to pursue lettering and illustration further and to try her hand at type design. Hische and her work have since been featured in many publications, she has traveled the world speaking about lettering and illustration, and she has probably consumed enough coffee to power a small nation. Hische spends most of her non-working hours at home watching *Battlestar Galactica* with her talented better half and their two kitties, or out and about consuming pork-fat-rich meals and fancy cocktails. To keep up with her day-to-day antics, you can follow her on Twitter, but be prepared for stupid cat videos and bizarro medical facts.

Among your peers in lettering design, whom do you admire and why?

I love Marian Bantjes's work. She was a huge inspiration for me when I was in college. I think what everyone admires about her work is that it looks impossible to actually do it. There are a lot of people who imitate different designers but no one has the patience that Marian has. I love Alex Trochut's work as well—his insane 3-D lettering work that is really beautiful and impressive. Seb Lester's work is always amazing. I always love everything that comes out of his studio. There are also a lot of illustrators that do excellent lettering that aren't in the type scene. I love cruising through illustration websites and seeing so many people integrating lettering into their work.

When did you discover typography as an art form, and when was it that you knew it would be your calling?

I'd probably have to reference the time in high school when I was the person who had to draw friends' names in graffiti type. I would think, "Yes. I'm the nerd that gets to be temporarily cool when asked to do artwork for the popular kids." In terms of as a career, it was later in college that I knew that I wanted to letter as a part of design work. I didn't really know that lettering existed as its own entity until after I had graduated and started incorporating it into my illustration work. The more I pushed lettering into my illustration, the more I started getting hired to do just lettering.

Where do you find your inspiration, and within that inspiration are there any influences in particular, such as people or art movements?

Working for Louise Fili was, of course, incredibly inspiring, and many of my stylistic inspirations are still in the back libraries of my brain because of my time with her. I had to work in a ton of different styles. She would put all kinds of crazy art books in front of me and I would then emulate different styles from different periods. As a young designer now, it's pretty easy to find inspirational stuff in print and online. It's important to look at what's new out there, but know that when you see some hot new designer making stuff, they are looking at older sources for inspiration—it's important to look back to historical sources sometimes rather than be the emulator of the emulator.

What would you say are the top three things you took away from working with Louise Fili?

It seems like such a no-brainer, but she never makes meetings with clients unless the work is done—she'll have an initial meeting to talk about design direction for the project, and she'll give kind of a ballpark schedule of when they will see the first round, but until the print outs are made, that meeting doesn't happen. I adhere to deadlines as much as humanly possible, but there's always that moment of panic two or three days before a deadline approaches, when I say, "Oh my God! I don't know if this is it. Maybe I should work on it longer." Then I think, "No, I'm jus them and see if we can schedule the meeting for a few days later." When there is no flexibility, I make the deadline, but if they have a bit of flexibility, it usually means that I will be happier with what I delivered and they will probably be happier with the result. Louise is also smart in that she doesn't feel the need to show the world every sketch and iteration of everything she's ever made—this allows her to be able to reuse bits of unapproved artwork for other clients, which is an amazing time saver and means that you can unearth artwork you never thought would see the light of day. It makes your future life easier because there is going to

be an instance when a client is going to need the *R* made of roses that you didn't show to the last client. If you don't blast it all over the Internet, you can reuse it.

I took a calligraphy class when I was in high school and I didn't really care about it at the time. If you're doing broad pen calligraphy it can look kind of '80s and dated because certain kinds of calligraphy were very popular during that time. (It's like how we all think that Cooper Black is a '70s font but really it was made ages ago and made popular in the '70s.) I was working on a letter *A* once and Louise asked me, "Why do you think

63 Bushwick. 64 Branding for the 2009 New to You lecture series. The type design was used on promotional materials and I letter-pressed these postcards to hand

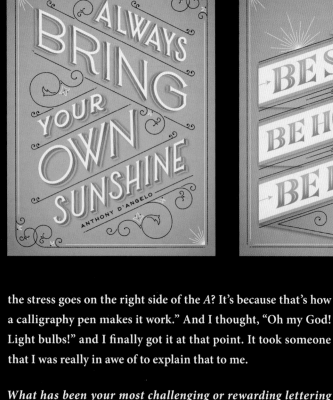

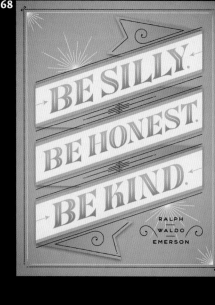

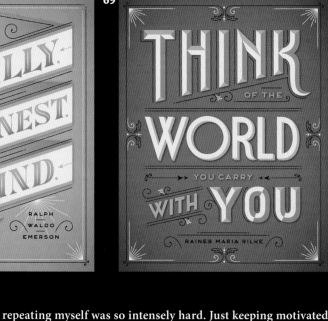

the stress goes on the right side of the *A*? It's because that's how a calligraphy pen makes it work." And I thought, "Oh my God! Light bulbs!" and I finally got it at that point. It took someone that I was really in awe of to explain that to me.

What has been your most challenging or rewarding lettering design to date?

Well, both challenging and rewarding has been the Daily Drop Cap project (dailydropcap.com). The project was to create a new drop cap every day with the final goal of twelve alphabets. I wanted a reason to experiment with type and do stuff where I'd have to mix up the styles. I was getting hired to do a lot of the same stuff—a common issue in illustration where you are hired to "play your greatest hits" over and over. I loved all that work, but I wanted to be able to mess around and do different things. I wanted to do very illustrative lettering too, which happened later in the project.

At the beginning of the project, it was easy to come up with new ways to draw the letters on the fly, but as the project reached it's eighth and ninth alphabets, I would sit at my desk in the morning and think, "I have to draw a *D* and I've already drawn ten *D*s. How am I going to make it work?" Mixing it up and not

repeating myself was so intensely hard. Just keeping motivated with the project after the seventh alphabet was really difficult. So it was a challenge of both my ability to stretch my style and try new things and my ability to stick with something. It went on for over a year and I have never done a project that long.

The biggest challenge in client work is doing something that's more in the masculine stylistic realm. There can be a snowball effect that happens once you get into any industry—if you do two or three pieces in a certain style, you just get asked over and over again to work in those styles. After working in more feminine styles for about four years, it was challenging for me to have to strip it down and make it masculine without it being too heavy handed.

How did you find the inspiration and sheer determination to continue posting on the Drop Cap project for so long?

Fortunately people were very forgiving about me not posting every day. It was hard to forgive myself the first couple of times that I lapsed a couple of days. The first five alphabets were done every day, even when I went on vacation. Then I began traveling so much, going to conferences and other events, that it became impossible to keep at it every day. I would come back and do four a day for five days in a row just so I could catch up. I began getting so burnt out catching up with the lapsed Drop Caps that the next couple of days after I caught up I'd find myself behind again. By the ninth or tenth alphabet I declared Drop Cap bankruptcy. I realized that I have other things going on. It's OK if I don't post regularly. As long as I finish the project I'll be OK with it.

How do you overcome creative blocks?

A lot of times with my lettering work, especially when I'm doing work for advertisements, I don't have to do all that much conceptualizing—it's pretty easy to not feel creatively blocked when you're just executing (if you love executing). It's easy to stay motivated, too, when you're surrounded by such amazing creative people all the time. I share a building with about fifteen of my close friends in the illustration community, and they keep me motivated and make me want to push myself. The only times that I feel very creatively blocked are when I'm overwhelmed with business tedium to take care of, which then limits the amount of time in a day that I can spend on actual work. Deadlines approach faster, and there are days that I actually can't start

making artwork until after 5 P.M. when the phone stops ringing and e-mails stop coming in. Finding the right balance between being busy but not too busy is tough.

Talk a bit about your process when approaching a lettering job.

I'm a big fan of word association lists, so my sketchbook looks like that of a crazy person. It's pages and pages of just lists. From there I'll pull the key words that are working and try to cross reference them to come up with something really fun and a bit off the wall that still works conceptually. After that, if it's a complicated layout, I'll do pretty intense pencil sketches. Once a pencil is approved by the client, I jump into Adobe Illustrator to bring it to final. I don't trace my sketches, just use them as a reference point and correct my mistakes as I translate them to the computer. Sketches are incredibly important for client work—they're a great way to flush out ideas and get the client to settle on something. I jump on the computer as soon as I can and a lot of further experimentation happens there. Type is an additive process for me, so what I'm doing on the computer isn't unlike what people are doing in sketchbooks. I'm deciding if I want it to be thick

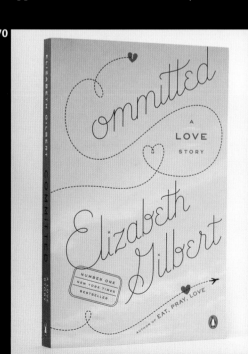

of them. Do I want it to be monoweight? Figure out the basic structure of it, and then I add all the fancy-pants stuff after that.

Do you approach creating a letter differently than how you approach a word or a phrase or a headline, or do you approach them all the same?

I approach them relatively the same. I would say that a letter might be slightly different than a word or a phrase, but I think a word or a phrase is pretty similar. When you show less, people expect more. If I'm doing just a letter, people will expect it to be more illustrative than if it's a word or a phrase.

What were the influences for the two fonts, Buttermilk and Snow-flake, that you created, and would you do it again?

I did a logo as a proposal while I was working for Louise. It needed a thick script, and I couldn't find anything I really liked online. I formulated my own and really liked it enough to turn it into a full alphabet. I had wanted to teach myself FontLab, as making fonts seemed like the natural next step in my lettering career, so I took this alphabet and made it into what is now Buttermilk. Snowflake, as it is a very decorative font that didn't need to connect in any way, was a bit easier to make. I drew the alphabet in a few days and translated it into FontLab in just under a week. It's based on a drop cap I did that looked like a cut paper snowflake. I thought about making full alphabets of some of the drop caps and, in a fit of procrastiworking, chose Snowflake to be my first experimental drop cap typeface. It was really fun to make and especially fun to see in use at the AIGA holiday party this past year.

Earlier this year I enrolled in the Cooper Union's Typeface Design certificate program. The program is a full year continu-ing ed program, and I was enrolled for the first six months. After making a revival typeface and starting a new text face, I decided that level of typeface design was not for me. It is much more akin to engineering than art at that point—you do have to have a mind for tedium because type design is so much more than the design of the alphabet. Creating the alphabet is probably only the first eighth of the work; after that you have to space it, kern it, hint it, do all of the extra characters no normal designer thinks about or will probably ever use. I'm going to stick with lettering for now.

I made a joke about it, saying that I'm still in the "fuzzy naver" stage of my career, and when I'm ready for "single malt scotch," I'll pick typeface design back up.

Do you have any advice for young designers who want to break into custom lettering or typography?

Incorporate lettering into as many projects as possible. One of the best ways to begin a career in anything is to just start mak-ing. Don't wait for clients to ask you to do it; create projects for yourself that allow you to do the work you really want to do. Don't think, "I'm going to quit my job and become a letterer." Instead think, "How can I do lettering for my job?" It makes your work so much more personal, refined and finished. If you're doing good stuff, people will start paying attention to the fact that you're doing that. Matteo Bologna gave a talk for my Cooper Union type class. He said he got into doing lettering because he needed a font for a project and was too lazy to look to find the best one. That's the way it ended up happening for me. I was too broke in college to buy good fonts, so I lettered instead. In and after college I was frustrated with how long it would take me to find a typeface that was even close to what I wanted for a project—instead I'd letter for it and be able to have more control over the end result.

How do you see custom lettering fitting into the invasion of more and more digital-based media? Do you think it's a part of the future or just a trend of the now?

I think there'll always be a reason for custom lettering. This is mostly because there's a lot of stuff that doesn't exist as fonts. Web fonts are awesome and they've got me really excited about designing for the Web, but I think there's still going to be a need for lettering, especially for things like logos where clients want to be as original as possible. You can't get the level of customization you get in lettering by using typefaces.

Do you see any trends emerging for type design, and do you think the introduction of more and more digital technologies have influence over this?

The newest trend will be making web fonts that are actually designed for the Web. You can't just retrofit anything for the

Web—it's a different environment and people treat it differently. As for type styles, it's going to be all over the map. I do love that so many people are interested in type and lettering right now. I think that's because it's super accessible compared to a lot of other art forms. You don't have to interpret it—you look at it, it says something (literally), and you decide whether or not that thing is communicated well through the style as well as the words.

72 Wrapping paper design for a bonds mailer. Jingle Bells Is Revamped to Suit the Aussie Summer Heat Near Christmas, Complete With Native Fauna in Underoos and Kangaroos on Surfboards.   73 The ADC Spring Paper Expo poster.

The only thing I hope for is that designers are aware of how the lettering industry works. I think that one of the biggest problems is that now that everything is moving digitally, there hasn't been quite enough of an outspoken movement to maintain pricing standards. Right now lettering is treated very much like illustration; it's all usage based and rights managed. Clients only have the rights to use it for a very limited amount of time and a very specific context. With clients hiring artists and designers for artwork that will be used in a digital realm only, they have very different expectations for what they should be paying, which I think is terrible. Artwork is artwork and if anything implies worldwide usage" it's the Internet.

What is your biggest lettering-related pet peeve?

There are a lot of people doing crazy swirly stuff that should not be doing crazy swirly stuff. That's not because they're infringing on my turf, it's because you don't add swirls just to add them. You add them appropriately when you need them. People should also have to apply for a license to be able to create curves on type. I see so many jerky curves on the Internet. You get x-ray vision for spotting that stuff after a while. I am more than happy to applaud anyone who is doing amazing lettering work. But when it's done terribly and everyone is golf-clapping them, I get angry about it.

TYPE TIDBITS

Serif or Sans Serif?
Serif.

Favorite letter?
K.

Favorite number/symbol?
5 •

Baskerville or Goudy?
Baskerville.

Favorite complementary font pair?
My own lettering and Sweet Sans.

Guilty pleasure font?
Alejandro Paul's fonts.

Mouse or Wacom tablet?
Mouse.

Mac or PC?
Mac.

Uppercase or lowercase?
Uppercase.

Design: Lifestyle or just a way to earn a living?
Lifestyle.

Bike or subway?
Subway in winter, bike in summer.

If you couldn't be a letterer/illustrator, what would you be/do?
Something medical or science-y.

Cats or dogs?
Cats.

SENTENCE GALLERY

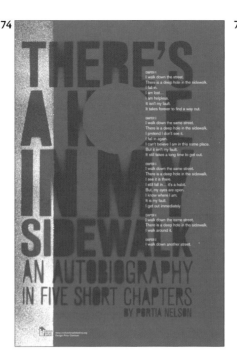

74 There's a Hole in My Sidewalk. **75** Me and You and Everyone We Know. **76** San Diego Latino Film Festival poster. **77** Rebuild. **78** *Tales Over Telephone* children's book cover. **79** Longfei postcard.

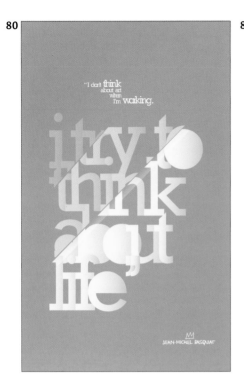

80 Jonathan Correa Art & Life poster. **81** Spike Heels poster. **82** Physique CD Release Show. **83** Whale in the Whirl. **84** Bumble in the Rumble. **85** Hawaiian destination wedding invitation suite.

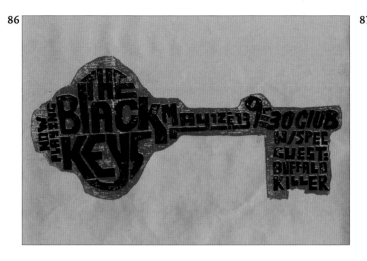

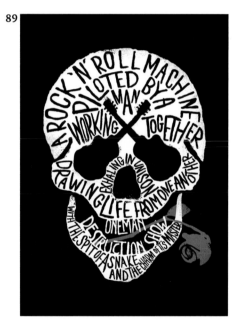

86 Black Keys poster. 87 Bad Decisions Make Great Stories. 88 Trim, Fold & Form Publicity. 89 OMDS Skull poster. 90 Atlas Copco Calendar. 91 PPO&S Holiday E-Card. 92 Emyy.

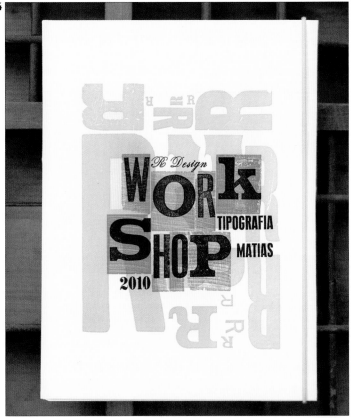

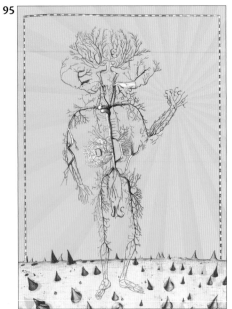

93 AIGA Get Involved. **94** R Design—Annual Student Conference. **95** Everybody Is Special. **96** I75 promo Christmas card. **97** Brèves De Trottoirs.

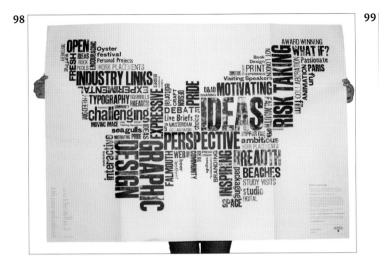

98 Butterfly poster. **99** Veseli Medvjedić/Joyful Teddy Bears. **100** Remember the Classics—Movie. **101** Postcards From Bookworms submission call poster design. **102** Time Doesn't Exist. **103** Fresh Beginnings.

ABOUT THE IMAGES IN THIS CHAPTER

Fig. 21
Typewriter keys. Photograph ©
Ilya Andriyanov

Fig. 35
TITLE: Zipcar—Get Off the Grid Boston!
UNIVERSITY: Texas A&M University—
Commerce
PROFESSORS: Brian Dunaway
& Kiran Koshy
DESIGNER: Derek Heinze
COPYWRITER: Mike Merritt
FONT USED: Hand lettering

Fig. 36
TITLE: Zipcar—Get Off the Grid
New York!
UNIVERSITY: Texas A&M University—
Commerce
PROFESSORS: Brian Dunaway
& Kiran Koshy
DESIGNER: Derek Heinze
COPYWRITER: Mike Merritt
FONT USED: Hand lettering

Fig. 37
TITLE: Zipcar—Get Off the Grid
San Francisco!
UNIVERSITY: Texas A&M University—
Commerce
PROFESSORS: Brian Dunaway
& Kiran Koshy
DESIGNER: Derek Heinze
COPYWRITER: Mike Merritt
FONT USED: Hand lettering

Fig. 38
TITLE: Fast Forward—Film Festival 2011
DESIGNER: João Loureiro
FONT USED: Helvetica Neue
CLIENT: Fast Forward Portugal

Figs. 39, 40
TITLE: FOU promotional ads
DESIGN FIRM: Cristina Martin Design
DESIGNER: Cristina Martin
PHOTOGRAPHER: Steven Piet
FONT USED: Neutra
CLIENT: Foundation Content

Figs. 41, 42, 43
TITLE: World Barista Games flagship
poster series
UNIVERSITY: Tyler School of Arts
PROFESSOR: Dustin Summers
DESIGNER: Justin Morris
FONTS USED: Hand-lettered Ribbon
Type, Gotham, Gotham Condensed

Fig. 44
TITLE: Business by Lily business card
DESIGN FIRM: Design Sense

DESIGNER: Katelijne De Muelenaere
FONT USED: Diavlo
CLIENT: Business by Lily

Fig. 45
TITLE: De Keukenkamer
business card
DESIGN FIRM: Design Sense
DESIGNER: Katelijne De Muelenaere
FONT USED: Eurostile
CLIENT: De Keukenkamer

Fig. 46
TITLE: Weddings by Lily business card
DESIGN FIRM: Design Sense
DESIGNER: Katelijne De Muelenaere
FONTS USED: Bickham Script Pro,
Bodoni Svtytwo Os Itc Tt
CLIENT: Weddings by Lily

Fig. 47
TITLE: MTV Scratch Identity
DESIGN FIRM: MTV Scratch
DESIGNER: Juan Carlos Pagan
FONT USED: Founders Grotesk
(slightly modified)
CLIENT: Self

Fig. 50
TITLE: AbcVille typeface
DESIGN FIRM: AbcVille Designs
DESIGNER: Dale Beisel
FONT USED: Custom lettering
CLIENT: www.abcville.com

Fig. 51
TITLE: Knit alphabet
DESIGN FIRM: Randi Meredith
Graphic Design & Illustration
DESIGNER: Randi Meredith
FONT USED: Hand lettering
CLIENT: Self

Fig. 52
TITLE: Construction alphabet
DESIGN FIRM: Little Utopia Design
DESIGNER: Alyssa Lang
FONT USED: Found Objects
CLIENT: Self

Fig. 53
TITLE: Urban type
DESIGN FIRM: D'emil
DESIGNER: Emil Holtoug
CLIENT: Gasværksvejen
Elementary School

Fig. 54
TITLE: Say What You Mean,
Mean What You Say
DESIGN FIRM: 55 Hi's
DESIGNER: Ross Moody

FONT USED: Buttermilk
CLIENT: Self

Fig. 55
TITLE: Helvetica Cuff
DESIGNER: Elaine Cunfer
FONT USED: Helvetica
CLIENT: Self

Fig. 56
Walter Feldman, *Circle Chart*, 1964,
oil on canvas, 48" × 48", Kutztown
University permanent art collection.

Fig. 57
TITLE: Don't Go
DESIGNER: Juan Carlos Pagan
FONT USED: Los Feliz
CLIENT: Self

Fig. 58
TITLE: Calligraphicow, Harrisburg, PA
ARTIST: Susan Leviton-Levworks
PHOTOGRAPH: Denise Bosler

Fig. 59
TITLE: Pixel blocks
DESIGNER: Ian Jamieson
FONT USED: Bit-based fonts
CLIENT: Self

Fig. 60
TITLE: Ciclista
UNIVERSITY: Esad Escola Superior De
Artes E Design, Matosinhos
PROFESSOR: João Lemos
DESIGNER: André Santos
FONT USED: Vitesse

Figs. 61, 62
TITLE: Letter-Box-Kite
CLIENT: Self Initiated
DESIGNER: Andrew Byrom
FABRICATION: Andrew Byrom,
Arian Franz
FONT USED: Letter-Box-Kite
CLIENT: Self

**Figs. 63, 64, 65, 66,
67, 68, 69, 70, 71, 72, 73**
Designed by Jessica Hische

Fig. 64
TITLE: Branding for the 2009 New
to You lecture series.
CLIENT: AIGA Philadelphia

Figs. 67, 68, 69
TITLE: Today Is the Day, lettering
and design for a day planner
ART DIRECTOR: Juanita Dharmazi
CLIENT: Galison

Fig. 70
TITLE: Paperback cover for Elizabeth
Gilbert's second novel, *Committed*
ART DIRECTOR: Paul Buckley
CLIENT: Penguin Books

Fig. 72
TITLE: Wrapping paper design
for a Bonds mailer
ART DIRECTORS: Lisa Sherry, Simon Cox
CLIENT: Bonds Underwear /
The Campaign Palace

Fig. 73
TITLE: The ADC Spring Paper
Expo poster
ART DIRECTOR: Laura Des Enfants
CLIENT: The Art Directors Club

Fig. 74
TITLE: There's a Hole in My Sidewalk
DESIGN FIRM: About Face Design
DESIGNER: Peter Camburn
FONT USED: Berthold Akzidenz Grotesk
CLIENT: Institute for Safe Families

Fig. 75
TITLE: Me and You and
Everyone We Know
UNIVERSITY: Yale University
PROFESSOR: Scott Stowell
DESIGNER: Ian Jamieson
FONT USED: Hand lettering

Fig. 76
TITLE: San Diego Latino Film
Festival poster
DESIGN FIRM: English Breakfast
DESIGNER: Matt Bonner
FONT USED: Delarge Bold
CLIENT: Media Arts Center San Diego

Fig. 77
TITLE: Rebuild
DESIGN FIRM: Sciencewerk
DESIGNER: Khendi Lee
FONT USED: Seismos
CLIENT: Red Cross Indonesia

Fig. 78
TITLE: *Tales Over Telephone*
children's book cover
UNIVERSITY: National Technical
University of Ukraine
PROFESSOR: A. Nechiporenko
DESIGNER: Olga Protasova
FONT USED: Hand lettering

Fig. 79
TITLE: Longfei postcard
DESIGN FIRM: Nanyang Polytechnic
ART DIRECTOR: Charles Lee

DESIGNER: Longfei Zhang
CLIENT: Self

Fig. 80
TITLE: Jonathan Correa Art & Life poster
UNIVERSITY: Concordia University
PROFESSOR: Andrew Foster
DESIGNER: Jonathan Correa
FONT USED: Rockewell

Fig. 81
TITLE: Spike Heels poster
UNIVERSITY: Kutztown University
PROFESSOR: Elaine Cunfer
DESIGNER: Kimberly Beyer
FONTS USED: Hand lettering,
	Neutraface Display Light

Fig. 82
TITLE: Dearling Physique
	CD Release Show
DESIGN FIRM: Im1984
DESIGNER: Samuel L Tapia
FONT USED: Politica
CLIENT: Dearling Physique

Fig. 83
TITLE: Whale in the Whirl
UNIVERSITY: Kutztown University
PROFESSOR: Denise Bosler
DESIGNER: Cheryl Sheeler
FONT USED: Hand lettering

Fig. 84
TITLE: Bumble in the Rumble
UNIVERSITY: Kutztown University
PROFESSOR: Denise Bosler
DESIGNER: Cheryl Sheeler
FONT USED: Hand lettering

Fig. 85
TITLE: Hawaiian destination
	wedding invitation suite
DESIGN FIRM: Kathy Mueller
	Graphic Design & Art Direction
DESIGNER: Kathy Mueller

FONTS USED: Custom lettering,
	Rotis Semiserif, Daisy Lau
CLIENT: Aida Galarza & Joe Sedon

Fig. 86
TITLE: Black Keys poster
UNIVERSITY: The Art Institute of Seattle
PROFESSOR: David Danioth
DESIGNER: Doug Sheets
FONT USED: Hand lettering

Fig. 87
TITLE: Bad Decisions Make Great Stories
DESIGN FIRM: 55 Hi's
DESIGNER: Ross Moody
FONT USED: Custom type inspired
	by Grotesque
CLIENT: Self

Fig. 88
TITLE: Trim, Fold & Form Publicity
DESIGN FIRM: Temasek Polytechnic
	School of Design
DESIGNER: Patricia Tan
FONTS USED: Lot, News Gothic Bold
CLIENT: Self

Fig. 89
TITLE: OMDS Skull poster
DESIGN FIRM: Dan Norris Ltd
DESIGNER: Dan Norris
FONT USED: Hand lettering
CLIENT: The One Man Destruction Show

Fig. 90
TITLE: Atlas Copco Calendar
DESIGNER: Tracy L. Kretz
FONTS USED: Dymaxion, Blue Highway
CLIENT: Atlas Copco

Fig. 91
TITLE: PPO&S Holiday E-Card
DESIGN FIRM: PPO&S
DESIGNER: Tracy L. Kretz
FONT USED: Disturbance
CLIENT: Self

Fig. 92
TITLE: Emyy
DESIGN FIRM: Tooco
DESIGNER: Francisco Miranda
FONT USED: Hand lettering
CLIENT: Canal Encuentro

Fig. 93
TITLE: AIGA Get Involved
DESIGN FIRM: TV Land In-House
	Brand Creative
DESIGNER/S: Marc Nahas,
	Alanna Siviero
FONT USED: Various "You Work
	for Them" Fonts
CLIENT: AIGA (National)

Fig. 94
TITLE: R Design—Annual Student
	Conference
DESIGNER: Rafael:Neder
FONTS USED: Antiga Grotesca Gorda
	Apertada, Bodoni, Clarendon,
	Manuscrita, and others
CLIENT: R Design

Fig. 95
TITLE: Everybody Is Special
DESIGN FIRM: L-Able
ART DIRECTOR: Thomas Scheiderbauer
DESIGNERS: Thomas Scheiderbauer +
	Pamela Campagna
FONT USED: Hand lettering
CLIENT: Self

Fig. 96
TITLE: I75 promo Christmas card
DESIGN FIRM: Sodavekt
DESIGNER: Andy Gibbs
FONT USED: Various
CLIENT: I75

Fig. 97
TITLE: Brèves De Trottoirs
UNIVERSITY: Ecv Nantes
PROFESSOR: Sophie Northam

DESIGNER: Lucie Rauer
FONT USED: Hand lettering

Fig. 98
TITLE: Butterfly poster
DESIGNER: Rebecca Alford
FONT USED: Woodblock Letters
CLIENT: Falmouth University

Fig. 99
TITLE: Veseli Medvjedić/
	Joyful Teddy Bears
DESIGNER: Marko Jovanovac
FONT USED: Manually arranged
	sugar cube type
CLIENT: Children's Theatre Branko
	Mihaljević; In Osijek

Fig. 100
TITLE: Remember the Classics—Movie
DESIGNER: Frederick Peens
FONT USED: Hand lettering
CLIENT: Chew Magazine

Fig. 101
TITLE: Postcards From Bookworms
	submission call poster design
DESIGN FIRM: Butawarna
DESIGNER: Andriew Budiman
FONT USED: Hand lettering
CLIENT: C2O Library

Fig. 102
TITLE: Time Doesn't Exist
DESIGN FIRM: Hello From Claire
DESIGNER: Claire Buchanan
FONT USED: Hand lettering
CLIENT: Self

Fig. 103
TITLE: Fresh Beginnings
DESIGN FIRM: James O'Connell |
	Design and Art Direction
DESIGNER: James O'Connell
FONT USED: Avant-Garde
CLIENT: Self

chapter five

{ PARAGRAPH }

Sentences come together to form a paragraph. It's as if the individual sentences want to become a group, because a group has more influence than an individual. Paragraphs explain. Paragraphs tell stories. Paragraphs use their influence to convince. While a sentence may hook the viewer into a design, it is the paragraph that keeps them there. This is a heavy load to bear, requiring appropriate paragraph arrangement in order to communicate effectively.

Few designs out in the market don't rely on paragraphs of text. A food package uses paragraphs to showcase the product, enticing the buyer to purchase the food. Over-the-counter drugs use paragraphs to communicate the correct dose of medicine. A play poster uses paragraphs to explain the who, what, when and where of a performance. The label on a fire extinguisher uses paragraphs to explain quickly and clearly how to put out a fire. Each of these examples requires a very different approach to designing a paragraph. Working with this volume of words is a critical skill for a designer.

VISUAL TONE

If you squint your eyes at a design, you will notice that different areas of text take on different tones (Figs. 1, 2). Headlines are dark while paragraphs look more gray. These blocks of text—the combination of words, tracking and leading—create the visual tone on the page that a viewer's eye perceives as color. Striking the right balance between different tones distinguishes the design and separates its various elements. For instance, a paragraph of black text on a white background gives the eye an impression of a gray tonal block that can be made lighter or darker with lighter or bolder typefaces, tighter or looser leading, or tighter or looser tracking. Used as a design element, visual tone brings interest and variety to the page's design.

The physical color of the type also gives a page varying degrees of tone and texture. In the past, black type on a white background was considered to produce optimal readability. It is now generally accepted that somewhat less contrast actually increases legibility, improving the design. Dark text on slightly tinted backgrounds and slightly shaded text on white backgrounds (e.g., black text on cream or charcoal gray text on white) have very high readability and add interest to a design (Fig. 3). This kind of color adjustment reduces eye strain and appears less stark. White text on dark background should be used sparingly and with care. This combination has a tendency to create a halo effect around the edges of the type, which quickly tires the eye (Fig. 4). Text and backgrounds that are similar in tonal value are also difficult to read; examples include blue on red, and lime green on purple (Fig. 5). If you are unsure whether your color combination has enough difference in tonal value, there

1

WE SHALL OVERCOME
Lyndon B. Johnson

2

WE SHALL OVERCOME

3

Maximum readability is the goal.

Maximum readability is the goal.

Maximum readability is the goal.

4

Maximum readability is the goal.

Maximum readability is the goal.

5

Maximum readability is the goal.

Maximum readability is the goal.

1, 2 Squinting at a design reveals the visual tone of a piece. Darker areas draw more attention than lighter, grayer areas. **3** Experiment with different text and background colors to create optimal readability. **4** Dark backgrounds with light text look dynamic but tend to tire a viewer's eye more quickly than dark text on a light background. **5** Don't let the color combination hinder readability. Colors that look "cool" together may not read well.

are several ways to test it. Bring your design into photo editing software and change your design into a grayscale color mode. Print it out on a black–and–white printer. Or print your design in color, then copy it with a black-and-white photocopier. If the colors come out the same or similar shades of gray, then the tonal values of your colors are too close.

VARYING SIZES

BODY COPY

The text that makes up a paragraph is referred to as *body copy*. Body copy reads best when set between 8 and 11 points in size (Figs. 6, 7). This is small enough so that a large amount of information can be presented on a page, but it's not too small to read. The x-height, weight, width and other typesetting variations affect the readability of body text, so designers must judge which size reads best. If the design is for young children or older adults, it is recommended that the body copy be set larger, to help those new to reading or with dwindling eyesight. It is also important to make sure your body copy size doesn't create lines that are too long or too short.

Because body copy constitutes the bulk of the communication in many documents, utilizing the correct size, font and alignment will optimize readability and communication. The correct combination of elements will vary from piece to piece, and it takes practice to determine the perfect mixture.

HEADLINES

Headlines are the first words readers notice. Headline type is often large, bold, colored and fun to look at. A headline is designed to stand out from the rest of the page and sets the tone for the document. Most designs have it set at 18–24 points in size, or larger. The look of the headline determines whether the design is viewed as serious or funny, cutting edge or traditional, or important or trivial (Figs. 8, 9). With so much riding on the headline, font choice is vital. While readability should always be the number one priority, one can use a wider variety of fonts for headlines. Fonts with quirks and personality can work quite well at the larger headline size, even though they may read poorly at smaller sizes. Keep in mind, however, that a headline font choice should always reflect the tone a document needs to portray. As mentioned in chapter 3, connotation is very important to the design. A good way to start

6

Gentlemen of the Jury: The best friend a man has in the world may turn against him and become his enemy. His son or daughter that he has reared with loving care may prove ungrateful. Those who are nearest and dearest to us, those whom we trust with our happiness and our good name may become traitors to their faith. The money that a man has, he may lose. It flies away from him, perhaps when he needs it most. A man's reputation may be sacrificed in a moment of ill-considered action. The people who are prone to fall on their knees to do us honor when success is with us, may be the first to throw the stone of malice when failure settles its cloud upon our heads.

–George Graham Vest

7

Gentlemen of the Jury: The best friend a man has in the world may turn against him and become his enemy. His son or daughter that he has reared with loving care may prove ungrateful. Those who are nearest and dearest to us, those whom we trust with our happiness and our good name may become traitors to their faith. The money that a man has, he may lose.
It flies away from him, perhaps when he needs it most. A man's reputation may be sacrificed in a moment of ill-considered action. The people who are prone to fall on their knees to do us honor when success is with us, may be the first to throw the stone of malice when failure settles its cloud upon our heads.

–George Graham Vest

6 Body copy set in 10-point Baskerville. **7** Body copy set in 8-point Century Gothic.

I am a
Serious Headline

I'M A LITTLE BIT MORE FUN!

a headline font search is by looking at fonts that reflect the tone of the design. You could also use a font that is the opposite style of the chosen body copy. If a serif is used for body copy, choose a sans serif for the headline and vice versa, as the contrasting styles of letterforms add visual interest to the page.

SUBHEADS

Subheads are brief lines of text that divide the body copy into sections between headlines and body copy. Subheads are used to give emphasis or clarify aspects of the text. Because this type falls in between paragraphs of text, it needs to be considered separately from the body copy. Subheads are slightly larger, bolder or colored differently than the body copy in order to help the reader distinguish them. Be careful not to create competition with the headline.

Subheads are there to help break up the text, not to steal the show from the headline. Be careful of floating heads, which occur when a subhead is vertically centered between the paragraph above and the paragraph below it. This equidistant spacing makes it difficult to distinguish the paragraph to which the subhead belongs. For clarity, position the subhead closer to the paragraph below it. You can do this by removing some leading or deleting a paragraph return. The goal for the space surrounding the subhead is to have two-thirds of the space above and one-third below (Figs. 10, 11).

CAPTIONS AND PULL QUOTES

There are two other classifications of text on a page: captions and pull quotes. *Captions* are text that appear next to an image for description or clarification (Fig. 12). They can also contain artist

8, 9 A headline sets the tone for a design. The serif headline connotes more reserve than the larger, stacked sans serif headline. Use the type to create the desired connotation and don't be afraid to experiment.

BAD

This is the paragraph avove the subhead. The subhead should not relate to me.

This is a Floating Subhead

This is the paragraph below the subhead. The subhead belongs to me. Adjust the space around the subhead so it forms a relationship the appropriate paragraph.

GOOD

This is the paragraph avove the subhead. The subhead should not relate to me.

This is a Correctly Placed Subhead
This is the paragraph below the subhead. The subhead belongs to me. Adjust the space around the subhead so it forms a relationship the appropriate paragraph.

PHOTOGRAPH BY DENISE BOSLER

A walk along the river yielded a great view of the Susquehanna River bridges.

We Have the Right

Susan B. Anthony

Friends and fellow citizens: I stand before you tonight under indictment for the alleged crime of having voted at the last presidential election, without having a lawful right to vote. It shall be my work this evening to prove to you that in thus voting, I not only committed no crime, but, instead, simply exercised my citizen's rights, guaranteed to me and all United States citizens by the National Constitution, beyond the power of any state to deny.

The preamble of the Federal Constitution says: "We, the people of the United States, in order to form a more perfect union, establish justice, insure domestic tranquility, provide for the common defense, promote the general welfare, and secure the blessings of liberty to ourselves and our posterity, do ordain and establish this Constitution for the United States of America."

> "It is an odious aristocracy; a hateful oligarchy of sex; the most hateful aristocracy ever established on the face of the globe."

It was we, the people; not we, the white male citizens; nor yet we, the male citizens; but we, the whole people, who formed the Union. And we formed it, not to give the blessings of liberty, but to secure them; not to the half of ourselves and the half of our posterity, but to the whole people—women as well as men. And it is a downright mockery to talk to women of their enjoyment of the blessings of liberty while they are denied the use of the only means of securing them provided by this democratic-republican government—the ballot.

For any state to make sex a qualification that must ever result in the disfranchisement of one entire half of the people, is to pass a bill of attainder, or, an ex post facto law,

and is therefore a violation of the supreme law of the land. By it the blessings of liberty are forever withheld from women and their female posterity.

To them this government has no just powers derived from the consent of the governed. To them this government is not a democracy. It is not a republic. It is an odious aristocracy; a hateful oligarchy of sex; the most hateful aristocracy ever established on the face of the globe; an oligarchy of wealth, where the rich govern the poor. An oligarchy of learning, where the educated govern the ignorant, or even an oligarchy of race, where the Saxon rules the African, might be endured; but this oligarchy of sex, which makes father, brothers, husband, sons, the oligarchs over the mother and sisters, the wife and daughters, of every household—which ordains all men sovereigns, all women subjects, carries dissension, discord, and rebellion into every home of the nation.

Webster, Worcester, and Bouvier all define a citizen to be a person in the United States, entitled to vote and hold office.

The only question left to be settled now is: Are women persons? And I hardly believe any of our opponents will have the hardihood to say they are not. Being persons, then, women are citizens; and no state has a right to make any law, or to enforce any old law, that shall abridge their privileges or immunities. Hence, every discrimination against women in the constitutions and laws of the several states is today null and void, precisely as is every one against Negroes.

10, 11 Subheads help to break up long text and add visual interest to a page, but make sure the viewer knows to which paragraph the subhead belongs. Use proper spacing to form a relationship with the paragraph below. **12** Captions let the viewer know more about an image that is not explained within the supporting paragraph. Captions are a great way to add to a story and give credit to the photographer or illustrator. Make certain, however, that the caption's typographic treatment does not distract from the surrounding body copy. **13** Use a pull quote to entice, shock, scare, surprise or seduce the viewer into stopping on a page.

or photographer credits. They can be as short as a few words or as long as an entire paragraph. Captions need to be set in a way that distinguishes them from the body copy without competing with it for attention. Captions are therefore generally smaller and less bold than the body copy. They are often set in italics. Captions still need to be readable, however, so make sure they aren't set too small.

A *pull quote* is text that has literally been pulled from the body copy and set separately to grab attention (Fig. 13). The most powerful pull quotes are ones that evoke feeling, causing a reader to stop and delve deeper to find out more from the document. Sometimes designers include quotation marks around the text; other times lines, boxes, different fonts, bold, italics or color are used to separate the text from the rest of the body copy. Pull quotes are found most commonly in magazines and longer brochures. While pull quotes should be important and attention grabbing, they should never become more significant than the headline (Fig. 14).

INITIAL CAPS

Initial caps are another element that can add visual interest to the text. *Initial caps* are found at the beginning of a paragraph to distinguish it from surrounding paragraphs. There are three types: drop caps, standup caps and hanging caps. A *drop cap* is a larger letter that drops down into the lines of text below it (Fig. 15). There is no rule about how far down it can go, but it should not hinder readability. Drop caps are commonly found at the beginning of a children's storybook. True to its name, a *standup cap* stands up from the top line of text (Fig. 16). The standup cap is several times larger than that of the surrounding text but shares the same baseline as the body copy. *Hanging caps* literally hang outside the edge of the paragraph. They can be positioned as a standup or drop down—or hover somewhere in between (Fig. 17). Hanging caps also work well if they are positioned slightly behind the paragraph

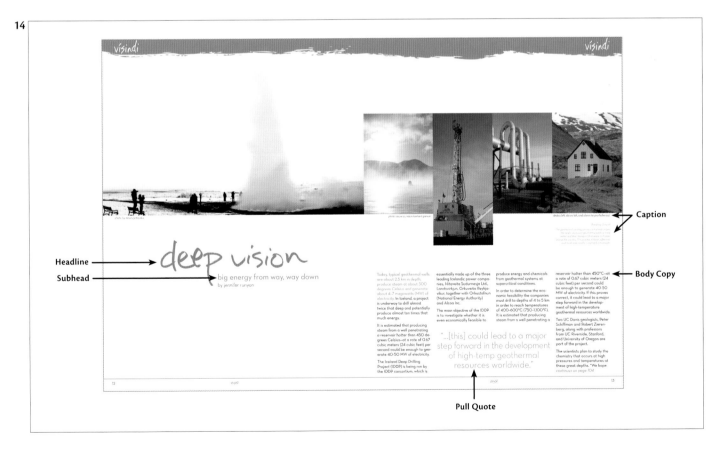

14

Headline
Subhead
Caption
Body Copy
Pull Quote

15

Hard by a great forest dwelt a poor wood-cutter with his wife and his two children. The boy was called Hansel and the girl Gretel. He had little to bite and to break, and once when great dearth fell on the land, he could no longer procure even daily bread. Now when he thought over this by night in his bed, and tossed about in his anxiety, he groaned and said to his wife, what is to become of us. How are we to feed our poor children, when we no longer have anything even for ourselves.

–The Grimms Brothers

16

Hard by a great forest dwelt a poor woodcutter with his wife and his two children. The boy was called Hansel and the girl Gretel. He had little to bite and to break, and once when great dearth fell on the land, he could no longer procure even daily bread. Now when he thought over this by night in his bed, and tossed about in his anxiety, he groaned and said to his wife, what is to become of us. How are we to feed our poor children, when we no longer have anything even for ourselves.

–The Grimms Brothers

17

Hard by a great forest dwelt a poor woodcutter with his wife and his two children. The boy was called Hansel and the girl Gretel. He had little to bite and to break, and once when great dearth fell on the land, he could no longer procure even daily bread. Now when he thought over this by night in his bed, and tossed about in his anxiety, he groaned and said to his wife, what is to become of us. How are we to feed our poor children, when we no longer have anything even for ourselves.

–The Grimms Brothers

18

Hard by a great forest dwelt a poor woodcutter with his wife and his two children. The boy was called Hansel and the girl Gretel. He had little to bite and to break, and once when great dearth fell on the land, he could no longer procure even daily bread. Now when he thought over this by night in his bed, and tossed about in his anxiety, he groaned and said to his wife, what is to become of us. How are we to feed our poor children, when we no longer have anything even for ourselves.

–The Grimms Brothers

of text. This is done by rendering the hanging cap in a lighter tone or color than the adjacent text, creating the illusion of depth on the page (Fig. 18).

There are several things you need to keep in mind when initial caps are part of a design. If you are using more than one initial cap on a page, do not allow them to line up with other initial caps horizontally across the page, as this will indicate to the reader that you are trying to spell something even if you aren't. This is especially important if it ends up spelling something embarrassing or contradictory to the text. Try to get the initial caps to disperse evenly throughout the page. Be creative with your initial caps. Consider using a contrasting font, a script or a decorative letter.

Try hand rendering the initial caps, especially if you are including other hand-rendered elements, such as an illustration, on the page.

COMPLEMENTARY TYPE PAIRS

It is important to strike the right balance of typographic elements to create a balanced visual tone. In addition to utilizing different text sizes, it is important to use a variety of fonts. The trick is finding the right number of different fonts. Too few and the design appears dull; too many and the result is chaotic.

As a rule, the majority of designs feature two fonts, a serif and a sans serif. Using two fonts that look different help distinguish

15 Drop cap example. **16** Standup cap example. **17** Hanging cap example. **18** Play with the arrangement of a hanging cap to create interesting visual relationships.

between different type elements such as headline, subhead, body copy and captions. Two serifs or two sans serifs will look like an editing error (Figs. 19, 20). It is good practice to choose one for the body copy and the other for headlines and additional text that needs to stand out (Fig. 21). Providing a contrast for the eye is important; at the same time, the two fonts should still complement each other. Using two fonts that look dramatically different makes the type feel out of place and the design disconnected. The goal is to communicate information, so make sure your choices are readable and legible.

The biggest challenge for many beginning designers is choosing the right combination. The options are unlimited; choosing the best pair depends on the desired design aesthetic. Start by making a list of ten serif and ten sans serif fonts (Fig. 22). Include several classic fonts: Garamond, Bodoni, Baskerville, Caslon, Goudy Old Style, Univers, Helvetica, Futura, Avant Garde and Gill Sans, for example. Set each font in both a headline size (around 24 point) and a short paragraph of body copy at 9 or 10 point (Fig. 23). Also set a few sentences in each style variation within the font families. Print them out. Place the prints side by side and compare each serif with each sans serif font. Look for similar qualities between them—x-height, weight, width, height, bias, counter sizes. It always comes down to a gut reaction in the end—do they work well together or do they conflict with each other? Note which combinations work. Over time, you will learn to identify suitable combinations at a glance. Now look closely

19

Serif Font One
Serif Font Two

20

Sans Serif Font One
Sans Serif Font Two

21

Serif Font One
Sans Serif Font One

Serif Font Two
Sans Serif Font Two

22

SERIF LIST	SANS SERIF LIST
Garamond	Helvetica Neue
Bodoni	Futura
Baskerville	Gill Sans
Times	Frutiger
Officina	News Gothic
Bembo	Univers
Rockwell	Optima
Walbaum	Franklin Gothic
Matrix	Meta
Sabon	Din

19, 20, 21 Good complementary type pairs match a serif with a sans serif. Using two serifs or two sans serifs creates a pair too similar in form and will look like a mistake.
22 Choose ten serifs and ten sans serifs to compare in order to generate a complementary type pair list.

at the matching sets. Within the pair, which looks better large as a headline and which one small as body copy? Does one look better bold or italic? Which complementary pair feels right for the job? Trust your instincts. If the pair reads well for you, then it will work for your viewer.

With experience, you will begin expanding your list. Keep it close by to reference when you need to design a page with body copy and headline. A word of caution: Do not rely on the same set for every design. It will make your work predictable and less creative. Remember to take into consideration the design requirements, client personality and chosen design style (Fig. 24).

The exception to the two-font rule is when the headline needs a special touch to enhance the communication of the design. A third font is permissible if a complementary pair is used for the rest of the piece. Continue to consider the entire design aesthetic when selecting the third font and make sure it, too, complements the chosen pair.

Garamond 9/13

Liberty or Death

No man thinks more highly than I do of the patriotism, as well as abilities, of the very worthy gentlemen who have just addressed the House. But different men often see the same subject in different lights; and, therefore, I hope that it will not be thought disrespectful to those gentlemen, if, entertaining as I do opinions of a character very opposite to theirs, I shall speak forth my sentiments freely and without reserve.

No man thinks more highly than I do of the patriotism, as well as abilities, of the very worthy gentlemen who have just addressed the House.

No man thinks more highly than I do of the patriotism, as well as abilities, of the very worthy gentlemen who have just addressed the House.

Bodoni 9/13

Liberty or Death

No man thinks more highly than I do of the patriotism, as well as abilities, of the very worthy gentlemen who have just addressed the House. But different men often see the same subject in different lights; and, therefore, I hope that it will not be thought disrespectful to those gentlemen, if, entertaining as I do opinions of a character very opposite to theirs, I shall speak forth my sentiments freely and without reserve.

No man thinks more highly than I do of the patriotism, as well as abilities, of the very worthy gentlemen who have just addressed the House.

No man thinks more highly than I do of the patriotism, as well as abilities, of the very worthy gentlemen who have just addressed the House.

Baskerville 9/13

Liberty or Death

No man thinks more highly than I do of the patriotism, as well as abilities, of the very worthy gentlemen who have just addressed the House. But different men often see the same subject in different lights; and, therefore, I hope that it will not be thought disrespectful to those gentlemen, if, entertaining as I do opinions of a character very opposite to theirs, I shall speak forth my sentiments freely and without reserve.

No man thinks more highly than I do of the patriotism, as well as abilities, of the very worthy gentlemen who have just addressed the House.

No man thinks more highly than I do of the patriotism, as well as abilities, of the very worthy gentlemen who have just addressed the House.

Helvetica Neue 8/13

Liberty or Death

No man thinks more highly than I do of the patriotism, as well as abilities, of the very worthy gentlemen who have just addressed the House. But different men often see the same subject in different lights; and, therefore, I hope that it will not be thought disrespectful to those gentlemen, if, entertaining as I do opinions of a character very opposite to theirs, I shall speak forth my sentiments freely and without reserve.

No man thinks more highly than I do of the patriotism, as well as abilities, of the very worthy gentlemen who have just addressed the House.

No man thinks more highly than I do of the patriotism, as well as abilities, of the very worthy gentlemen who have just addressed the House.

Futura 8/13

Liberty or Death

No man thinks more highly than I do of the patriotism, as well as abilities, of the very worthy gentlemen who have just addressed the House. But different men often see the same subject in different lights; and, therefore, I hope that it will not be thought disrespectful to those gentlemen, if, entertaining as I do opinions of a character very opposite to theirs, I shall speak forth my sentiments freely and without reserve.

No man thinks more highly than I do of the patriotism, as well as abilities, of the very worthy gentlemen who have just addressed the House.

No man thinks more highly than I do of the patriotism, as well as abilities, of the very worthy gentlemen who have just addressed the House.

Gill Sans 8/13

Liberty or Death

No man thinks more highly than I do of the patriotism, as well as abilities, of the very worthy gentlemen who have just addressed the House. But different men often see the same subject in different lights; and, therefore, I hope that it will not be thought disrespectful to those gentlemen, if, entertaining as I do opinions of a character very opposite to theirs, I shall speak forth my sentiments freely and without reserve.

No man thinks more highly than I do of the patriotism, as well as abilities, of the very worthy gentlemen who have just addressed the House.

No man thinks more highly than I do of the patriotism, as well as abilities, of the very worthy gentlemen who have just addressed the House.

23 Set the fonts in similar headline and body copy sizes to both see how the individual fonts appear in these formats and compare side-by-side with each other.

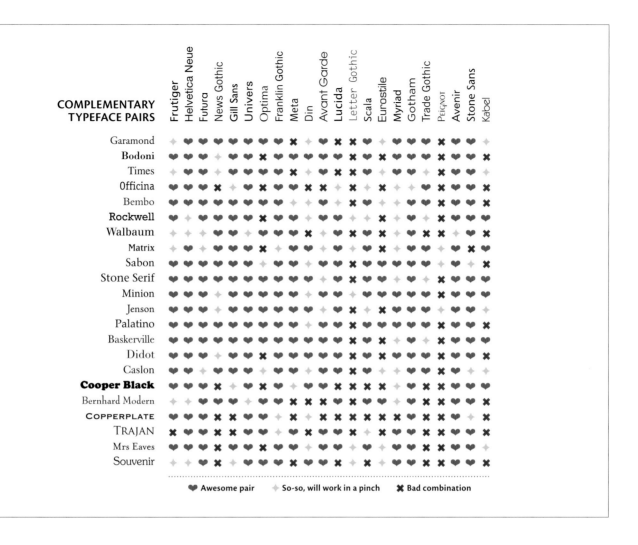

24 A "cheat-sheet" chart depicting complementary serifs and sans serifs.

TYPE ISSUES

Designing with larger amounts of text requires greater attention to detail. Type issues are more likely to crop up when dealing with paragraphs of text as opposed to individual sentences. A designer must be extra diligent and conscious of the words on the page in order to make the text as readable as possible, because readability is what contributes most to a design's communication. This attention to detail separates a conscientious designer from one who just goes through the motions. Thoroughness goes a long way in a client-designer relationship.

When designing with large amounts of text, the first step is to format it in the chosen font, point size, leading, tracking and column width. Do not worry about fine-tuning details before the overall design is decided. This will only lead to unnecessary work when designs change, sometimes several times, in the development phase. When the initial formatting is complete and a design is approved, the text needs to be analyzed and adjusted according to the following rules.

WIDOWS

Words don't like to be widowed any more than people do. A *widow* is a line at the end of a paragraph that is one-third the length of the other lines in the paragraph or less (Figs. 25, 26). It often consists of one or two lonely leftover words. This breaks the flow of text

25

BAD

Four score and seven years ago our fathers brought forth on this continent, a new nation, conceived in liberty, and dedicated to the proposition that all men are created equal.

Now we are engaged in a great civil war, testing whether that nation, or any nation so conceived and so dedicated, can long endure. We are met on a great battlefield of that war. We have come to dedicate a portion of that field, as a final resting place for those who here gave their lives that that nation might live. It is altogether fitting and proper that we should do this.

GOOD

Four score and seven years ago our fathers brought forth on this continent, a new nation, conceived in liberty, and dedicated to the proposition that all men are created equal.

Now we are engaged in a great civil war, testing whether that nation, or any nation so conceived and so dedicated, can long endure. We are met on a great battlefield of that war. We have come to dedicate a portion of that field, as a final resting place for those who here gave their lives that that nation might live. It is altogether fitting and proper that we should do this.

from one paragraph to the next and creates awkward negative space between the paragraphs.

There are several options for fixing widows, depending upon the chosen design and how much control the designer has over text edits. The easiest fix is to add or delete a few words from the paragraph. This option only works when the designer is also responsible for the text. If the text comes from an outside source, such as the client or a copywriter, it cannot be changed without their permission, though there are other options when text cannot be edited. The width of the paragraph column can be adjusted slightly, increasing it until the word or words pop up onto the line before it, or decreasing the paragraph column width until other words drop down to join the widow. This solution works when the design layout is not set in stone, thus allowing the designer to tweak paragraph width. The same goes for adjustments in type size. If the text formatting can still be changed, the designer can increase or decrease the size of type slightly, perhaps .5 points, until the widow disappears. The designer can also tighten or loosen tracking within the paragraph to bring the words up to the previous line or push other words down to join the last line, respectively. This solution is best, as it doesn't affect editing or overall design. Be careful not to tighten or loosen the tracking too much or the words may lose readability. Remember to adjust tracking on the entire paragraph, not just the widowed line, so that the adjustment flows well with the rest of the paragraph.

There are rare occasions when all these efforts fail. The following option should only be used when absolutely necessary: horizontally scale the type ever so slightly, 1 or 2 percent at the most. More than that and the integrity of the typeface is at risk.

ORPHANS

An *orphan* is one or two lines of a paragraph at the end of a column separated onto the top next column of type (Figs. 27, 28). It can also be the opening line of a paragraph stuck at the end of a column while the remainder of the paragraph is in the next column. Like widows, orphans break the flow of text and create readability issues. The same methods used to fix widows can be used for orphans, with the added option of lengthening the paragraph's space at the bottom or top to allow the words to rejoin the original paragraph. This option is only available when there is sufficient flexibility in the design.

25, 26 Widows break the flow of text and must be addressed even in the shortest document.

BAD

Four score and seven years ago our fathers brought forth on this continent, a new nation, conceived in liberty, and dedicated to the proposition that all men are created equal. Now we are engaged in a great civil war, testing whether that nation, or any nation so conceived and so dedicated, can long endure. We are met on a great battlefield of that war. We have come to dedicate a portion of that field, as a final resting place for those who here gave their lives that that nation might live. It is altogether fitting

and proper that we should do this.

But in a larger sense, we cannot dedicate—we cannot consecrate—we cannot hallow—this ground. The brave men, living and dead, who struggled here, have consecrated it, far above our poor power to add or detract. The world will little note, nor long remember, what we say here, but it can never forget what they did here. It is for us the living, rather, to be dedicated here to the unfinished work which they who fought here have thus far so nobly advanced. It is rather for

28

GOOD

Four score and seven years ago our fathers brought forth on this continent, a new nation, conceived in liberty, and dedicated to the proposition that all men are created equal. Now we are engaged in a great civil war, testing whether that nation, or any nation so conceived and so dedicated, can long endure. We are met on a great battlefield of that war. We have come to dedicate a portion of that field, as a final resting place for those who here gave their lives that that nation might live. It is altogether fitting and proper that we should do this.

But in a larger sense, we cannot dedicate—we cannot consecrate—we cannot hallow—this ground. The brave men, living and dead, who struggled here, have consecrated it, far above our poor power to add or detract. The world will little note, nor long remember, what we say here, but it can never forget what they did here. It is for us the living, rather, to be dedicated here to the unfinished work which they who fought here have thus far so nobly advanced. It is rather for us to be here dedicated to the great task remaining before us—that from

29

BAD

At this second appearing to take the oath of the presidential office there is less occasion for an extended address than there was at the first. Then a statement, somewhat in detail, of a course to be pursued seemed fitting and proper. Now, at the expiration of four years, during which public declarations have been constantly called forth on every point and phase of the great contest which still absorbs the attention and engrosses the energies of the nation, little that is new could be presented. The progress of our arms, upon which all else chiefly depends, is as well known to the public as to myself, and it is, I trust, reasonably satisfactory and encouraging to all. With high hope for the future, no prediction in regard to it is ventured.

–Abraham Lincoln

30

GOOD

At this second appearing to take the oath of the presidential office there is less occasion for an extended address than there was at the first. Then a statement, somewhat in detail, of a course to be pursued seemed fitting and proper. Now, at the expiration of four years, during which public declarations have been constantly called forth on every point and phase of the great contest which still absorbs the attention and engrosses the energies of the nation, little that is new could be presented. The progress of our arms, upon which all else chiefly depends, is as well known to the public as to myself, and it is, I trust, reasonably satisfactory and encouraging to all. With high hope for the future, no prediction in regard to it is ventured.

–Abraham Lincoln

HYPHENATION

Hyphenation is the splitting of a word at the end of a line and continuing onto the next line. Hyphenation within body copy is a subject of debate. Some designers feel words should never be divided and so eliminate hyphenation completely, while others believe it is acceptable if its use is limited. As a general rule, you should avoid using too many hyphens in a single paragraph, two or fewer (Figs. 29, 30). Also, there should never be more than two hyphens on consecutive lines, as they disrupt the readability of the text. Hyphens also create unsightly rag in left-aligned and justified text. Most computer programs have adjustable justification and hyphenation (H&J) settings to refine the rules you want your document to follow.

27, 28 An orphan can falsely indicate that a sentence or sentences belong to the next paragraph or next column. **29, 30** Fix hyphenation whenever possible to avoid the feeling of broken text.

BAD BREAKS

Multiple-line headlines need to break in a way that flows with natural pauses in speech and makes sense to the reader. The easiest way to figure out where to break a headline is by speaking the headline aloud. Where does the natural pause occur? If the headline needs to be broken onto several lines, read it with pauses for each line. Use different emphasis. Which one sounds "right"? The fastest way to cause confusion is to break a headline in an awkward location. For example, if the headline "Katie bites into the Big Apple" is broken after the word "bites" then it appears as though Katie is someone we should avoid lest we end up with teeth marks on our arm. Better to break this headline after the word *into* so that the

reader's natural inclination is to read the next line to see where the bite takes place (Figs. 31, 32).

Body copy can also suffer from bad breaks. Although these breaks are subtler, they still disrupt the flow of readability. One classic bad break in body text is hyphenating a proper name at the end of a sentence. Lack of hyphenation will also create bad breaks, particularly if the paragraph contains many lengthy words, resulting in poor rag that diminishes readability. At the opposite end of the spectrum, leaving small words such as *I, to, it, an* and *of* dangling at the end of a long line causes that word to separate visually from the body copy. This is more pronounced when the lines before and after it are shorter (Figs. 33, 34). The same fixes for

31

BAD

Katie bites
into the Big Apple.

32

GOOD

Katie bites into
the Big Apple.

33

BAD

The habit of reading is one of the greatest resources of mankind; and we enjoy reading books that belong to us much more than if they are borrowed. A borrowed book is like a guest in the house; it must be treated with punctiliousness, with a certain considerate formality. You must see that it sustains no damage; it must not suffer while under your roof. You cannot leave it carelessly, you cannot mark it, you cannot turn down the pages, you cannot use it familiarly. And then, some day, although this is seldom done, you really ought to return it.

–William Lyon Phelps

34

GOOD

The habit of reading is one of the greatest resources of mankind; and we enjoy reading books that belong to us much more than if they are borrowed. A borrowed book is like a guest in the house; it must be treated with punctiliousness, with a certain considerate formality. You must see that it sustains no damage; it must not suffer while under your roof. You cannot leave it carelessly, you cannot mark it, you cannot turn down the pages, you cannot use it familiarly. And then, some day, although this is seldom done, you really ought to return it.

–William Lyon Phelps

31, 32 A headline can be misleading if broken after the wrong word. Break for good readability. **33, 34** Fix small dangling words to assist readability and clean up the appearance of body copy.

widows all work to fix bad breaks. Another solution is to manually force the offending word or words down to the next line.

PARAGRAPH SEPARATION

Creating a document with multiple paragraphs of body copy requires attention to the way the individual paragraphs separate from each other. In word processing programs, it is common to hit the return key twice to separate paragraphs. This technique is fine for term papers and text-only documents, but is not considered correct in a typographically designed piece. The vast space created by the double return breaks the flow of text, creating an unsightly gap. Two acceptable solutions to separating paragraphs while maintaining good design aesthetics are either indentation or adding space between the paragraphs, but not both. Either method is completely acceptable. Which one you choose depends upon your personal design sensibilities.

An *indent* is a small space before the first word of a paragraph equal to an em space, the space occupied by a capital *M*, which will vary from font to font. Indents are used in all paragraphs on a page except for the first one, which, because it is first, stands sufficiently alone. You should never, under any circumstances, use the space bar to create an indent, as it is inaccurate and amateurish, causing uneven spacing that is difficult to fix if the indent size later needs to be adjusted (Fig. 35). To create an indent, either use a tab designated for the correct distance or adjust the first line indent measurement in a programmable paragraph style found within your design layout computer program. Do your best to input a measurement that is equivalent to the size of a capital *M*. Start with ⅛ of an inch (.125") (Fig. 36).

Adding space between paragraphs is an alternative method for creating separation; however, as mentioned, this is not as simple as hitting the return key twice. The return key is programmed to create a gap equivalent to the leading within the paragraph. This works well to separate individual lines, but twice its depth is too large a gap for paragraph separation. The goal is to keep paragraphs close enough together for flow but not so far apart as to hinder readability (Figs. 37, 38). This space, called *space after*, can be set in the programmable paragraph styles found within a design layout computer program. A good starting point is to insert the measurement for half of the leading used within the paragraph. For instance, if the paragraph leading is 14 point, then assign the space after to 7

35

BAD

       Mr. President, Mrs. Clinton, members of Congress, Ambassador Holbrooke, Excellencies, friends: Fifty-four years ago to the day, a young Jewish boy from a small town in the Carpathian Mountains woke up, not far from Goethe's beloved Weimar, in a place of eternal infamy called Buchenwald. He was finally free, but there was no joy in his heart. He thought there never would be again.
       Liberated a day earlier by American soldiers, he remembers their rage at what they saw. And even if he lives to be a very old man, he will always be grateful to them for that rage, and also for their compassion. Though he did not understand their language, their eyes told him what he needed to know —that they, too, would remember, and bear witness.

–Elie Wiesel

36

GOOD

Mr. President, Mrs. Clinton, members of Congress, Ambassador Holbrooke, Excellencies, friends: Fifty-four years ago to the day, a young Jewish boy from a small town in the Carpathian Mountains woke up, not far from Goethe's beloved Weimar, in a place of eternal infamy called Buchenwald. He was finally free, but there was no joy in his heart. He thought there never would be again.
Liberated a day earlier by American soldiers, he remembers their rage at what they saw. And even if he lives to be a very old man, he will always be grateful to them for that rage, and also for their compassion. Though he did not understand their language, their eyes told him what he needed to know —that they, too, would remember, and bear witness.

–Elie Wiesel

35, 36 Space indents so that they are they are similar in size to a capital *M*. This space will provide separation from other paragraphs but not hinder readability.

BAD

Mr. President, Mrs. Clinton, members of Congress, Ambassador Holbrooke, Excellencies, friends: Fifty-four years ago to the day, a young Jewish boy from a small town in the Carpathian Mountains woke up, not far from Goethe's beloved Weimar, in a place of eternal infamy called Buchenwald. He was finally free, but there was no joy in his heart. He thought there never would be again.

Liberated a day earlier by American soldiers, he remembers their rage at what they saw. And even if he lives to be a very old man, he will always be grateful to them for that rage, and also for their compassion. Though he did not understand their language, their eyes told him what he needed to know —that they, too, would remember, and bear witness.

–Elie Wiesel

GOOD

Mr. President, Mrs. Clinton, members of Congress, Ambassador Holbrooke, Excellencies, friends: Fifty-four years ago to the day, a young Jewish boy from a small town in the Carpathian Mountains woke up, not far from Goethe's beloved Weimar, in a place of eternal infamy called Buchenwald. He was finally free, but there was no joy in his heart. He thought there never would be again.

Liberated a day earlier by American soldiers, he remembers their rage at what they saw. And even if he lives to be a very old man, he will always be grateful to them for that rage, and also for their compassion. Though he did not understand their language, their eyes told him what he needed to know —that they, too, would remember, and bear witness.

–Elie Wiesel

39

BAD

Fans, for the past two weeks you have been reading about a bad break I got. Yet today I consider myself the luckiest man on the face of the earth. I have been in ballparks for seventeen years and have never received anything but kindness and encouragement from you fans.

Look at these grand men. Which of you wouldn't consider it the highlight of his career to associate with them for even one day?

Sure, I'm lucky. Who wouldn't consider it an honor to have known Jacob Ruppert—also the builder of baseball's greatest empire, Ed Barrow—to have spent the next nine years with that wonderful little fellow Miller Huggins—then to have spent the next nine years with that outstanding leader, that smart student of psychology—the best manager in baseball today, Joe McCarthy!

–Lou Gehrig

40

GOOD

Fans, for the past two weeks you have been reading about a bad break I got. Yet today I consider myself the luckiest man on the face of the earth. I have been in ballparks for seventeen years and have never received anything but kindness and encouragement from you fans.

Look at these grand men. Which of you wouldn't consider it the highlight of his career to associate with them for even one day?

Sure, I'm lucky. Who wouldn't consider it an honor to have known Jacob Ruppert—also the builder of baseball's greatest empire, Ed Barrow—to have spent the next nine years with that wonderful little fellow Miller Huggins—then to have spent the next nine years with that outstanding leader, that smart student of psychology—the best manager in baseball today, Joe McCarthy!

–Lou Gehrig

point. Adjust the space up or down until the distance promotes the best readability. Just remember that when using indents you do not need an extra space separating paragraphs, and vice versa.

JUMPING HORIZONS

When paragraphs of text are side by side on a page, the baselines must align horizontally. Failure to do so creates jumping horizons, poor alignment that makes the page appear off-balance and unfinished (Figs. 39, 40). Special attention should also be paid

to paragraph breaks. Adjust the spacing between paragraphs to continue even horizons. Please note, however, that in order for the majority of the page's baselines to align, it is acceptable for the last lines in the paragraphs and columns to be uneven.

TOMBSTONING

As previously discussed, subheads are a great way to divide the text of a document into sections. However, it is important to consider their arrangement on the page. *Tombstoning* occurs when

37, 38 Space after works well to create differentiation between paragraphs but be careful not to leave too much space or it will create unsightly gaps in the design. If after entering measurements for the "space after" an unusually large space appears, check the text for extra returns and delete them. A well-intentioned typist probably hit the return key twice. **39, 40** Don't let horizons jump. Misalignment causes the page to look sloppy and unfinished.

the subheads align on similar baselines across the page or pages, an effect that produces a stagnant flow and can also make two subheads look like one long headline (Figs. 41, 42). To create a more dynamic look, and to eliminate any confusion, make sure the subheads vary in position on the page.

BURIED SUBHEAD

Variation in subhead position is important to keep an interesting layout. However, if a subhead is positioned too low on the page, it will be overlooked. It can appear to separate from the paragraph to which it belongs, particularly if it stands alone as an orphan or has only a few

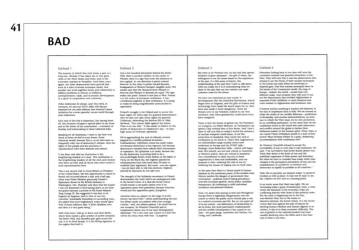

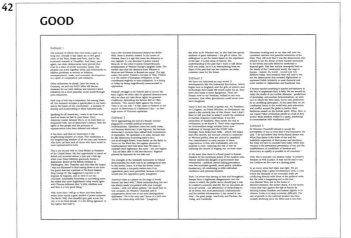

43 BAD

This is a day of national consecration. And I am certain that on this day my fellow Americans expect that on my induction into the Presidency I will address them with a candor and a decision which the present situation of our people impels. This is preeminently the time to speak the truth, the whole truth, frankly and boldly. Nor need we shrink from honestly facing conditions in our country today. This great Nation will endure as it has endured, will revive and will prosper.

So, first of all, let me assert my firm belief that the only thing we have to fear is fear itself—nameless, unreasoning, unjustified terror which paralyzes needed efforts to convert retreat into advance. In every dark hour of our national life a leadership of frankness and of vigor has met with that understanding and support of the people themselves which is essential to victory. And I am convinced that you will again give that support to leadership in these critical days.

BURIED SUBHEAD
In such a spirit on my part and on yours we face our common difficulties. They concern, thank God, only material things. Values have shrunken to fantastic levels; taxes have risen; our ability to pay has fallen; government of all kinds is faced by serious curtailment of income; the means of exchange are frozen in the currents of trade; the withered leaves of industrial enterprise lie on every side; farmers find no markets for their produce; and the savings of many years in thousands of families are gone.

More important, a host of unemployed citizens face the grim problem of existence, and an equally great number toil with little return. Only a foolish optimist can deny the dark realities of the moment.

And yet our distress comes from no failure of substance. We are stricken by no plague of locusts. Compared with the perils which our forefathers conquered because they believed and were not afraid, we have still much to be thankful for. Nature still offers her bounty and human efforts have multiplied it. Plenty is at our doorstep, but a generous use of it languishes in the very sight of the supply.

–Franklin D. Roosevelt

44 GOOD

This is a day of national consecration. And I am certain that on this day my fellow Americans expect that on my induction into the Presidency I will address them with a candor and a decision which the present situation of our people impels. This is preeminently the time to speak the truth, the whole truth, frankly and boldly. Nor need we shrink from honestly facing conditions in our country today. This great Nation will endure as it has endured, will revive and will prosper.

So, first of all, let me assert my firm belief that the only thing we have to fear is fear itself—nameless, unreasoning, unjustified terror which paralyzes needed efforts to convert retreat into advance. In every dark hour of our national life a leadership of frankness and of vigor has met with that understanding and support of the people themselves which is essential to victory. And I am convinced that you will again give that support to leadership in these critical days.

BETTER SUBHEAD PLACEMENT
In such a spirit on my part and on yours we face our common difficulties. They concern, thank God, only material things. Values have shrunken to fantastic levels; taxes have risen; our ability to pay has fallen; government of all kinds is faced by serious curtailment of income; the means of exchange are frozen in the currents of trade; the withered leaves of industrial enterprise lie on every side; farmers find no markets for their produce; and the savings of many years in thousands of families are gone.

More important, a host of unemployed citizens face the grim problem of existence, and an equally great number toil with little return. Only a foolish optimist can deny the dark realities of the moment.

And yet our distress comes from no failure of substance. We are stricken by no plague of locusts. Compared with the perils which our forefathers conquered

–Franklin D. Roosevelt

41, 42 Subheads that align across the entire design don't let the viewer's eye move throughout the page. Stagger them for better organization and visual interest.
43, 44 Make sure the viewer can find subheads. Burying them at the bottom of a page only serves to create confusion.

45

BAD

This Headline Whispers

We dare not forget today that we are the heirs of that first revolution. Let the word go forth from this time and place, to friend and foe alike, that the torch has been passed to a new generation of Americans, born in this century, tempered by war, disciplined by a hard and bitter peace, proud of our ancient heritage and unwilling to witness or permit the slow undoing of those human rights to which this Nation has always been committed, and to which we are committed today at home and around the world.

–John F. Kennedy

46

GOOD

No Whispering Headlines

We dare not forget today that we are the heirs of that first revolution. Let the word go forth from this time and place, to friend and foe alike, that the torch has been passed to a new generation of Americans, born in this century, tempered by war, disciplined by a hard and bitter peace, proud of our ancient heritage and unwilling to witness or permit the slow undoing of those human rights to which this Nation has always been committed, and to which we are committed today at home and around the world.

–John F. Kennedy

47

BAD

The best book I have read this year is titled, <u>Of Mice and Men</u>. It is a great work of art.

48

GOOD

The best book I have read this year is titled, *Of Mice and Men*. It is a great work of art.

sentences after it before splitting into the next column (Figs. 43, 44). This is called a *buried subhead*. A buried subhead is distracting to the reader and can hurt the readability of the text. Fix a buried subhead by adjusting the column length, manually forcing the subhead to the top of the next column or editing the text, if permitted.

WHISPERING HEADLINE

A *whispering headline* is one that fails to attract the attention of the viewer because it is too small, blends in with the text to which it is assigned or is of insufficient boldness or color contrast (Figs. 45, 46). A headline needs be more important than the rest of the text. The goal is to create contrast between the headline and text, guiding the viewer and creating a tonal difference on the page. Make the headline at least

double the size of the surrounding text. Consider using a complementary font, bolding the headline text or using a color that is striking.

UNDERLINING

Underlining text diminishes readability. Horizontal lines that run under text interfere with the space between lines, making the eye work harder to distinguish the tops of letterforms of the line below an underlined sentence. As discussed in chapter 3, the eye differentiates letters by following the upper contour of letters. An underline also interferes with descenders, makes it difficult to separate one line from the next and adds unnecessary clutter. Underlining is the non-designer's way of highlighting text. The more elegant and designerly way to accomplish this is to italicize or bold the text,

45, 46 Viewers want to make sure they are in the correct place. Show them by letting the headline be noticeable among the rest of the text on a page. **47, 48** Underlining is only for term papers and bibliographies. Bring sophistication to a design by using italics, bold or color to create differentiation.

which calls attention to the text without hindering readability. Underlining is only permissible in term papers and academic bibliographies. Replacing the underline of a title to a book, magazine or article with bold or italicized type in a designed text is completely acceptable (Figs. 47, 48).

DESIGNING WITH PARAGRAPHS

Paragraphs do the heavy lifting of communication. They explain in detail what an individual sentence cannot. Paragraphs tell the full story, completing the communication begun by the headline, rounding up the rest of the information and presenting it in a way that is legible and easy to understand. You would be hard-pressed to design anything whose purpose is to communicate detailed information without using paragraphs.

POSTER DESIGN

Most posters rely on an image to draw a viewer's attention, followed by a catchy sentence to keep it. The paragraph is there for support. In the instance of a play or performance poster, the paragraph's job is to give the viewer the rest of the information (date, time, theater company or performance venue) and additional text to describe

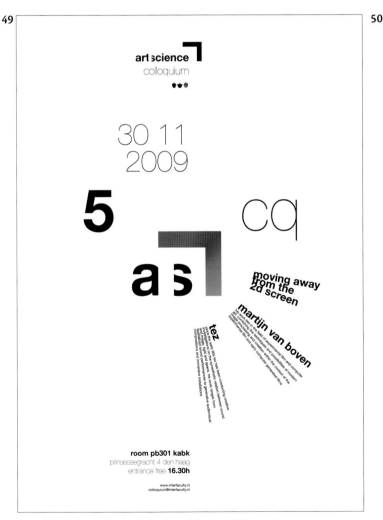

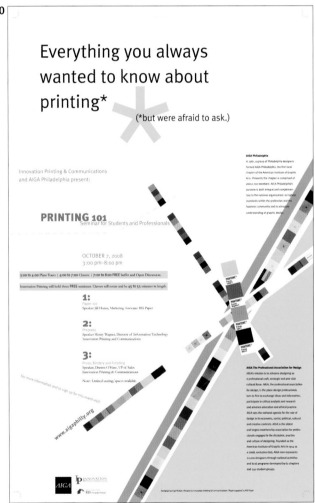

49 Artscience Colloquium poster. **50** Printing 101 seminar.

51 Frequency North posters.

the poster's purpose. Sometimes a poster is informational, such as an educational poster hanging in a classroom, and provides facts about the subject matter. On a poster designed to sell a product, the paragraph does its best to persuade, seducing the viewer into desiring the product. By filling out the headline and the visual, the paragraph completes the design (Figs. 49, 50, 51).

DESIGNING POSTERS

A poster is similar to an advertisement in that the designer has a very short time to make an impression, as viewers view most posters quickly while walking past. Unlike an advertisement, though, it can have a longer "shelf life" if its impact and attractiveness encourages someone to hang it in their home, thereby extending its life.

The first order of business when designing a poster is to determine the focus. A poster needs to be simple and grab attention; it must communicate the connotation of the events or information and it must be readable from a distance. Don't fall into the trap of automatically assuming that the visual must be the main element. It is easy for the typography to become the dominant feature of a poster. All of the techniques and advice for designing headlines (in this chapter) apply. This is an opportunity to create hand-rendered typography, as the title or headline is often short. The typography can actually become the image if the entire space is taken up with letters. If the image is dominant, make sure it can be seen well from a distance. A poster works best, though, when there is a complementary relationship between the typography and the visual. If the headline creates a pun that is then supported by the image, it produces a synergy that makes for a more powerful poster.

In the midst of all of this remains the paragraph text. It is all too easy to forget that these words of support must be incorporated into the overall design. It is tempting to take the block of text and plop it down into a corner, but because these words complete the poster, they should not be treated as an afterthought. Try placing the paragraph in various places. Put it directly below the headline; incorporate it into the image; try stretching it out along the bottom of the poster reversed in a block of color; set it large and put it in the background of the poster; let it run beside the entire image of the poster by using loose leading; angle it to either conflict with or complement the headline. Let the paragraph be obvious.

BROCHURE DESIGN

Brochures are typically used as marketing tools. We have all seen the giant racks of brochures in hotel lobbies or visitors' centers. Each one vies for attention, screaming as loudly as possible to compete against the brochure next to it. Too often, no single brochure grabs the viewer's attention, and all of its creator's efforts to make it stand out result in nothing but confusion.

Brochures differ from posters because they are more tangible. Brochures are meant to be picked up and held, while posters typically remain at arm's length up on a wall. The goals of communication are also very different. A poster needs a quick and powerful hit. It should slug the viewers and make them say "wow." A brochure can take more time to communicate with the reader, who has the luxury of either reading it all at once or saving it for later. The proximity of viewing makes for a more personal experience. Therefore, designing for a piece viewed in such close quarters requires a different set of design techniques.

DESIGNING BROCHURES

The most common format for brochure is a *tri-fold*—an 8½ × 11 piece of paper folded into thirds (Figs. 52, 53, 54). This format maximizes available design space and still fits into a standard #10 business envelope, allowing businesses to easily send out marketing information without investing in different stationery sizes. The front panel of the tri-fold is considered the cover, so it must make an impact. The design approach is the same as with any other design—headline and image work together to create a wow factor that should entice the viewer to pick it up. Because tri-folds are commonly found in holders that typically obscure the lower half to two-thirds of the brochure, all of the important information and attention-getting design must appear on the exposed top portion of the brochure, a challenge that rivals that of designing a business card.

Many designers make the mistake of putting the company's logo at the top. Unless the logo is very well known, this hinders response to the brochure, as all the important information is pushed down and left hidden. Better to put the headline at the top, followed by the image and then the logo. People want to know the brochure's "what" before its "whom." It is best to keep the information simple, enhancing clarity and eliminating visual clutter among other brochures that may surround it.

Good flow, ease of readability and clarity of information are critical for the brochure's interior. The panel on the left is considered to be part of the interior. The right-hand panel is more independent because it folds out to expose the interior. It still must maintain a relationship with the rest of the interior, however, because they are seen together. Information that stands alone can be placed on the independent right panel. It is a good place to state facts, show pictures, provide testimonials, insert a stand-alone chart or give an overall introduction to the company. The bulk of the information should appear on the left and remaining interior panels. Be careful of headlines and imagery that traverse the crease between the left and center panels, as these will be effectively cut off by the independent right panel folded over the center when the tri-fold is first opened. All of the rules of design concerning column width, type size, leading, tracking, widows, orphans, quotation marks, jumping horizons, tombstoning, buried subheads, whispering headlines and so on, apply here. Because the folds in the

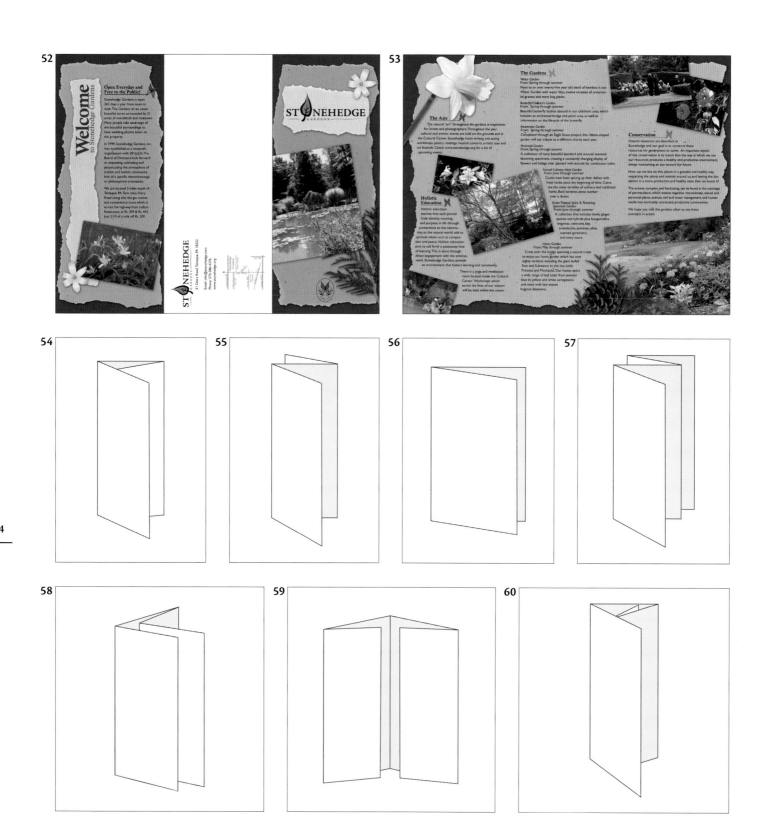

52, 53 Stonehedge Gardens brochure.   **54** Tri-fold.   **55** Z-fold, also known as an accordion fold.   **56** Booklet fold.   **57** Accordion fold.   **58** Parallel fold.   **59** Gatefold.   **60** Barrel fold.

brochure act as a visual barrier from panel to panel, the paragraphs should break logically. Never allow text to cross over a fold, because the crinkling of the paper along the fold line will obscure the letters. Always remember the audience and desired connotation.

The back panel of the brochure typically contains information such as hours of operation, the company address and phone number and other contact information, and sometimes a map. If the brochure contains a form to be filled out by the viewer, be sure to leave enough space to fill in the requested information. Test it by filling the form out yourself. Did you leave enough room

to allow for the idiosyncrasies of handwriting? Be careful not to include important information the customer will need to retain on the reverse of the form if this will be torn off and given back to the company.

There are other brochure formats available for different design approaches. An 8½ × 11 sheet of paper can be folded into a *z-fold* (Fig. 55), also called an *accordion fold*, creating two uninterrupted surfaces on which to design. If a company has access to a 6 × 9 booklet-style envelope, the same piece of paper can be folded in half instead of thirds, creating the appearance of a booklet (Fig. 56).

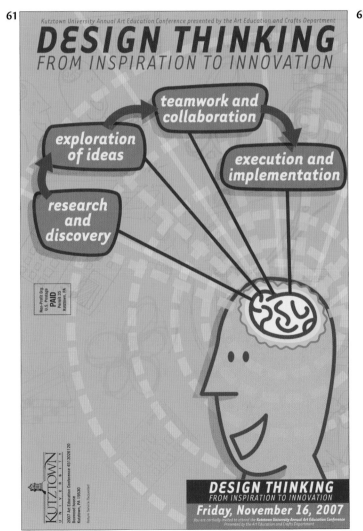

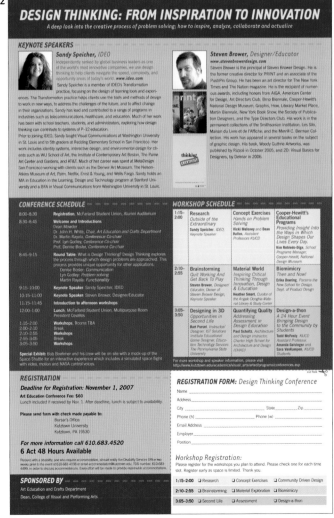

61, 62 Design Thinking conference mailer.

Sometimes an 8½ × 11 sheet of paper is not quite large enough to contain all of the necessary information, in which case legal-size paper, 8½ × 14, can be used. Folded into fourths, this sheet will still fit into a #10 business envelope. Folding methods include accordion (Fig. 57), parallel (Fig. 58), gate (Fig. 59) and barrel folds (Fig. 60). Although this larger size allows for more interesting folding and more space for design, it can incur greater printing costs. In the event legal-size paper is still not large enough, 11 × 17 paper can be used. The most common method of folding 11 × 17 for a brochure is to fold it in half lengthwise and then in half again. This size fits into a booklet-style envelope or can be arranged to leave a clear panel for self-mailing information (Figs. 61, 62).

AN INTERVIEW WITH AMANDA GEISINGER

Amanda Geisinger precociously declared in kindergarten that she was going to be a graphic designer, and never looked back. She was single-mindedly obsessed. Geisinger and crayons fell madly in love at an early age—although at first it was a relationship that seemed doomed to fail. As she was born blind, you'd think someone might have gently advised her that one needed to be able to see in order to dedicate one's life to work in a visual field. But fortunately, no one ever brought this to her attention. Through a childhood marked by what seemed like an endless succession of surgeries, Geisinger stubbornly colored on—even though she can remember not being able to see the lines in her coloring book (Fig. 63). Fortunately those surgeries worked out; by the time she hit college, she had enough functional vision to make a serious go of the art thing. Magnifying glass in one hand and colored pencil in the other, Geisinger attacked her major in communication design with a triple concentration: illustration, graphic and web design.

As she made her way through her formal design education, Geisinger's vision for her career began to come more sharply into focus. She discovered a passion for children's design and illustration, a knack for publication design and a fascination with the wide world of web. Today her magnifying glass and her Photoshop magnifying glass still play a significant role in her work, but she is indeed doing what she set out to do in kindergarten. After graduating, Geisinger moved to Manhattan and has had incredibly exciting experiences working professionally with amazing people and products both in children's publication and children's web design.

Who or what are your influences?

Like all designers, I have heroes that I admire from afar. However, I find that I have been most strongly influenced by the people that I have personally worked with—professors that patiently guided me through projects, designers and art directors that have taken me under their wing during internships and my present extremely talented colleagues. For me, seeing how someone else successfully handles the same problem that I'm facing has a much bigger impact than just looking at good design.

How do you overcome creative blocks? Where do you go for inspiration?

For small-scale project-based block, there are two solutions. The fail-proof for me is to walk away for at least three hours (or even better, overnight) and completely forget about the project. If I can just get away, when I come back I see what the problem was right away and I'm off and running. Unfortunately, in an office situation you don't typically have this option. In that case, I tend to suck it up and do rapid-fire options—I'll force myself to do several (or many) versions really, really quickly. Typically they're absolutely horrendous, but eventually one will hit on something that inspires me, and that will set me merrily off in the right direction.

For large-scale, longer-lasting, I-don't-want-to-be-a-designer-I-should-have-gone-to-med-school type situations (which I have experienced with some frequency), I think it's been most helpful for me to engage in something creative that is completely out of my comfort zone and not at all related to my work. For example, I found a stained glass class refreshing (I made a monster, woo!). More recently, poking at the world of cartooning has been filling that role. Also helpful is creating something for someone you love—even something simple like making a card for a friend. Your affection for that person can give quite a boost to your feelings for what you are doing, which in turn impacts the success of your efforts. Or, for the same reason, find content you're passionate about and find an excuse to work with it. When I'm only creating for money, my creative juices can go sour pretty quickly. I need other sources of motivation.

What are the differences and similarities in your experiences between the print and web environments?

The biggest difference for me has been the process. In the world of print, there was a small, focused amount of content, and that

content came before design. I never worked with *lorem ipsum* or placeholder images—design always began and was based on the actual copy and art. After the layout was designed, it would route through a team of about ten editors—about four or five times—and every single letter, punctuation mark, space and image would be scrutinized intensely. After the file finally got handed to the printer, we'd get proofs and repeat the process, this time with a lightbox. Once a magazine went to press, the content couldn't be changed.

In web, because there is a huge amount of constantly changing content, design has to come before that content. Now, instead of joyfully agonizing over each and every letter, I'm designing the broader framework with placeholder content. When design is complete, a developer pushes the work live and hooks that framework up to a content management system, a web-based application that allows producers and editors to feed the actual content (like copy, videos and games) straight into that framework in real time without the help of a designer or

programmer. The downside is that design is forced to surrender some control of the appearance of the final product. The upside is that this kind of system allows for an incredible amount of data, flexibility, error correction, automation and extremely fast content production.

Also, a magazine is focused on relatively independent content creation, while the goal of the websites I've worked on is to support the ventures of an entire company. So, while working in print I got to hire illustrators to create original art, in web I work primarily with pre-existing style guides. One of the most similar things is working within a visual system. At a magazine, a lot of pages can be based off of a template: The department pages are always laid out and styled a certain way, the table of contents follows a form, and so on. Body copy is always a particular font size and color. Etcetera. In web, we work primarily out of templates, too. This allows the artwork on each page to vary, while maintaining consistency and establishing a brand across the site

66

With the infusion of digital technologies into the publication world, where do you see magazine design heading for the future?

You know, I'm not sure. I think that there is still a lot of interest out there in the general public for the traditional magazine form. People like interacting with traditional books and magazines, and engagement time seems to be significantly longer with paper media. However, where the Internet waddles in and makes a mess is that, while there is no strong opposition to the magazine form, people are now more reluctant to pay for content. Another huge part of the problem for magazines is also the trend in advertising right now. Despite having what (I think) research shows to be a significantly lower engagement level, digital advertising is seen as having more value than print because of the high traffic a website can generate.

I'm personally rooting for the survival of the traditional paper-based magazine. I love working in the digital environment, but it so far has not been able to create an experience that successfully replicates, replaces or compels me to abandon my devotion to the world of printed material.

What do you feel are the most important skills for a young designer to develop?

Type. I kind of feel like this is a no-brainer. If you're not good at type, you're not good at design. I also feel like it can be one of the most difficult aspects of design to learn. I still have very little confidence in my own type skills.

Composition. Also a no-brainer.

Which goes hand in hand with *hierarchy*. It's important to know what's important and to treat it accordingly.

Concepting. Any monkey with Photoshop can do something stylish; smart and thoughtful sets you apart.

And yet… *software skills.* If you're not comfortable with the tools in your hands, it's going to show in the work you make with them.

66 Hand-lettered wedding invitation for Darbie Boswell and Jon Pelachick.

You incorporate hand lettering in your design work, such as the wedding invitation created for Darbie and Jon, as well as in your illustration work. Please describe your process when approaching a job that requires hand lettering (Fig. 66).

Usually when I hand letter something it's because I know exactly what I want it to look like and I know that a font can't do that. Rarely do I not start without a pretty clear vision in my head. If the letterforms are complex or I have a very specific goal, I'll do my version of type-research—I'll scour my font collections for letterforms that have elements of what I'm going for. For example, when I was working on the piece for Craig and Lisa, I know that I wanted the letters to fairly closely resemble a classic serif; I just needed them to be a bit more flexible (Figs. 67, 68, 69). So I took a tour of my serif folder before settling into my drawing. If I don't have a clear enough vision of where I'm going, I'll do some sketchy thumbnails for layout. From there it's straight to the tight full-size sketch. When I am reasonably happy with it I'll ink right on to the sketch. Typically I'll work in pen, and if I need color I'll add it digitally.

67

70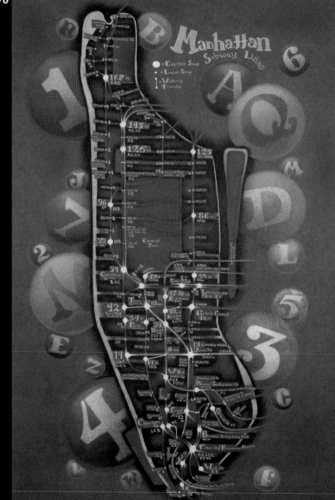

68

69

67, 68, 69, 70 Samples of Amanda Geisinger's work.

What influence does typography have in your web design work?

The primary audience for my work is children. They have the expectation that they won't have to read much to accomplish that (or they're just not old enough to be able to read), and so consequently they have a low tolerance for text in all of its forms—be it headlines, body copy and even navigation. I think this is a fun challenge—both from a stylistic and content perspective. Making type entertaining/intriguing while maintaining extreme ease of use is an interesting balancing game. The less fun challenge comes from having less control over the styling of individual instances of copy, because almost all of it is automated or entered by non-designers into the content management system and then dynamically styled. (I have nightmares about not being able to kern some of our headlines.) I think as the Web evolves, we'll see this issue get more resolution. I'm pretty excited for the widespread implementation of HTML5 and Typekit.

Has there been a particular job you found to be the highlight of your career to date?

My jobs have all been absolutely amazing—and really fit my interests and skill set I think as well as perhaps professional work can. I would definitely say that designing for children is really where my passion (and aesthetic sensibility) lies, and I'm fortunate to be employed in that area. I would say that the job I have now is definitely a dream job. However, discovering new kinds of work that I can do just for fun has been just as much of a highlight. I got introduced to the strange new world of comics when part of one of my professional jobs became to work with amazing editors and artists to help in the purchasing, creation and editing of work for a comic book. Going in, I knew nothing about comics (well, I liked Garfield as a kid, but that was not particularly useful knowledge)—and it was really exciting to get to learn so much from some of the greatest talent in the business. Through them I became enchanted with the medium, and trying to pick it up on my own for fun has been an engaging and

refreshing process that consistently forces me out of my technical and creative comfort zones.

What would be a dream job for you?

Illustrating textbooks or nonfiction for children! My favorite projects have been illustrations that explain how things work to kids—I had a lot of fun with nuclear power and viral replication. I'd also like to write a book at some point, but I am still undecided as to the subject matter.

In your opinion, what separates a good designer from a great designer?

On top of a solid technical and conceptual skill set, I think what really impresses me is the ability not just to deal with the details but to be subtle with them. I'm always surprised at the power of soft touches—like a .25 stroke, a 5% drop shadow or just knocking back text from black to 90% gray.

What is one (or several) of your biggest typography-related pet peeves?

Using a font to mimic a hand-done look. This causes me pain. Mental anguish. Distress. I die inside every time I see it. "Handwriting" fonts are an abomination. Pens are your friends, people.

Beauty before function. The designer was trying so pretentiously hard to get the pretty on that type that was meant to be read that it is not actually legible. One of the things that I really appreciate about designing for kids is that it's a little harder to fall into this trap. Because they're new to reading, there tends to be a lot more of sensitivity on the part of everyone involved in the design process to the usability of the type.

Large unformatted chunks of body copy. Headlines are not the only type that needs designer-love! Paragraphs can be beautiful, too!

Papyrus. I have a sense of humor about Comic Sans, but Papyrus is just not funny. EVER. Please don't use it. EVER. Thanks.

TYPE TIDBITS

Serif or Sans Serif?
I think serifs are beautiful!

Favorite letter?
Definitely ö. I just got back from Sweden, and I have such letterform envy! I love that mark! Also, I am totally addicted to the em dash. Swoon. And these things { }.

Guilty pleasure font?
I don't know about a font, but I'm all about cheesy effects—on headline-size type, load me up with the strokes, gradients, drop shadows, textures ... I'm lucky that I design primarily for children, so I can get away with a lot more cheese than the average type designer.

Helvetica or Verdana?
Definitely Helvetica; but I appreciate Verdana in the appropriate context, too!

Favorite complementary font pair?
You know, I don't think I've ever used them together, but at the moment my two favorite fonts are Cochin and Gotham. Hmmm ...

Paper or screen?
Paper for sure!

Mac or PC?
Mac.

Uppercase or lowercase?
Lowercase. Uppercase is loud, and despite working in Times Square, I like things quiet.

Design: Lifestyle or just a way to earn a living?
It's more like a chronic disease. There's no cure—once you've learned how to kern, you'll never be able to stop.

Illustrating or creating design?
Definitely illustrating—although I would argue that there is quite a bit of design involved in illustration.

Subway or taxi?
The subway system here is kind of like my magic carpet—a crowded, unpredictable and colorfully populated magic carpet—that takes me almost anywhere I could want to go. While it occasionally does break down and break my heart, my affection for it knows no bounds.

PARAGRAPH
GALLERY

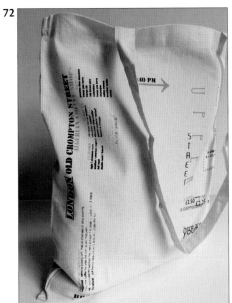

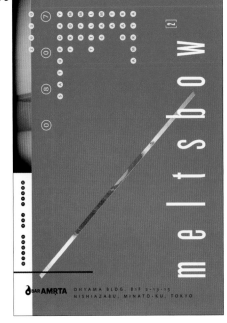

71 Benjamin Wiley Partnership Program. **72** Coffee Bean screenprint on bag. **73** The Metamorphosis: Conventional Book. **74** Carlson & Keller wedding invitations.
75 Meltsbow poster #02.

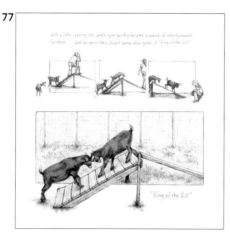

76, 77, 78 Best Wedding Present Ever. **79, 80, 81, 82** Les 10 Ans Du Café Zinette posters. **83** "29 Things Young Designers Need to Know" poster. **84** Memories book.

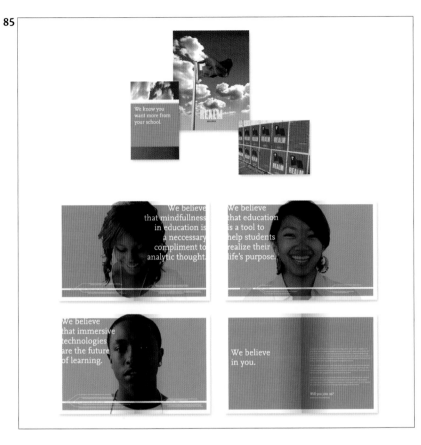

85 Realm Charter School Application. **86** Pellegrino event poster. **87** Projection Typography. **88** Verba et Voces poster. **89** Young Widows at Kung Fu Necktie poster.

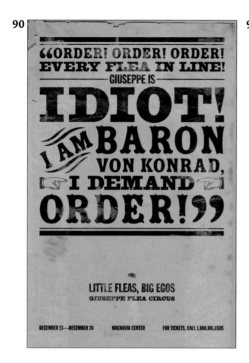

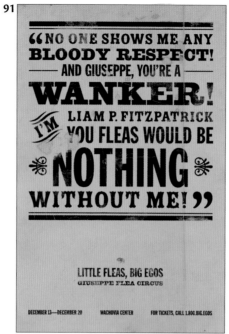

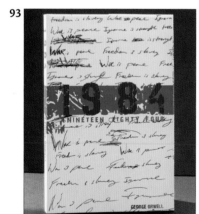

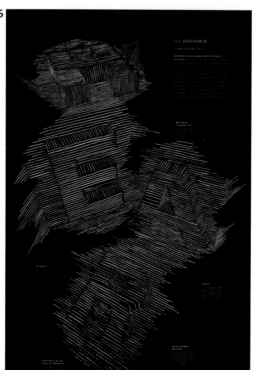

90, 91, 92 Guiseppe Flea Circus posters. **93** *1984*, by George Orwell, book cover. **94** Cross-cultural wedding invitation. **95** Audio Visualize poster. **96** Children Learn What They Live mural.

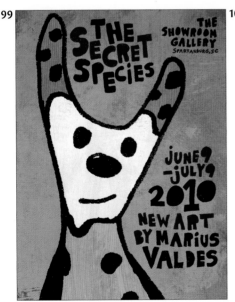

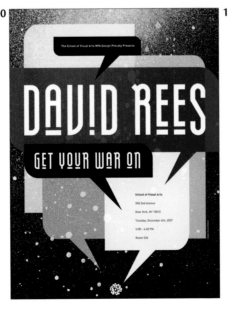

97 Burroughs typographic poster. **98** Misspent: The Poster. **99** The Secret Species poster. **100** David Rees lecture poster. **101** Seu Jorge's poster.

102, 103 Istanbul Deko Etiquette.   **104** Music for Toys 3 festival poster.   **105** Lettering page.   **106** SS-Japandroids poster.   **107** The Krea Art & Design School poster.

ABOUT THE IMAGES IN THIS CHAPTER

Fig. 14
TITLE: Strjall Magazine
UNIVERSITY: Kutztown University
DESIGNER: Matt Twombly
FONTS USED: Hand lettering,
NeutraText

Fig. 49
TITLE: Artscience Colloquium poster
DESIGN FIRM: Formalism
DESIGNERS: Sietske Sips, Taconis Stolk
FONT USED: Helvetica Neue
CLIENT: Artscience Interfaculty,
University of the Arts, The Hague

Fig. 50
TITLE: Printing 101 seminar
DESIGN FIRM: Gigi McGee Design
DESIGNER: Gigi McGee
FONT USED: Meta
CLIENT: Innovation Printing

Fig. 51
TITLE: Frequency North posters
DESIGN FIRM: The College of Saint
Rose Office of Creative Services
and Marketing
DESIGNER: Mark Hamilton
FONT USED: LLRubberGrotesque,
Helvetica Narrow, Franklin
Gothic Condensed
CLIENT: The College of Saint Rose

Figs. 52, 53
TITLE: Stonehedge Gardens brochure
UNIVERSITY: Kutztown University,
Designathon event
DESIGNER: Greg Christman
FONTS USED: Gill Sans, Calisto, Cochin
CLIENT: Stonehedge Gardens

Figs. 61, 62
TITLE: Design Thinking
conference mailer
FONTS USED: Tarzana Narrow,
Trade Gothic
CLIENT: Kutztown University Art
Education and Crafts department

Figs. 63, 64, 65, 66, 67, 68, 69, 70
© Amanda Geisinger

Fig. 71
TITLE: Benjamin Wiley
Partnership Program
DESIGN FIRM: PPO&S
DESIGNER: Tracy L. Kretz
FONTS USED: Fury, Garage Gothic
CLIENT: Pennsylvania State System
of Higher Education

Fig. 72
TITLE: Coffee Bean screenprint on bag
UNIVERSITY: Middlesex University
PROFESSOR: Andy Gossett
DESIGNER: Dimitra Karagiannakou

Fig. 73
TITLE: The Metamorphosis:
Conventional Book
UNIVERSITY: University of Lincoln
PROFESSORS: Barrie Tullet,
Philippa Wood
DESIGNER: Charlotte Middleton
FONTS USED: Letter Press Type, Calibri

Fig. 74
TITLE: Carlson & Keller
wedding invitations
DESIGN FIRM: IM1984
DESIGNER: Samuel L Tapia
FONTS USED: Politica, Alright Sans
CLIENTS: Kara Carlson, Steven Keller

Fig. 75
TITLE: Meltsbow poster #02
DESIGN FIRM: Meltsbow
DESIGNER: Norifumi Yoshida
FONT USED: Knockout,
Whitney Index & Scala San
CLIENT: Meltsbow

Figs. 76, 77, 78
TITLE: Best Wedding Present Ever
UNIVERSITY: Kutztown University
PROFESSOR: Denise Bosler
DESIGNER: Cheryl Sheeler
FONT USED: Hand lettering

Figs. 79, 80, 81, 82
TITLE: Les 10 Ans Du Café
Zinette posters
DESIGN FIRM: GVA Studio
DESIGNERS: GVA Studio
CLIENT: Café Zinette

Figs. 83
TITLE: "29 Things Young Designers
Need to Know" poster
DESIGN FIRM: id29
DESIGNER: Doug Bartow
FONTS USED: Pf Din Text Condensed
Pro, Ff Scala and Ff Scala Sans, Ocrb
CLIENT: HOW Magazine

Figs. 84
TITLE: Memories book
UNIVERSITY: Moore College
of Art & Design
PROFESSOR: Daniel Sipe
DESIGNER: Lindsay M Deisher
FONT USED: Garamond

Fig. 85
TITLE: Realm Charter School
Application
ART DIRECTOR: Christopher Simmons
DESIGNER: Christopher Simmons,
Justin Holbrook, Nathan Sharp
FONTS USED: Nexus, Vitesse,
Tungsten, Cyclone
CLIENT: Realm Charter School

Fig. 86
TITLE: Pellegrino event poster
DESIGN FIRM: The College of Saint
Rose Office of Creative Services
and Marketing
ART DIRECTOR: Mark Hamilton
DESIGNER: Chris Parody
FONTS USED: Wide Latin, Medicine,
Bleeding Cowboys, Digital 7,
Carnival, Rosewood, Allstar, Army,
Ironwood, Back to 1982, Bellerose,
Saddlebag, Paisley, Old English,
Bauer Bodoni
CLIENT: The College of Saint Rose

Fig. 87
TITLE: Projection Typography
DESIGN FIRM: Claude Bossett
DESIGNER: Claude Bossett
FONT USED: Impact

Fig. 88
TITLE: Verba et Voces poster
DESIGNER: Kamil Kamysz
FONT USED: Mixed
CLIENT: Capella Cracoviensis

Fig. 89
TITLE: Young Widows at
Kung Fu Necktie poster
DESIGN FIRM: Underground America
DESIGNER: Justin Renninger
FONT USED: Avenir
CLIENT: R5 Productions

Figs. 90, 91, 92
TITLE: Guiseppe Flea Circus posters
UNIVERSITY: Tyler School of Art,
Temple University
PROFESSOR: Dermot MacCormack
DESIGNER: Neha Agarwal
FONTS USED: Cg Egiziano,
Franklin Gothic, Zebrawood

Fig. 93
TITLE: 1984 book cover
UNIVERSITY: University of
Wisconsin-Whitewater
PROFESSOR: Renee Melton
DESIGNER: Dan Schunk
FONT USED: 28 Days Later

Fig. 94
TITLE: Cross-cultural wedding invitation
DESIGN FIRM: Latrice Graphic Design
DESIGNER: Vicki L. Meloney
FONT USED: Bickham Script Pro
CLIENTS: Stacey and Kostia Peki

Fig. 95
TITLE: Audio Visualize poster
UNIVERSITY: California College
of the Arts
PROFESSORS: Brett MacFadden,
Scott Thorpe
DESIGNER: Nicholas Navarro
FONT USED: Univers 47 Light Condensed,
Univers 57 Condensed, Univers 67
Bold Condensed

Fig. 96
TITLE: Children Learn
What They Live mural
DESIGN FIRM: About Face Design
DESIGNER: Peter Camburn
FONTS USED: Helvetica, Garamond,
Futura, Gill Sans, Rotis Semi
Serif, Bodoni Roman, Baskerville,
Courier, Cooper Black, Basetwelve,
Frutiger, Univers 47
CLIENT: Institute for Safe Families

Fig. 97
TITLE: Burroughs typographic poster
UNIVERSITY: Moore College
of Art & Design
PROFESSOR: John Burns
DESIGNER: Jamie L. Blank
FONTS USED: Helvetica Neue
(Bold, Regular, Light)

Fig. 98
TITLE: Misspent: The Poster
DESIGNER: Ervin Esen
FONTS USED: Knockout, Archer,
Numbers Depot, Soho, Sarah
Script, Eames Century Modern

Fig. 99
TITLE: The Secret Species poster
DESIGN FIRM: Zoo Valdes
DESIGNER: Marius Valdes
TYPE DESIGNER: Bob Wertz, Sketchbook B
FONT USED: Hand-rendered version
of Valdes Poster Sans
CLIENT: The Showroom Gallery

Fig. 100
TITLE: David Rees lecture poster
DESIGN FIRM: Masood Bukhari LLC
ART DIRECTOR: Steven Heller
DESIGNER: Masood Bukhari
FONTS USED: Modula (customized), Meta
CLIENT: School of Visual Arts MFAD

Fig. 101
TITLE: Seu Jorge's poster
PROFESSOR: Mario Moura
DESIGNER: Diego Henrique
    Oliveira De Paiva
FONT USED: Sr Jorge

Figs. 102, 103
TITLE: Istanbul Deko Etiquette
DESIGN FIRM: Istanbul Deko
ART DIRECTOR: Geray Gençer

DESIGNER: Geray Gençer
FONT USED: Various
CLIENT: Istanbul Deko

Fig. 104
TITLE: Music for Toys 3 festival poster
DESIGN FIRM:
    www.sergiomembrillas.com
DESIGNER: Sergio Membrillas
FONT USED: Hand lettering
CLIENT: Monster K7

Fig. 105
TITLE: Lettering page
UNIVERSITY: UCN
PROFESSOR: Rikke Kjær
DESIGNER: Ana-Gabriela Stroe
FONT USED: Hand lettering

Fig. 106
TITLE: SS-Japandroids poster
DESIGN FIRM: Straightsilly
ART DIRECTOR: Mig Reyes

DESIGNERS: Mig Reyes, Kyle Stewart
FONT USED: Alright Sans
CLIENT: Schubas

Fig. 107
TITLE: The Krea Art & Design
    School poster
DESIGN FIRM: Fabergraph
DESIGNER: Béla Frank
FONT USED: Clarendon
CLIENT: Krea Art & Design School

chapter six

{ PAGE }

The headline is written; the imagery is selected; the body copy is set to Garamond 9/13; the complementary font for the remainder of the text is Trade Gothic; the color palette is lime green, orange and brown; the size is an 18 × 24 inch poster. All the decisions have been made and it is now time to put it all together as a designed page. Think of this page as a container that holds all of the information. How it accomplishes this is up to the designer. It can be neat and orderly or fluid and organic. Think about all of the designed materials you see on a daily basis. Start in the bathroom: toothpaste, mouthwash, maybe a magazine beside the toilet. All of these are information containers that are designed in very different ways. Making your way into the kitchen for breakfast reveals a plethora of new sources of information: a box of breakfast cereal, a coffee canister, the daily newspaper, yesterday's mail, a child's permission slip—all inundate us with information. According to the article "Our Rising Ad Dosage: It's Not as Oppressive as Some Think," from *Media Matters* (February 15, 2007), the average person is exposed to six hundred advertisements or more every single day. If the total number of all forms of designed materials were added up, these exposures would reach into the thousands or tens of thousands. With this much exposure, it is important to understand how to turn letters, words, sentences and paragraphs into pages.

LAYOUT, DESIGN AND COMMUNICATION

The challenge to creating a successful design is knowing where, when and how to use different design techniques to place information, visuals and other design elements to make the final page communicate the necessary information. The viewer doesn't want to have to work when he sees a page, and he shouldn't have to. The headline, imagery, subheads, body copy, captions and other information need to present themselves in a way that logically supports the communication goal.

The process of placing information on a page and organizing it is called *creating a layout*. The goal is to arrange all of the elements that belong on the page in such a way as to form relationships. Layout relationships are important because this is how a viewer gathers information from a page. A headline that relies on an image for meaning does not work well if the image and the headline are too far apart. Elements that belong together should be positioned in proximity to one another. However, layout alone does not a successful page make. Design is the process that gives the page personality and artistic value. Decisions about the font, color, image and placement of these items are what create the design.

Communication comes from the layout and design working well together. Good communication will always be a top priority for any client and should be the top requirement for every designer. A page

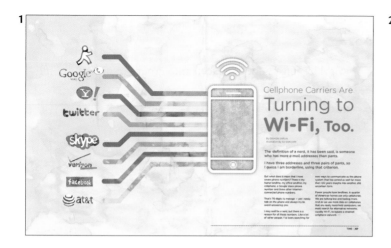

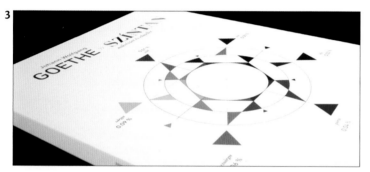

1 Magazine spread. **2** Christmast typo poster. **3, 4, 5, 6** *The Theory of Colors* book redesign.

must look good, of course, but it cannot sacrifice communication for appearance. The design must still communicate to the viewer that the item is on sale; the dose of the drug should be two pills every six hours; the company made a 10 percent increase in profits in a particular year; the car comes in red, blue or silver paint selections; or that this camera will make her child look perfect in every picture. Knowledge of relationship principles, grid, hierarchy and visual concept will allow the designer to make appropriate decisions in creating a well-designed layout for optimum communication (Figs. 1, 2, 3, 4, 5, 6).

GESTALT THEORY

Gestalt is a form of psychology that focuses on cognitive behaviors. Designers are influenced by the visual perceptual aspect of this,

particularly the theory that the whole is greater than the sum of its parts. The mind copes with the visual confusion of our everyday world by consolidating objects into groups in order to simplify input. For instance, when our eyes see a tail, paws, legs, a body, fur, a collar, ears and nose, our mind brings these parts together to register a cat. The mind effectively simplifies the parts by making it into a single object. Applying this theory to design creates unity within a piece. The stronger the relationship between elements on a page, the better the communication. This theory also helps the designer influence the viewer by controlling how the design is viewed. Five design principles derive from the Gestalt theory: proximity, similarity, continuity, closure and figure/ground. Each employs different methods to create unity within the whole.

7

P r o x i m i t y

Proximity

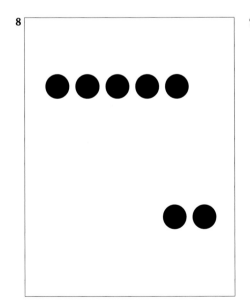

8

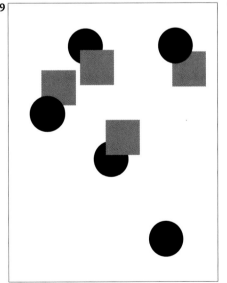

9

10

Proximity

7 The closer the objects, the more proximity. **8** The five circles at the top of the page and two circles at the bottom of the page have proximity to each other, respectively. The two groups do not have proximity with each other. **9** Overlapping objects creates the strongest proximity. **10** The headline and image have proximity, while the body copy remains separate.

PROXIMITY

Proximity refers to objects placed close together being perceived as a group. When spaced far apart, objects are perceived as separate (Fig. 7). Proximity occurs when objects are closer to each other than to any other object. Proximity spacing can be as close objects in direct contact, or as far apart as opposite sides of a page (Fig. 8). The strongest proximity relationship is when objects overlap, leaving no doubt that they belong together (Fig. 9). Using other design elements, such as lines or shapes to surround objects, also creates strong proximity. Lines and shapes can also link objects by passing through them or by underlining them (Fig. 10).

SIMILARITY

Shared visual characteristics automatically create relationships. The more alike objects appear, the more likely they are to be seen

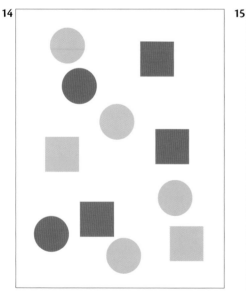

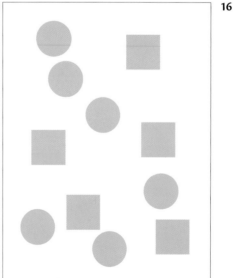

11 These two dogs have no similarity other than in species name. **12, 13** These two dogs have similarity in species name, color and adornment. **14** The objects of like color have similarity. **15** The objects of like shape have similarity. **16** The headline and subheads maintain similarity through color, whereas the body copy maintains similarity through color and shape.

as a group. Note that similarity is based upon what an object looks like, not what an object is. Two dogs on a page do not automatically have similarity because they are dogs. One could be a Great Dane and the other a Chihuahua—dogs that have very little in common (Fig. 11). However, similarity would be created if both were brown and wearing red collars (Figs. 12, 13).

Similarity can be achieved in many different ways, including size, color and shape. Objects of a like size have similarity, illustrated by the fact that on a page filled with big circles and little circles, the mind will see all the big circles as belonging in one group while all the little circles are in another, even if they are evenly dispersed on the page. Color and shape have the same effect. On a page filled with similar-sized circles and squares in two different colors, the mind will separate them into two groups based upon color (Fig. 14). However, if the circles and squares are all the same size and color, the mind will group them according to shape (Figs. 15, 16).

CONTINUITY

The principle of *continuity* dictates that once the eye begins to follow something, it will continue traveling in that direction until it encounters another object (Fig. 17). A good example is a line with an arrow at the end of it (Fig. 18). This symbol indicates that a viewer should follow the line to the end to see where the arrow is pointing. Symbols and objects that are similar to arrows, such

as a hand with a pointing finger, are used frequently in design to create continuity.

Other ways to lead the eye include a photograph or illustration containing an eye. A common design rule is that if an image of a person is used, make sure the person is looking toward the rest of the design (Fig. 19). This helps the viewer move through the information instead of looking off the edge of the page, turning away from the information. A designer can also create a path through the page, either literally or figuratively. An image of a road, a path, a fence, a row of flowers or a tunnel can all guide the eye across a page. For readers from Western cultures, the natural inclination is to lead the viewer's eye from left to right. Continuity gives the designer significant control over the viewer. The mind can't help but follow the path.

CLOSURE

Closure is related to continuity in that it asks the eye to complete a path. As long as enough essential information is present, the mind supplies the missing pieces of an object (Fig. 20). Closure works best with objects that are recognizable. For example, an outline of a triangle that slowly has pieces taken away is still recognizable as a triangle even when down to a bare minimum of pieces. Complex objects are trickier for the mind to complete (Figs. 21, 22, 23). The designer must strike a balance between what

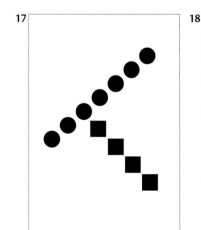 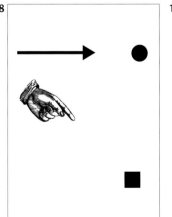  

17 The eye naturally follows a path, which can be a useful tool in establishing continuity in a design. **18** Directing a viewer with visual cues, such as arrows and pointing hands, gives control over how a design is viewed. **19** The dog's eye directs a viewer to follow its gaze to the headline.

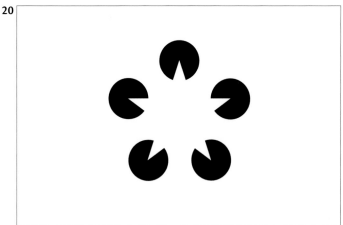

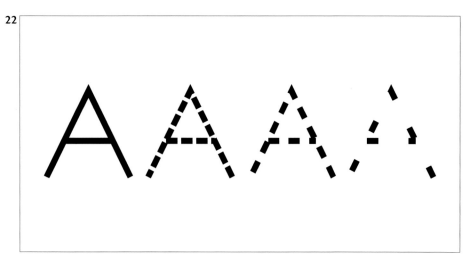

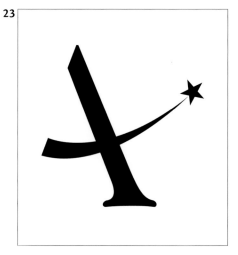

is taken away and what remains. The mind cannot complete the object if too much of it is missing. Closure can be found quite often in paintings, mosaics and sculptures through the ages. Classical artists have long recognized the ability of the mind to fill in the blanks.

FIGURE/GROUND

The *figure/ground principle* is based upon the relationship between an object and the surrounding space. Figure/ground is also referred to as positive and negative space, the positive being the object and the negative referring to the space around it (Fig. 24).

This principle gives the illusion of depth, and is a fundamental principle used in almost every design. Figure refers to more than just imagery; type is considered figure as well (Fig. 25). Figure/ground can be used quite creatively when both the figure and ground form recognizable shapes at the same time. There are many examples of this, one of the most common being the optical illusion of two opposing faces on opposite sides of the page with the negative space in between them forming a lamp, spindle or another recognizable shape (Fig. 26).

20 It is easy to discern the star shape even though the star is formed only by negative space. **21** Completing the lines around the head and back is unnecessary for determining that the image is a panda. **22** Experimentation needs to occur when taking pieces away from an image. Taking away too much will result in an unrecognizable form. **23** Even though the left stroke is missing, the logo is still recognizable as an *A*.

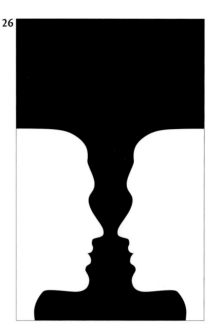

RELATIONSHIPS

Understanding how page relationships work is vital to the creation of a successful design. Balance, unity, contrast and rhythm are design principles that reflect the basic human need to create order. These relationship principles are always combined to create a design layout. They also complement the Gestalt principles for arranging content on a page.

BALANCE

There are two types of balance: symmetrical and asymmetrical. *Symmetrical balance* has a central axis, with both halves having the same visual weight. *Asymmetrical balance* also has a central axis, but with unequal visual weight. People like balance and seek it out. Human beings have symmetrical balance around an axis down the center of our bodies, the left side of our body reflecting the right side. Although nature prefers symmetrical balance, the two sides are never an identical duplication. Radial symmetry, symmetry that extends from a central point instead of off a central axis, is also found frequently in nature. All forms of balance are applicable to design layouts, though radial symmetry is seen in fine art more often than in design.

Symmetrical balance gives the feeling of being orderly and formal. The weight of the page contents is evenly distributed across the layout (Figs. 27, 28). This doesn't mean that the halves must be identical, however. It means that the visual weight of one item needs to be equal to the visual weight of another. The central axis can run horizontally, vertically or diagonally. For instance, a large bold headline can easily have the same visual weight as a photograph filling a similar sized space. Similarly, a headline positioned as a block of text is balanced by an equally weighted column of body copy (Figs. 29, 30). Another example would be a large image on one half that is balanced by a headline plus two blocks of body copy on the other half. The only rule is that the same visual weight must be generated by the elements in both halves (Fig. 31).

Asymmetrical balance feels dynamic, tense and expressive. It can't be cut neatly in half, which provides many more possibilities for content arrangement. Asymmetrical balance can be achieved in two ways. The first is a carefully planned layout that intermingles

24 Simple figure/ground relationship. The blue background is the ground and the dog silhouette is the figure. 25 In this example, the figure is the headline type while the dog photo is the ground. 26 This image, showing both a lamp and human faces, plays with the idea of competing figure/ground relationships.

large and small text and images with no obvious effort at maintaining balance on each half, but which strikes a solid visual relationship between all the elements (Fig. 32). The second asymmetrical balance style is to purposely create tension on the page by placing elements so as to severely throw off the balance (Fig. 33). For instance, grouping the headline, imagery and body text all on the left side of the page and leaving the right side blank makes the page feel heavily weighted on the left. Asymmetrical balance is best used for dramatic visual effect (Figs. 34, 35).

27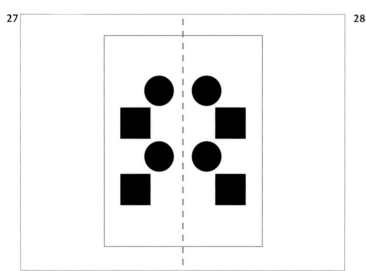

28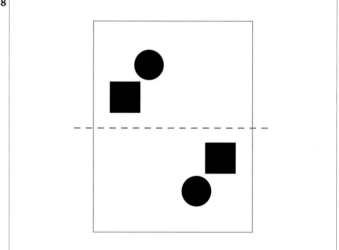

29

30

31

27, 28 As long as a page has equal weight distribution on either side of its axis, the image is considered to have symmetrical balance. **29, 30** The headline and image with body copy occupy the same amount of space and generate the same visual weight, therefore creating symmetrical balance even though they are not exactly the same objects. **31** The visual weight of the Pez candy topper is heavy, and even though it is smaller than the type area, the lighter weight of the type creates equal visual weight.

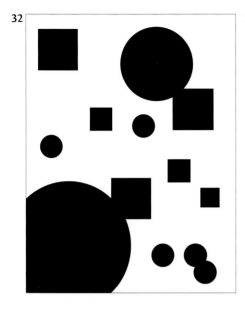

32

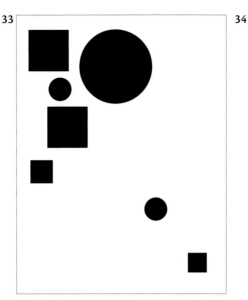

33

34

ASYMMETRICAL

Lorem ipsum dolor sit amet, consectetur adipiscing elit. Aliquam aliquam, velit eu vehicula convallis, libero velit varius tellus, vel lacinia libero dui vel lorem. Donec nisl tellus, posuere eget semper vel, auctor eu odio. Maecenas urna quam, viverra in congue non, pretium eget ante. Vivamus dui magna, lacinia nec suscipit non, posuere quis diam. In id sem condimentum augue lacinia venenatis nec eget dui. Etiam volutpat porta tellus, at interdum ipsum vulputate sit amet. Proin a odio at nibh pellentesque pharetra rutrum ut mi. Nunc mollis odio non arcu feugiat placerat. Donec vulputate mauris id felis faucibus id suscipit sapien

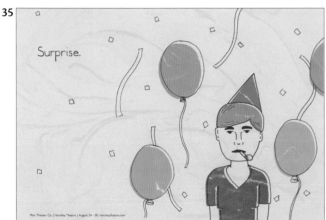

35

Surprise.

Mix Theater Co. | Hershey Theatre | August 24 - 28 | hersheytheatre.com

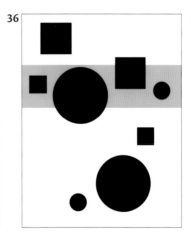

36

37

UNITY

Lorem ipsum dolor sit amet, consectetur adipiscing elit. Aliquam aliquam, velit eu vehicula convallis, libero velit varius tellus, vel lacinia libero dui vel lorem. Donec nisl tellus, posuere eget semper vel, auctor eu odio. Maecenas urna quam, viverra in congue non, pretium eget ante. Vivamus dui magna, lacinia nec suscipit non, posuere quis diam. In id sem condimentum augue lacinia venenatis nec eget dui. Etiam volutpat porta tellus, at interdum ipsum vulputate sit amet. Proin a odio at nibh pellentesque pharetra rutrum ut mi. Nunc mollis odio non arcu feugiat placerat. Donec vulputate mauris id felis faucibus id suscipit sapien. In in lectus ipsum, auctor elementum purus. Cras quis mauris sed diam feugiat ullamcorper non nec arcu. Aenean rutrum ultrices mauris, vel euismod justo tincidunt eu. Aliquam dignissim consectetur nibh, ut dapibus nisi pellentesque nec. Vestibulum vitae lorem nulla. Integer porta nisl quis risus cursus auctor vel non ante. Integer tempus mattis lectus, ut auctor neque varius in. Duis eu libero nec ipsum auctor dictum.

Donec purus justo, vestibulum sed dapibus ac, ornare id lorem. Nam in nibh dolor, congue consectetur augue. In aliquet augue ligula. Integer aliquet posuere sem nec

UNITY

Unity is the quality of maintaining consistency by forming a visual relationship between the page elements, to prevent a design from spiraling into a chaotic mess. There are many ways to bring unity to a design layout. Using any of the Gestalt principles discussed above automatically forms relationships between elements on the page, resulting in unity. Similar aesthetic qualities such as color, shape, texture and line quality forge relationships between the common similar elements. The use of a single font, or of a complementary pair, gives the design consistency over the page. Size also creates unity, in that elements that are either very large or very small are perceived by the viewer as related. A subtler sense of unity is conveyed by underlying graphic elements, such as fields of color, lines and shapes surrounding other design components (Figs. 36, 37).

32 Evenly distributing elements on a page with no thought to balance usually results in an asymmetric format. **33** Purposefully created tension can add a dynamic zing to a page. **34** The severe negative space on the right side of the page forces the viewer's eye to bounce back to the left side elements. **35** Heavy imagery on the right side of the page is asymmetrically balanced by the small type. **36** Size, shape, color and underlying connective elements all help create unity. **37** The yellow of the headline, image and graphic flowers create unity even though they are separated.

CONTRAST

Contrast between elements creates interest and emphasis. Without sufficient contrast, a viewer will see the page as monotonous and unexciting. Size, color, texture, type, alignment and other properties are used to create contrast. The greater the differences in these properties, the more contrast the page will have. For instance, a large headline and small imagery, or vice versa, use contrasting sizes to create visual interest (Figs. 38, 39). A complementary type pair is also a great way to create contrast. Combined with contrasting color, this gives the page an instant spark. The goal is to create enough contrast

38

39

40
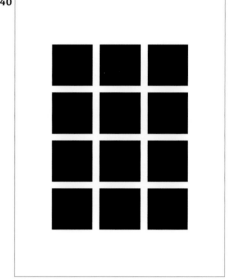

41

42
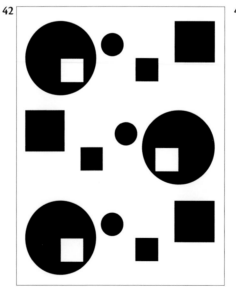

43

38, 39 Working with opposites, large type and small image or large image and small type, creates contrast. All elements being the same size results in a dull and monotonous layout. **40** Repetition is used to create movement. The series of squares encourages a viewer to move along the page from one square to the next. **41** The repeated flowers create movement and excitement. **42** Rhythmic patterns create movement in the same way a tune would; it gives the highs and lows of a tune. **43** The large to small flower pattern at the top leads the viewer into the page, and the small to large flower pattern at the bottom brings the viewer back in, creating a circular eye movement.

for the viewer to become engaged with the page, but not so much that the viewer's eye bounces back and forth between too many elements with nowhere to focus. The differences must be obvious.

MOVEMENT

Movement is the culmination of both Gestalt and relationship principles. All of these principles create a relationship that allows a designer to control a viewer's eye on a page. The eye will follow large elements to smaller ones, from one grouping to another, and from one side of the page to the other. A good design will have clear movement through the page, tying it all together.

Repetition is strategically placed repeating design elements that create a visual connection for the eye to follow (Fig. 40). Repeated elements also enhance consistency within a design. Shapes, lines, images, colors and fonts all can be used as repeated elements (Fig. 41). This can also be accomplished on a larger scale by repeating elements across several pages. Be careful, though; repetition can backfire, creating monotony if overused.

Rhythm is what creates the flow through a page. To understand this concept, envision a favorite song as shapes flowing across a page. The highs and lows within the tune will generate a rhythm that is repeated over and over. This effect can be replicated with type and imagery in design (Figs. 42, 43). For instance, using varying sized images across the top of a page and repeating the same image size variation pattern again at the bottom of a page will create a rhythmic flow.

GRID

The *grid*, a matrix of vertical and horizontal lines that come together to create a two-dimensional structure, is a key element of design that allows for the systematic organization of information on a page. It is a guide to help the designer bring order to both small and large amounts of information while maintaining consistency throughout a design. It is analogous to the skeletal structure of the human body, in which muscles, nerves, blood vessels and skin follow along the bones, joints and ligaments that make up the skeleton. A grid is essentially the skeletal structure of the page.

Grids can be rigid or loose, simple or complex. Whatever form they may take, grids assist in the laying out of the page. A grid should make the process of design easier by streamlining decision-making, therefore saving time. Remember, though, that a grid is a design tool like any other, which needs to be mastered and used properly.

GRID ELEMENTS

A grid is made up of a group of standard elements: margins, columns, alleys, gutters, rows and modules (Fig. 44). The selection and arrangement of these elements are what give grids their personality.

Margins are the spaces between the edge of the page and the start of the content. They serve several purposes. By allowing the eye to rest in an area outside the content, margins allow the content to break from one page to the next. In a practical sense, they keep content away from the edge of the page so that nothing is inadvertently cut off when the paper is trimmed after printing. The left and right margins are also called the *thumb space* because it is where a page is typically held. Margin space here prevents a viewer's thumbs from covering important content.

Columns are vertical spaces that run top to bottom in between the margins. They typically hold the bulk of the content, both text and imagery. There is no set number of columns that can be on a page, and there is no rule stating that all columns must be the same width. Variety in column width can sometimes lead to interesting divisions on the page.

The small vertical space separating columns is called an *alley*. The alley prevents text or imagery in one column from interfering with the content of an adjacent column.

The interior margins where a left and right page meet are called *gutters*. (Note that some design software also uses the term gutters to refer to alleys.) The binding that holds the pages together obscures this area and the designer should avoid placing important content there. Just as you would not want to fall into the gutter, neither does type or imagery. Gutter size will vary depending on the binding being used.

Rows are secondary organization elements in a grid. They run horizontally across columns and allow the designer to align items between columns. A design can have one or many rows, and like columns, they can also vary in size. Many longer documents have a row set a specific distance down from the top of a page called a *sink*. It acts as the starting point for each page in the design. A sink creates consistency, producing a coherent look across multiple pages.

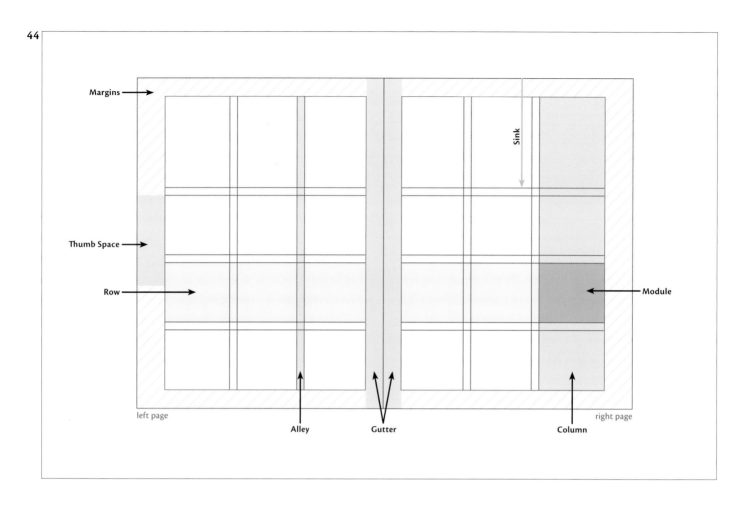

44

Margins

Sink

Thumb Space

Row — Module

left page — right page

Alley — Gutter — Column

A *module* is the space created when a column and row cross. It may seem that dividing up a grid into smaller and smaller spaces makes for a more limited grid, but in fact, it does the opposite. The more spaces there are in a grid, the more options are available for type and image placement. This means that a four-column grid with four rows begins with sixteen modules in which to place content. Combining modules in various ways pushes the number of options to well over one hundred. While a grid doesn't necessarily have to use modules, they do create more flexibility in a layout.

GRID ARCHITECTURE

The type of grid system used depends on a number of variables, as there is no set standard. The size of the page, the amount of text and imagery, the number of pages available for the total design, the aesthetic design requirements and the audience all influence the number of columns and rows, the size of margins and the use of modules. The design also needs open space to allow the viewer's eye room to move about the page.

MANUSCRIPT GRID

A *manuscript grid* is the simplest of all the grids and is used for a continuous flow of text, such as a book or long essay. The main area of the grid contains one column, with margins forming the negative space (Fig. 45). The gutter is generous, as this type of document almost always has a significant binding. The biggest issue with a manuscript grid is determining the proper line length

44 A grid is made up of a group of standard elements: margins, columns, alleys, gutters, rows and modules.

for comfortable reading over the course of many pages. Text that flows too close to the edge of the page creates tension and allows the document's physical surroundings to distract the reader. Wider margins help to keep the lines at an optimal length, providing enough space around the text to help focus the eye. Wider margins on the outside edges—the left side of the left page and the right side of the right page—will also give adequate thumb space, as this document will be in a readers' hands for a longer period of time. Be sure to leave enough space in the upper and lower margins for other information, such as chapter headings and page numbers (Fig. 46).

COLUMN GRID

The *column grid* is best used for text that is discontinuous or is divided into many articles or sections, examples of which would include a magazine, annual report, newspaper or corporate brochure (Figs. 47, 48, 49). The number and width of columns depends upon the text, imagery and other information that needs to be included on the page. A too-narrow column creates short line

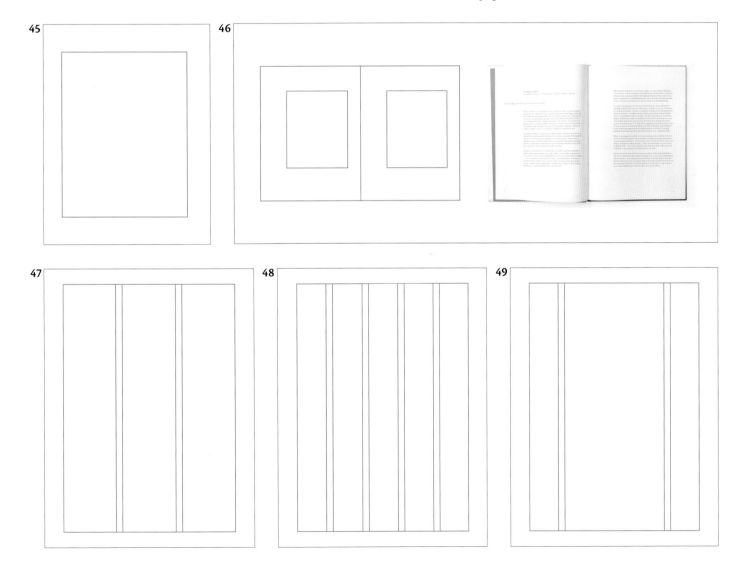

45 Experiment with margin width to create different visual connotation. 46 Dramatic left margins allow for callouts to set out from the rest of the text. 47, 48, 49 Column grids can have both even and uneven column widths. Let the content help determine grid layout.

lengths that are choppy to read. Conversely, columns that are too wide will also hinder readability by making line lengths too long. The optimal setup is such that the text flows smoothly from one column to the next, and so can be easily followed by the reader.

A design may have any number of columns per page, in widths that may vary or be exactly the same. Multiple columns can be combined to create a compound column (Fig. 50). The rule regarding creating compound columns is: Text may span more than one

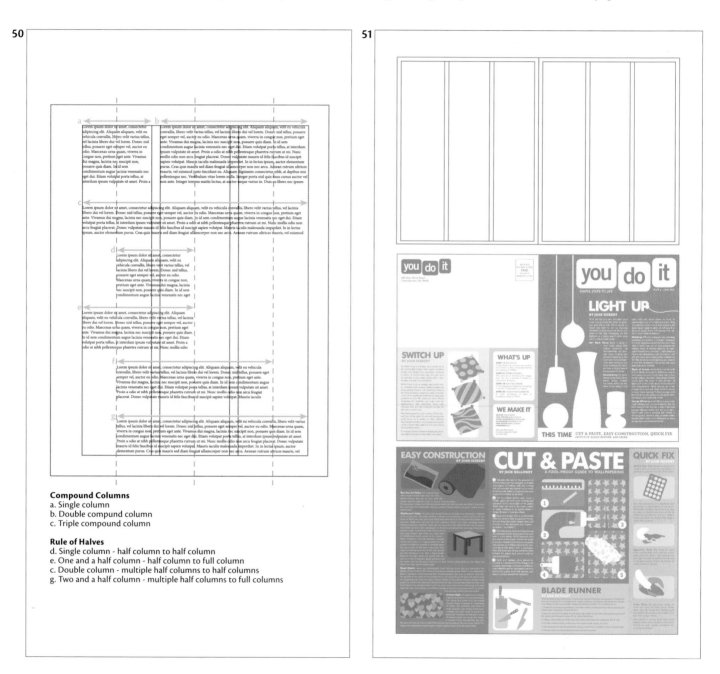

Compound Columns
a. Single column
b. Double compund column
c. Triple compound column

Rule of Halves
d. Single column - half column to half column
e. One and a half column - half column to full column
c. Double column - multiple half columns to half columns
g. Two and a half column - multiple half columns to full columns

50 Multiple columns can be combined to create a compound column. **51** Even though the newsletter is created with three simple columns, visual interest was added by breaking the columns up with color blocks.

column as long as the line length does not hinder readability. If the designer has created a three-column grid, the text may flow in each column independently, span across two columns, or span across all three columns. In addition, a designer can apply the Rule of Halves. This means that columns may be divided in half and text may flow from half column to half column, or half column to full column. Compound columns create interest by introducing variability within a long document, maintaining the reader's interest. The flexibility that comes with a column grid makes it a clear choice for many designers (Fig. 51).

MODULAR GRID

A *modular grid* is a column grid that also contains rows, resulting in a series of modules (Fig. 52). As previously mentioned, modules produce the greatest degree of flexibility within a grid, although they can create more confusion than clarity if used incorrectly. A modular grid is best used for pages that contain large amounts of complex text and imagery or for pages that contain more than one article or section. All the rules for compound columns apply to modular grids (Fig. 53). The only difference is that compound modules can be formed by combining modules horizontally, vertically or

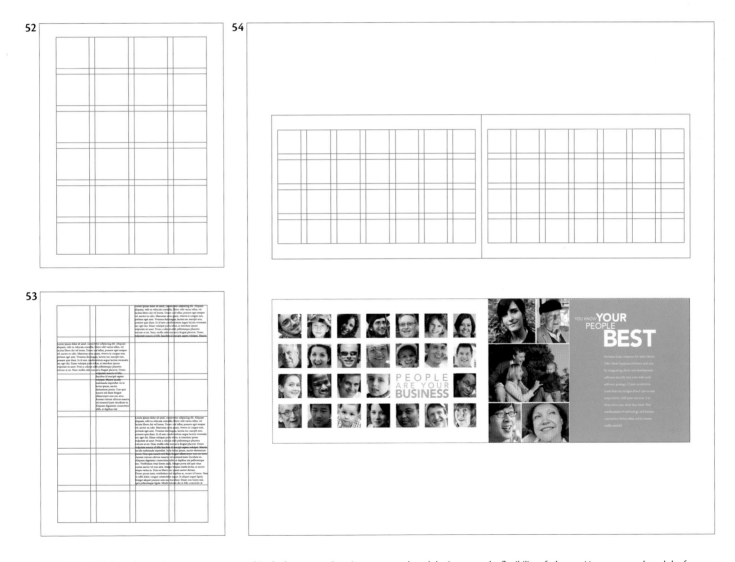

52

53

54

52 Modular grids lend themselves to great variety within the layout. **53** Creating compound modules increases the flexibility of a layout. Use compound modules for type, imagery and graphics. **54** Modules can be obvious or subtle with a layout.

both. This ability to combine spaces both horizontally and vertically gives the designer infinite possibilities for laying out a page. The Rule of Halves applies to modules as well. With so many choices for organizing information, it is essential to adhere to a visual system to ensure consistency in the use of modules throughout the design. Utilizing modules different ways on each page of a continuous document will create confusion, infusing the design with chaos. Consistency in the use of modules will streamline the execution of the design and maintain order (Fig. 54).

HIERARCHICAL GRID

A *hierarchical grid* is used when a page contains different sections of information that must be viewed completely separately from one another (Fig. 55). Physical lines that divide the sections are almost always a part of the design. This style of grid is more common in digital than in print design. It helps the viewer navigate quickly across a complex website or digital application. The content dictates the grid, which very often has an irregular pattern of columns and rows that allows for a more organic flow to the information while maintaining organization (Fig. 56).

NONTRADITIONAL GRID

This is a category of grid that does not fall within the standard realm of columns and rows (Figs. 57, 58, 59). A nontraditional grid is for the designer who wants to experiment with the layout. It is also an opportunity to incorporate influences from historical design movements, such as the strong diagonals from Russian Constructivism, or the non-design randomness of Dada. Diagonals, curves and shapes can create interesting gridlines. This kind of grid is extremely appealing to many designers, but it must be used with caution, as it can be very tiring to view for long documents. Content layout can also be more difficult with a nontraditional grid (Fig. 60).

BREAKING THE GRID

There will be occasions when a grid does not work, or elements within a grid don't fit, as a grid relies on content and page format. For example, one or two elements within a grid structure can purposely extend outside the vertical and horizontal guidelines. This can be done to create a dynamic visual statement or to draw the viewer's eye to a focal point. Artistic expression and strong conceptual design will lead a designer to break the grid on purpose. Accidental composition can also break a grid. A headline, type or image is placed on a page early in the layout process, only to have it land in a spot that creates contrast or good hierarchy, or forms a relationship with other elements on the page. There's nothing wrong with happy accidents.

Sometimes the content "just feels right" in its placement, even when it breaks the grid; this is called *intuitive designing*. A word of warning: Many young designers think that intuitive designing is easy. It is not. It takes time to develop the skills needed to properly

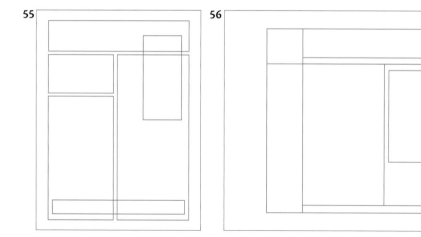

55 Hierarchical grids are best used to unify a layout when separate sections need their own hierarchy or grid. **56** Hierarchy within navigation and text areas benefits from the hierarchical grid.

57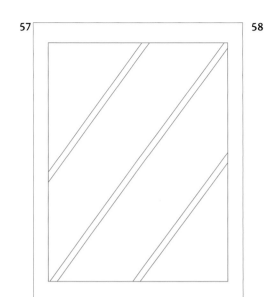

58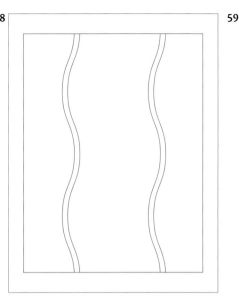

59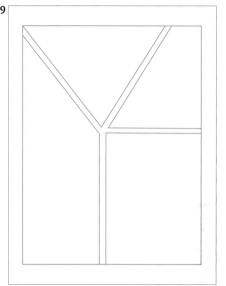

60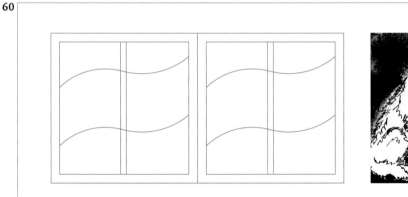

communicate the page's content. Even intuitive design has an underlying grid structure, although it may be a simple baseline grid. An effective design maintains readability and communicates its goals to the viewer. Sacrificing either of these objectives, no matter how cool it may look, fails as an effective design (Figs. 61, 62, 63, 64).

USING A GRID

Deciding which grid to use is not easy. The right grid will communicate eloquently, while the wrong grid will fail miserably. The best grids bring design efficiency, creative guidance and order to the content. The grid needs to allow for placement of all of the information in the design, including imagery, body copy, headline, captions and subheads. Following are things to consider when establishing a grid:

- The grid should not be so simple that the design becomes monotonous.

- Allow the smallest images to define the size of columns, rows and modules.

57, 58, 59 Non-traditional grids work well to surprise the viewer, but be careful because if used too much, they can tire the eyes. **60** Wavy rows create movement across the page, leading the viewer from page to page.

- Leave room for flexibility, especially for the headline.

- Allow for adequate white space, to help the eye flow through the content.

- Using the Rule of Halves is acceptable.

- The more information that needs to go on a page, the more flexibility is required in the grid.

- Make sure the grid reflects the connotation of the content being presented. A crazy, non-linear grid may not be the best decision for a Fortune 500 brochure.

- A grid should work with the content, not fight it.

- A grid is merely the framework for a design. Ultimately it is the designer's abilities and sensibilities that bring the design to life.

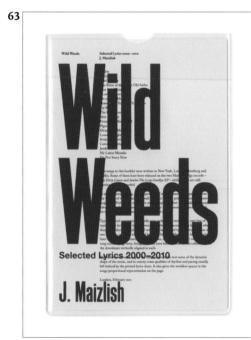

61, 62 Instead of columns and modules, the images themselves dictate the placement of the text. **63, 64** A typographical songbook that visually conveys the lyrical structure of each track.

HIERARCHY

Once a grid has been established, the content can be inserted to create the design. Content is composed of different types of information of varying degrees of importance, known as *hierarchy*. Hierarchy is determined by size, position, visual weight and color. Hierarchy gives the designer control over the viewer when used well. The wrong hierarchy, or its lack, will confuse or alienate a viewer. The designer dictates what the viewer sees and when the viewer sees it. Hierarchy says to the viewer, "Look at me and start here!"

The first step is to look at all the information on the page and determine which is the most important, followed by the second-most important and so on. The viewer needs direction about what she should garner from the page, and if everything has the same emphasis, or if the wrong emphasis is applied, she will abandon her efforts without having properly absorbed the information.

Once hierarchy has been determined, placement and design attributes are applied. It is only natural to assume that the largest element on the page is the most important. It stands to reason, therefore, that the headline should be the largest element. This is true in the majority of design layouts, although if the headline's visual weight and color give it more emphasis than the rest of the information, it could actually be the smallest element on the page. The same goes for positioning. Western readers naturally view a page from the top down, and from left to right. Type appearing at the top of the page will have more emphasis than type at the bottom, unless other hierarchy-influencing attributes are applied. The powerful principles of Gestalt can also be applied to the arrangement and positioning of type and other elements on the page to help give the page a focal point. Visual weight is easily achieved with typography by using the variations found within a font's family. Black and extra

65 The whispering headline, lack of color contrast and hidden pull quote don't assist a viewer in knowing what is of importance. **66** Switching color, placement and size of type and visuals, emphasis is now given to what is important within the hierarchy.

bold create heavy visual weight that command attention. Narrow, light and book weights connote lesser visual importance and help regulate the degree of hierarchy. Color also plays an important role in hierarchy. Dark, bold or vibrant colors tend to stand out more than soft, dull or pastel colors. Contrasting colors also create emphasis. Combining any or all of these influencing attributes gives the designer more control and a more interesting and creative solution for hierarchy (Figs. 65, 66).

NEGATIVE SPACE

Much attention is paid to the design elements that are placed on the page. Less is paid to the space left over, called *negative space*. This negative space has just as much influence over how a viewer perceives the page as the content does. Many new designers feel the need to fill every inch of space on the page (Figs. 67, 68). This not only detracts from the readability of the page, but it creates a design that feels crowded. Negative space on the page does several things: It allows the viewer's eye to flow around the content, it provides a resting place for the eye and it helps the viewer differentiate sections of content from each other.

Here are ways to avoid a cluttered page:

- Keep the margins open.

- Make sure the alleys are of a sufficient width so that columns of text do not appear to run together.

- Give the space around an image the same distance as the alley width.

- Provide either an indent or space after each paragraph.

- Eliminate all unnecessary borders, boxes, rules or any other symbols that do not benefit the design.

- Make sure the background, whether a solid color or an image, does not interfere with the text.

- Resist the urge to place something in every corner of the page.

- Format the text so it does not contain rivers.

- Consider using left-aligned text instead of justified, as justified alignment fills columns completely.

- Rearrange text or imagery to eliminate oddly shaped or trapped negative spaces within the page, and reallocate that space to be above, below or to the outside of the other page elements.

- Use well-executed hierarchy.

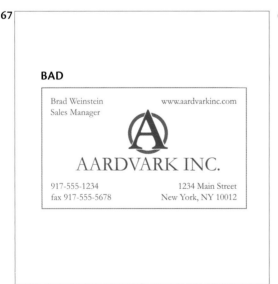

67 A common layout mistake is to fill the entire card with information. While it may seem that leaving negative space hurts a design, the opposite is true. **68** Adding negative space by shrinking and realigning text helps give focus to the card. A solution in horizontal and vertical layout is shown.

VISUAL CONCEPT

Multi-page designs need careful attention throughout the design to establish order, maintain consistency and ensure readability, especially when dealing with a variety of text and image content.

This is called creating a *visual concept*; it can also be thought of as establishing a game plan for the design. Assembling all of the type and imagery can be daunting—there is a lot to think about. Keeping in mind the type, the images, the Gestalt principles, the design relationship principles, the grid—all while maintaining the

69

70

71

72

73

69, 70, 71, 72, 73 A cool, sophisticated, yet earthy color palette captures the feeling of this Icelandic magazine. Crisp, clean lines and Neutra Text are offset by hand-lettered headlines. The simple four-column grid has a deep sink that creates an image showcase.

accidentally fabulous
An impromptu dialogue
with Iceland's Sigur Rós.

design's readability and communication—can be stressful. Decisions about the design's look, grid, type formatting and image creation made prior to executing the design itself will simplify the design process.

Always carefully consider the client's objective and target audience as a part of the decision-making process. Sketching and research are good ways to begin developing a visual concept. Create a type palette that contains a complementary type pair plus one or two interesting headline fonts. Narrow down a color palette to four or five colors that work well with the design concept. Devise a plan for image usage—choose a similar style of photography, or use all images from the same artist. Develop a strategy for the grid system and establish the hierarchy within the grid. The overall goal is to make sure the pages feel as though they are part of the whole, as opposed to individual pieces (Figs. 69, 70, 71, 72, 73, 74, 75).

Don't be afraid to make alterations to the visual concept if something isn't working as expected. Break the grid when necessary.

Finally, avoid the use of "bells and whistles" to jazz up a design. Drop shadows, glows and other extras distract the viewer. Allow the design elements to speak for themselves. When the design has a solid visual concept, these extra features are purposeless.

DESIGNING WITH PAGES

Pages are the last stage in communication. They are where all of the content and elements come together. They pull the whole story together into a cohesive thought. Therefore, it is crucial to develop a design that communicates properly and is aesthetically pleasing. A designer wants the reader to immerse herself in the page. It should continue to hold a reader's attention until the last word is read.

PUBLICATION DESIGN

Multi-page documents such as annual reports, books and corporate brochures require particular attention to design in a way that single-page documents do not. The visual concept must flow from page to page, from front to back. Keeping the idea fresh, especially in long, multiple-page documents, is one of the biggest challenges a designer will face. If the designer pays close attention to the typography and the grid, and works hard to create unity and consistency, the document will come together well (Figs. 76, 77, 78, 79, 80).

DESIGNING PUBLICATIONS

The first step in designing any publication is to be organized. A designer should have all text and imagery before developing a visual concept. Starting to design a multiple-page document without key elements causes unnecessary work and will likely result in the document being redesigned several times. Many clients think

74, 75 Further examples of Icelandic magazine. The feature story continues the strong horizontal and vertical of the grid. The entire magazine has clear visual concept that allows for variation in design.

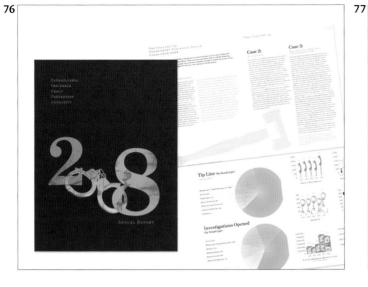

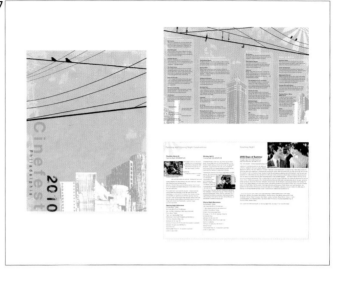

76 IFPA 2008 Annual Report. **77** Cinesfest Program Booklet. **78, 79, 80** Legal Leaf Annual Report.

nothing if parts of a document are missing at the design stage. In reality, missing imagery or text will throw off the balance of an entire design. Trying to add additional content into a fully designed document can generate significant issues by causing the information to reflow. It is not unrealistic to ask a client to be prepared to provide all of the information at the beginning of the project. Once the information is received, take the time to read through all of the text and analyze all of the imagery. Clues to the visual concept can be found in the text. Pay close attention to the tone of the writing. Formal writing requires a formal concept, while casual writing allows for an organic or expressionistic concept. All of the elements should then follow this chosen concept.

Take into consideration the type of publication when finalizing the visual concept. Books are meant to be read in their entirety and should be designed for maximum readability; therefore, they need a visual concept that helps the pages flow well. Let's look at the differences in visual concept for two similar, yet different, types of publications: corporate brochures and annual reports. Both provide detailed information about the company. Corporate brochures communicate essential information that a reader needs to know about the company. They are all about presenting the company in a favorable light and tend to be information-heavy. The visual concept should emphasize clarity. Be sure to follow a company's style guide to make sure that the company is being represented properly. Annual reports also disseminate information about a company, including progress the company has made, changes within the company, and financial information, but they are viewed by investors and potential investors, providing an opportunity to highlight special aspects of the company. Information graphics—visual representations of numerical data—help make sense of complicated numbers and add interest. For both annual reports and corporate brochures, clarity is important so readers can access information easily. This does not mean that the design needs to be boring, though. Visual excitement creates a positive atmosphere, imparting a favorable and profitable impression even if the opposite is true.

When designing a publication, start by developing the grid. The grid is what carries the design through multiple pages. Once a grid has been established, begin the process of creating a visual concept by analyzing and deciding upon fonts, colors and imagery. Maintain consistency throughout the document by limiting font choice to the complementary pair and assuring that it harmonizes with the visual tone. Add variety to the layout by using a flexible grid. Vary the placement of images and body text enough that it gives interest—but not so much so that the pages seem to separate from each other. Maintain strong headlines and subheads, as these will help break up large amounts of text and give the eye a break. Information graphics should be clear, easy to understand and visually stimulating. Imagery should enhance the tone set by the visual concept. Consider using silhouetted images in addition to boxed images. Utilizing continuance, unity and other Gestalt and relationship principles will help the reader's eye flow from one page to the next.

MAGAZINE DESIGN

Magazine design relies heavily on visual concept. Magazines are a challenge in that they are composed of many different types of pages, each of which needs its own design style while still maintaining the feel of a cohesive whole. The main parts of the magazine are the cover, the table of contents, departments and features. These are the same for both print and digital platform magazines. The cover and table of contents are well-known parts of a magazine. *Departments* are one- to two-page articles related to a particular subject presented in each issue of the magazine; examples include health, beauty, fitness, gadgets, travel, advice or food. The articles change from issue to issue but the general subject remains the same. *Features* are main articles, typically listed on the cover, which are unique to each issue. Feature articles are what draw a reader to a magazine. A magazine is often purchased because a particular article reaches out to a given reader. Advertisements are not included, as they are designed by outside sources instead of the designer who creates the magazine (Figs. 81, 82, 83, 84, 85, 86, 87, 88, 89).

DESIGNING MAGAZINES

The cover, table of contents and departments represent the backbone of design for a magazine, as these elements are present in each issue. The cover is the first thing the reader sees, so it must make the appropriate impact. It should be strong, simple and enticing. Faces sell best. The parts of the cover are the *nameplate* (the title

81

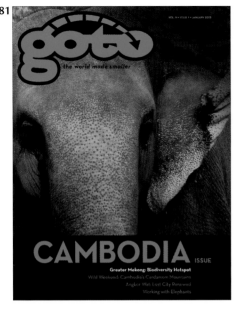

82

83

Cambodia

Nation, Religion, King

The Kingdom of Cambodia, formerly known as Kampuchea, is a country in South East Asia with a population of over 13 million people.

Get ready for your next exciting trip to exotic and historic Cambodia. Once inaccessible because of the rule of the Khmer Rouge and despite severe shrinking due to logging, the rainforests of Cambodia are being rediscovered, explored and protected. Join feature writer Monibuth Chheng as she describes her experience in the rainforests on two separate visits—one in the wilderness and one in the Rainbow Lodge, a green resort situated in the forest. The resort was implemented to have the smallest ecological disruption with a goal of creating educational opportunities available to local workers, the community and tourists.

Located at the mouth of the Mekong River, is a tangle of small houseboats, fishing boats and even a school boat—you must be able to swim to attend. These are the Villages of Tonle Sap Lake. Their adaptations to life on the water are intense and creative.

The Artisans de Angkor is a high-end craft market comprised of Cambodian artisans. It is a French owned company with the goal of creating a viable industry with Cambodian exclusivity. The artisans—selected from around the country—are paid to learn a trade.

Explore this issue before you explore your next destination and get ready, it's time to **goto** Cambodia.

Romilda Vane
Editor

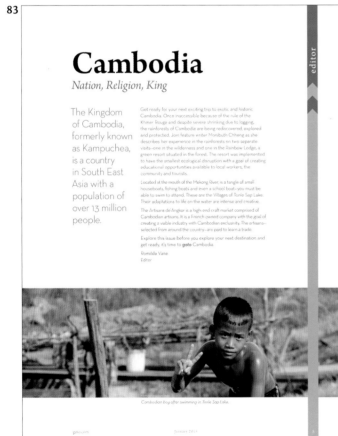

Cambodian boy after swimming in Tonle Sap Lake.

84

GREATER MEKONG

BIODIVERSITY HOTSPOT

175

PAGE

85

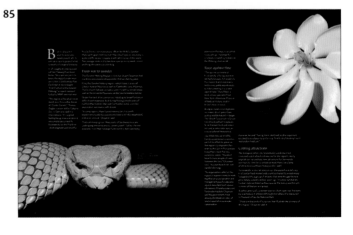

81, 82, 83, 84, 85 *Goto* magazine.

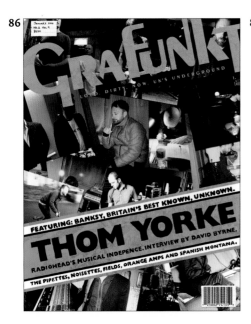

86

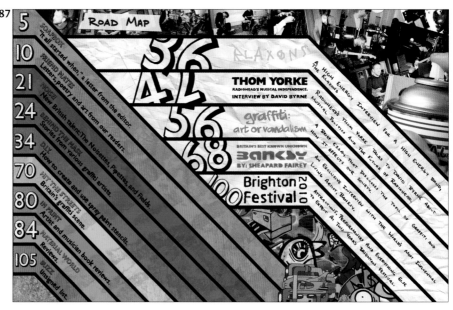

87

88

89

of the magazine), imagery and *cover lines*, which are the titles of articles found inside. The nameplate is the face of the magazine and it must make the magazine stand out from all the others on the shelf. Nameplate design is a variation of logo design, so all of the same rules apply. The tone set by the cover should be a good indication as to what the reader will find inside. Crazy, chaotic cover lines in screaming hues of yellow and fluorescent orange will lead a reader to believe the magazine will be crazy and chaotic on the inside as well. Look at your cover design next to the covers of competing magazines. Is the nameplate noticeable? Does the cover seem lost among the competition? Are the cover lines visible from several feet away? Does the imagery interfere with the nameplate?

86, 87, 88, 89 *Grafunkt* magazine.

The *department pages* set the tone for the rest of the magazine. They need to have a consistent look, although they do not have to be identical. A solid visual concept will ease the process of designing the department pages. A well-designed grid plus good font and color palettes create a solid foundation. The departments should also use similar image styles to enhance consistency among pages. Designing department pages is no easy task. A designer must come up with a visual concept that can flourish even with exposure to the public—issue after issue, year after year. The designer should never feel dissatisfied or, worse yet, bored by the visual concept after a month or two. A modular grid works quite well for magazines because it allows the most versatility while still maintaining a horizontal and vertical system of organization. Consider creating compound modules as designated areas for headlines, imagery and body copy. Placing these elements in the same place on the various department pages creates consistency, while varying the size, color and shape within those areas prevents the design from becoming dull.

The *table of contents* is the reader's guide to navigating the magazine. It should be easy to find information in it without confusing the reader. There should be a clear division between departments and features. The page locations of departments and features should also be clear. It is helpful to include short descriptions of the articles so that a reader may better find what he is looking for. Images that relate to the interior articles will also entice a reader, so long as it's obvious to which article the image belongs. The table of contents should have a very transparent hierarchy, using the hierarchy of the cover lines as a guide in determining article importance.

The *features* are the magazine's wow factor. These articles are the most dramatic and are generally the most expensive to produce in terms of imagery, photographers, artists and other people involved. Many times the article is the work of a guest writer instead of someone on the magazine's staff. Because of this, features have permission to break the visual concept in order to make more of an impact, although they should not go completely against the overall tone. A magazine with a clean and classic look should not have a chaotic or messy feature, though it may use alternative fonts, alternative colors and article-appropriate imagery. Feature articles are the perfect venue for creative and expressive headline typography. Don't be afraid to fill the entire page with a headline. The feature article is supposed to make a statement. Try hand lettering or creating your own font to match the artistic vision of the article. Use the same type style to create pull quotes and subheads. To make the feature article more special, create imagery with qualities similar to the typography. You can take risks with features you wouldn't otherwise be able to take with departments.

Steven Brower was born on the Lower East Side of Manhattan but raised in the Bronx. Always artistic, he was the art director for his junior high school yearbook in the ninth grade. He attended the High School of Music & Art in Harlem as an art student and, upon graduation, studied at the School of Visual Arts. Brower did the only logical thing he could with such an intensive art background: He dropped out and played in rock and roll bands for the next decade. Brower then returned to school and graduated from California State University, Fullerton with a degree in graphic design. He returned to New York and worked in book publishing but left his full-time job as art director at a publishing house in 1995 to go freelance, and he became an associate of the Push Pin Group. In 1999, Brower was hired as a freelancer to redesign *Print* magazine, and he then became their full-time art director and was promoted to creative director. He left in 2004 to create books that he has written and designed—sometimes with others, sometimes solo—and also to teach full time.

In 1999, you were brought on staff to redesign Print *magazine. What was the need for the redesign? How did you approach the redesign of such an iconic magazine?*

Andrew Kner, who had been art director for thirty-five years, decided to retire. The publisher wanted a fresh look. There had been a redesign a few years earlier by Andy, but essentially the look hadn't changed in decades. One of my challenges was to try to keep the spirit of the magazine, while at the same time creating a current look. Since the editor, Martin Fox, remained on, there was a consistency in the editorial content that I wanted to be reflected in the design. I was a tremendous fan of *Print* and very much wanted this to be an extension of what had gone before, not a reinvention (Figs. 90, 91).

What are the differences between designing for a magazine versus designing for a book? What are the similarities?

Both need to flow and be paced cinematically. Magazines can be more informal and are a great place to experiment, which I did often at *Print*. If you screw up there's always the next issue. Since a book has permanence, it has to be more formal.

Content often determines the format of a publication. Your books Woody Guthrie: Art Works, Breathless Homicidal Slime Mutants: The Art of the Paperback, From Shadow to Light: The Life & Art of Mort Meskin, *and* Satchmo: The Wonderful World and Art of Louis Armstrong *are heavy with visual art along with text (Figs. 92, 93, 94). How did the content of your books influence the final design looks?*

Each book has been different in format, beginning with *Woody Guthrie: Art Works*. For that book I wanted to establish an intimacy to give the reader the experience of looking in on Guthrie's personal journals. The cover was cloth with stamping and no jacket, so there was a tactile experience holding the book. I utilized Guthrie's own typography as initial caps. I wanted *Satchmo* to be oversized and square, like a record album and also reel-to-reel tape box. He posed more of a challenge, as he didn't letter much. I used his type for his name on the cover, but there was little more. So I created an entire typeface for the title of the book and all the chapter headings (Fig. 95). I cut it out of paper and I think I captured the feel of both the man and the period. For *Breathless*, it was important for it to be the same proportions as a mass-market paperback, slightly oversized, and to look and feel like one. And for *From Shadow to Light* I wanted it to look substantial, a "coffee table" book, since the subject, Mort Meskin, is little known but is an important comic book artist.

What strategies do you employ to create good pagination and flow?

Whether a magazine or book, I strive to achieve cinematic flow. I want the reader to be surprised, enthralled, while at the same time informed. I believe I tend to err on the conservative side with this, although I have been known to experiment. It's a fine balance between adventurous and over the top.

How do you determine your font choices? What characteristics do you look for in fonts that will be used as part of multi-page designs?

Interesting question. First I should state that 90 percent of the time I use Garamond and Trade Gothic in my work. However, sometimes I either get bored or the material calls for something different. For example, other than my handcrafted type, *Satchmo* is typeset completely in Gill Sans. Now, that can be a very noisy face, but by using the lightest weight and open tracking, it gained a surprising elegance and was the correct face to use considering the Jazz Age time period. For *2D: Visual Basics for Designers*, a textbook I designed and co-authored, I chose Melior, a face I hadn't used before or since. It had a slight quirkiness, while at the same time it looked studious and was highly legible (Fig. 96).

91

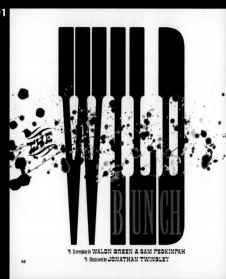

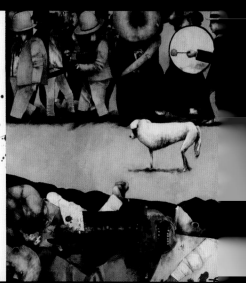

93

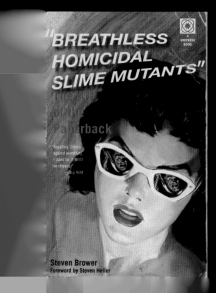

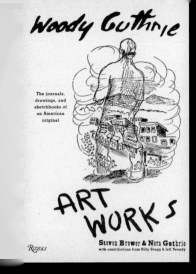

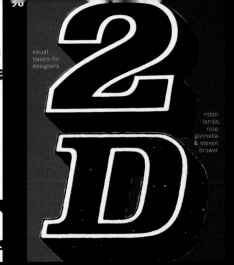

t role do novelty fonts have in publication design?

n, just the term bugs me—I think of hand-buzzers and fake . Of course, they could be used for magazine heads, depend-
n the content.

t role does the cover play in magazine and book design?

are posters that are meant to attract a potential reader over. covers have remained pure, while contemporary magazines r for the table of contents and UPC code on their covers. I s in our busy world we no longer have time to open a maga-
to read the contents.

t are the most important publication design theories you : young designers should know?

they are telling a story—whether it is one story, as in most s, or several brief conversational stories, as in a magazine. efore, it is the designer's responsibility to keep the conver-
n lively and interesting. The material determines the level mplexity.

With the infusion of digital technologies into the publication world, where do you see magazine and book design heading for the future? How will this influence the internal structure? The cover design?

Everything will change. I love books and printed matter, but future generations will not view it as a necessity. As the nine-teenth-century English philosopher Alfred North Whitehead said, "The major advances in civilization are the processes that all but wreck the societies in which they occur." Personally I have been exploring eBooks and find them wanting, but they are rife with possibilities. I think simply trying to mimic a printed book is the wrong way to approach it; rather, it should be viewed as a new way to tell your story.

What are your influences? Where do you go for inspiration?

My two main influences from childhood were the comic book creator Jack Kirby and Push Pin Studios, primarily Milton Glaser and Seymour Chwast. As for inspiration, I find it everywhere. In recent years I like looking at aging ephemera. Every now and

TYPE TIDBITS

Serif or Sans Serif?
Sans.

Favorite letter?
A.

Helvetica or Futura?
Futura.

Favorite complementary font pair?
Garamond, Trade Gothic.

Pen and paper or Wacom tablet?
Pen and paper.

Mac or PC?
Mac.

Uppercase or lowercase?
LOWERCASE.

Design: Lifestyle or Just a way to earn a living?
Lifestyle.

If you could start your own magazine, what would be the subject matter?
Forgotten and little-known artists, musicians, writers, film makers. (Any backers out there?)

Real book or digital book?
You have to ask!

Jazz or blues?
Both! All roots music.

PAGE
GALLERY

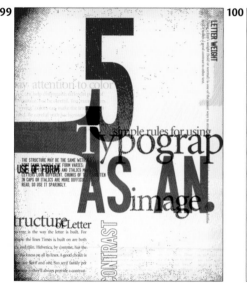

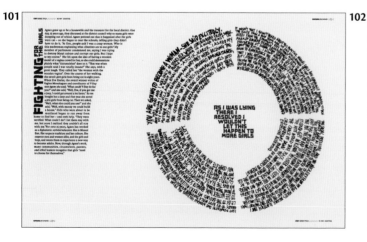

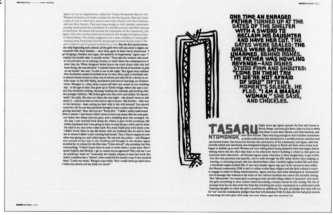

97, 98 Bayard Brochure. **99** 5 Simple Rules for Using Typography as an Image poster. **100** Gotham specimen poster series. **101, 102** Strength Selection book.

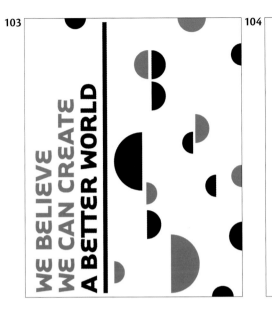

**WE BELIEVE
WE CAN CREATE
A BETTER WORLD**

104

EVER SINCE IT HAS HAD THE RESOURCES TO FOLLOW ITS DREAMS AND TO PRESENT SHOWS AROUND THE WORLD, CIRQUE DU SOLEIL HAS CHOSEN TO BE INVOLVED IN COMMUNITIES, AND MORE PARTICULARLY WITH YOUTH AT RISK. IN COOPERATION WITH ITS PARTNERS, CIRQUE DU SOLEIL IS INVOLVED IN NEARLY 80 COMMUNITIES WORLDWIDE, IN SOME 20 COUNTRIES SPANNING FIVE CONTINENTS.

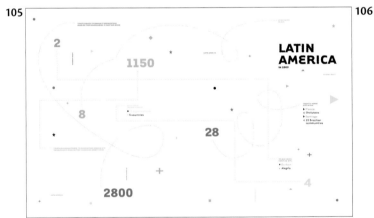

105

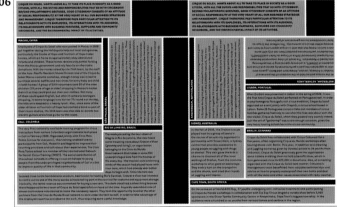

106

He created artscience.

107

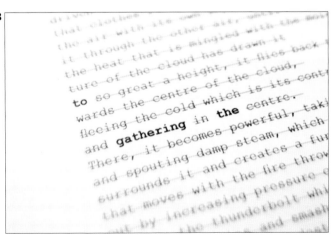

108

183

PAGE

103, 104, 105, 106 Cirque du Soleil Report. **107, 108** DA VINCI.

109

110

111

112

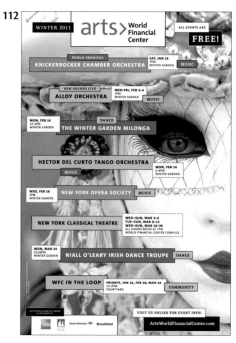

113

114

115

116

117

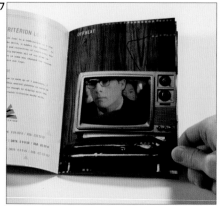

109, 110, 111 SIA 55 architecture projects. **112** Arts > World Financial Center poster. **113, 114** Book design adapted from *The Wolf and the Seven Young Kids* by the Brothers Grimm. **115, 116, 117** Whiting AAT logo manual.

118, 119 Comme il Faut Social and Environmental Responsibility Report.   120, 121, 122 John Mortonson's funeral.   123 Americana specimen poster series.   124 The Movable Book of Letterforms.

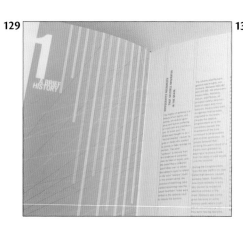

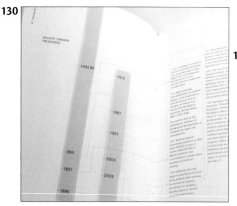

125 ArtScience poster-flyers for the final exam exhibition 2009. **126** Typ09 Conference Program. **127, 128, 129, 130** *Prison of the Mind* book cover. **131, 132** 2009 Parsons Communication Design Book.

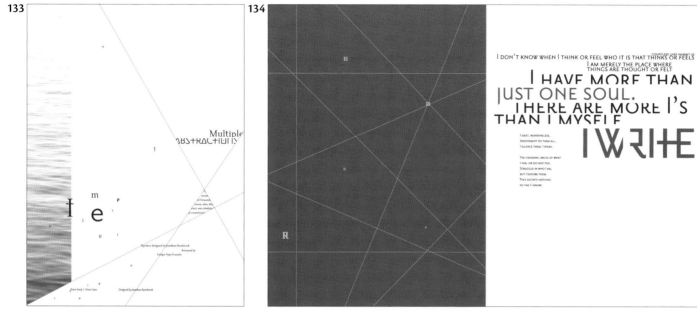

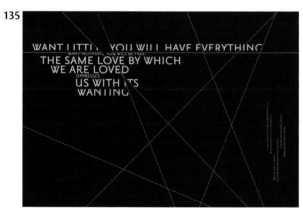

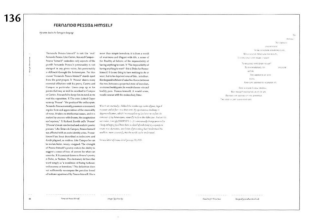

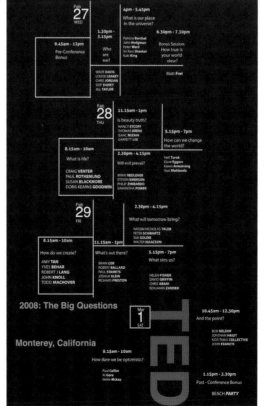

133, 134, 135, 136 Multiple Abstractions book.   **137** TED poster of events.

ABOUT THE IMAGES IN THIS CHAPTER

Fig. 1
TITLE: Magazine spread
UNIVERSITY: La Roche College
PROFESSOR: Neha Agarwal
DESIGNER: So-Eun Ahn
FONT USED: Gotham Rounded

Fig. 2
TITLE: Christmast typo poster
DESIGNER: Filip Zajac
FONT USED: RePublic Book CE
CLIENT: Self

Figs. 3, 4, 5, 6
TITLE: *Goethe: The Theory of Colors* book redesign
UNIVERSITY: Hungarian University of Fine Arts
PROFESSOR: Attila Auth
DESIGNER: Réka Diósi
FONTS USED: Didot, Din

Fig. 11
PHOTOGRAPH: Eric Isselée

Fig. 12
PHOTOGRAPH: Marcin Pikula, Lisa Thornberg

Fig. 13
PHOTOGRAPH: Vitaly Shabalyn, Lisa Thornberg

Fig. 31
TITLE: Collector Toy Exhibition invitation postcard
UNIVERSITY: Kutztown University
PROFESSOR: Denise Bosler
DESIGNER: Laura Dubbs
FONTS USED: Helvetica Neue UltraLight, RNSCamelia

Fig. 35
TITLE: Surprise Play poster
UNIVERSITY: Kutztown University
PROFESSOR: Denise Bosler
DESIGNER: Matt Gorlaski
FONTS USED: Hand lettering, Gill Sans

Fig. 46
TITLE: 2009 Parsons Communication Design book
UNIVERSITY: Parsons the New School for Design
PROFESSORS: Julia Wargaski, Juan Carlos Pagan, Cindy Rodriguez
FONTS USED: Futura, National

Fig. 51
TITLE: You Do It newsletter
UNIVERSITY: Kutztown University
PROFESSOR: Denise Bosler

DESIGNER: Josh Seibert
FONTS USED: Rockwell, Futura

Fig. 56
CLIENT: Montgomery County Public Libraries
FONTS USED: Alita, Verdana

Fig. 60
TITLE: The Devil and His Grandmother
UNIVERSITY: Kutztown University
PROFESSOR: Denise Bosler
DESIGNER: Cara Ray
FONTS USED: Hand lettering, Baskerville

Figs. 61, 62
TITLE: *Riot!* magazine
UNIVERSITY: Kutztown University
PROFESSOR: Denise Bosler
DESIGNER: Corey Reifinger

Figs. 63, 64
TITLE: Wild Weeds songbook
PROGRAM: Typography Summer School
INSTRUCTOR: Fraser Muggeridge
DESIGNER: Emma Williams
FONT USED: Adobe Caslon Pro, Block Gothic, Helvetica Neue
CLIENT: J. Maizlish Mole / Marseille Figs

Figs. 69, 70, 71, 72, 73, 74, 75
TITLE: *Strjall* magazine
UNIVERSITY: Kutztown University
PROFESSOR: Denise Bosler
DESIGNER: Matt Twombly
FONTS USED: Hand lettering, Neutra Text

Fig. 76
TITLE: IFPA 2008 Annual Report
DESIGN FIRM: PPO&S
ART DIRECTOR: Tracy L. Kretz
DESIGNER: Tracy L. Kretz
FONT USED: TBD
CLIENT: Pennsylvania Insurance Fraud Prevention Authority

Fig. 77
TITLE: Cinesfest Program Booklet
UNIVERSITY: Moore College of Art & Design
PROFESSOR: Rosemary Murphy
DESIGNER: Jamie L. Blank
FONTS USED: Helvetica Neue (Bold, Regular)

Figs. 78, 79, 80
TITLE: Legal Leaf Annual Report
UNIVERSITY: University of Stevens Point
PROFESSOR: Marcia Pastorius

FONTS USED: Frutiger, InaiMathi
CLIENT: Legal Leaf

Figs. 81, 82, 83, 84, 85
TITLE: *Goto* magazine
UNIVERSITY: Kutztown University
PROFESSOR: Denise Bosler
DESIGNER: Randi Meredith

Figs. 86, 87, 88, 89
TITLE: *Grafunkt* magazine
UNIVERSITY: Kutztown University
PROFESSOR: Denise Bosler
DESIGNER: William Riedel
FONTS USED: Hand lettering, Gill Sans

Figs. 93, 94, 95, 96
© Steven Brower

Fig. 90
TITLE: *Print* Magazine
ART DIRECTION/DESIGN: Steven Brower
PHOTOGRAPHER: Barnaby Hall

Fig. 91
TITLE: *Print* Magazine
ART DIRECTION/DESIGN: Steven Brower
ILLUSTRATOR: Jonathon Twingley

Fig. 92
TITLE: *Breathless Homicidal Slime Mutants: The Art of the Paperback*
DESIGN: Steven Brower
ILLUSTRATION: Norman Saunders

Figs. 97, 98
TITLE: Bayard Brochure
DESIGN FIRM: The O Group
ART DIRECTORS: Jason B. Cohen, J. Kenneth Rothermich
DESIGNER: J. Kenneth Rothermich,
PHOTOGRAPHER: Greg Kinch
COPYWRITERS: Alex Ammar, Jennifer Eggers
FONT USED: Neutraface, Blockhead, Clarendon, Logger, Rubino, Shelly, Thunderbird, Toolbox, Vandoesburg
CLIENT: North Development Group

Fig. 99
TITLE: 5 Simple Rules for Using Typography as an Image poster
DESIGN FIRM: Peter Quamme
DESIGNER: Peter Quamme
FONTS USED: Go Long, Minion
CLIENT: Self

Fig. 100
TITLE: Gotham specimen poster series
UNIVERSITY: Kutztown University
PROFESSOR: Denise Bosler

DESIGNER: Peter Hershey
FONT USED: Gotham

Figs. 101, 102
TITLE: Strength Selection book
UNIVERSITY: Academy of Art University
PROFESSOR: Ariel Grey
DESIGNER: Clara Silva
FONT USED: Malaga, Expos

Figs. 103, 104, 105, 106
TITLE: Cirque du Soleil Report
UNIVERSITY: Academy of Art University
PROFESSOR: Kelly Conley
DESIGNER: Clara Silva
FONT USED: Tarzana

Figs. 107, 108
TITLE: DA VINCI
UNIVERSITY: Rhode Island School of Design
PROFESSOR: Akefeh Nurosi
FONTS USED: Courier, Courier Sans

Figs. 109, 110, 111
TITLE: SIA 55 architecture projects
DESIGN FIRM: GVA Studio
DESIGNERS: GVA Studio
FONT USED: Helvetica Neue
CLIENT: SIA

Fig. 112
TITLE: Arts > World Financial Center poster
DESIGN FIRM: Think Studio, NYC
DESIGNER: John Clifford
FONTS USED: Corpid, Serifa
CLIENT: World Financial Center

Figs. 113, 114
TITLE: Book design adapted from *The Wolf and the Seven Young Kids* by the Brothers Grimm
UNIVERSITY: Kutztown University
PROFESSOR: Denise Bosler
DESIGNER: Sara Smith
FONT USED: Garamond

Figs. 115, 116, 117
TITLE: Whiting AAT logo manual
UNIVERSITY: Chicago Portfolio School
PROFESSOR: Tim Lapetino
DESIGNER: Matthew Whiting
FONTS USED: Knockout, Courier New
CLIENT: Criterion Collection

Figs. 118, 119
TITLE: Comme il Faut Social and Invironmental Responsibility Report
DESIGN FIRM: Dina Shoham Design
ART DIRECTORS: Dina Shoham, Michal Granit

DESIGNER: Dina Shoham
FONTS USED: Hand lettering,
Hebrew fonts: Lueeza, Narkis New
CLIENT: Comme il Faut

Figs. 120, 121, 122
TITLE: John Mortonson's funeral
UNIVERSITY: Kutztown University
PROFESSOR: Denise Bosler
DESIGNER: Matt Aialo
FONT USED: Hand lettering

Fig. 123
TITLE: Americana specimen
poster series
UNIVERSITY: Kutztown University
PROFESSOR: Denise Bosler
DESIGNER: Jordan Gehman
FONT USED: Americana

Fig. 124
TITLE: The Movable Book of Letterforms
UNIVERSITY: Indiana University
DESIGNER: Kevin Steele
FONT USED: Arno Pro

Fig. 125
TITLE: ArtScience poster-flyers
for the final exam exhibition 2009
DESIGN FIRM: formalism
DESIGNERS: Sietske Sips, Taconis Stolk
FONT USED: Helvetica Neue
CLIENT: ArtScience Interfaculty of the
University of the Arts, The Hague

Fig. 126
TITLE: Typ09 Conference Program
UNIVERSITY: School of the Art
Institute of Chicago (SAIC)

PROFESSOR: Daniel Morgenthaler
DESIGNER: Youngwook Nam
FONTS USED: Black Oak, Adobe
Wood Type, Wide Latin, Rockwell,
Mesquite, Clarendon, ITC Officina
Sans, Egyptienne

Figs. 127, 128, 129, 130
TITLE: *Prison of the Mind* book cover
UNIVERSITY: Academy of Art University
PROFESSOR: Carolina de Bartolo
DESIGNER: Lisa Schneller
FONT USED: Trade Gothic

Figs. 131, 132
TITLE: 2009 Parsons
Communication Design Book
UNIVERSITY: Parsons the
New School for Design

PROFESSORS: Julia Wargaski, Juan
Carlos Pagan, Cindy Rodriguez
FONTS USED: Futura, National

Figs. 133, 134, 135, 136
TITLE: Multiple Abstractions Book
UNIVERSITY: Academy of Art University
PROFESSOR: Ariel Grey
DESIGNER: Clara Silva
FONT USED: Priori Serif, Priori Sans

Fig. 137
TITLE: TED poster of events
DESIGN FIRM: Creative Circus
DESIGNER: Alex Brannon
FONT USED: Helvetica
CLIENT: TED

chapter seven
{ SCREEN }

There has been a debate going on for years about print design versus screen design. Some say that print is dead and that paper documents are no longer needed in a plugged-in, turned-on world. Why carry around a single printed book when you can carry two thousand of them in your digital device? Proponents of print design say that the screens can never replace the touch and feel of paper in the hands, and that there will always be a need for printed designs. Some people do not like to read text on a screen, and many enjoy turning pages manually.

Despite all of these arguments, the digital environment has become an integral part of our lives. Our computers, smartphones, tablets and other digital devices are constantly in use, never far from reach. These devices are often the first things we check when we arise in the morning and the last things we look at before we go to bed at night. Everything from e-mail and the weather to medical diagnosis and online magazines can be accessed on a screen. The goal of everything we view on a screen is exactly the same as that which we see on paper: It must communicate. Communication requires sound typographic decisions. This is why the theories and principles behind typography design are the same for both print and screen, although there are differences in how the typography is ultimately executed.

GOING DIGITAL

Going digital is not as simple as using the "save as" or "export" option in a favorite page layout software program. Although many programs now offer the option of translating a printed page directly into a coded webpage, the results are not optimal for a screen environment or a digital reader. The way in which a reader views a page on a screen is influenced by several factors, including resolution, lighting and the device on which it is being viewed. Finally, digital versions of a print design open up options for interactivity (Fig. 1).

LIGHT
Printed documents rely on reflected light to make the content visible. Light waves stream from a light source, hit the page, are diffused and are reflected back to the eye, where they are perceived as color and shape. Screens depend on backlighting to emit light waves rather than rely on reflected light; the device contains its own light source. Because the light waves don't bounce back and forth between the light source and the page before reaching the eye, they are less diffused and are therefore more tiring to the eye. Color, contrast, typeface choice and visual concept work together to create a digital environment that is visually pleasing.

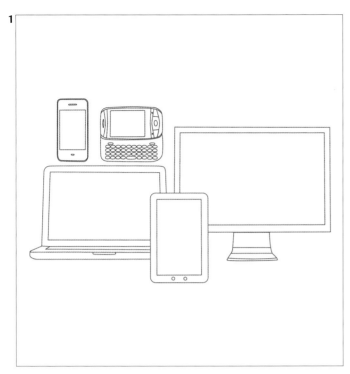

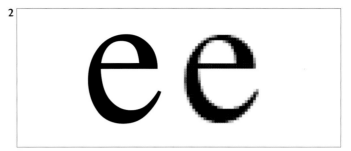

RESOLUTION

Quality print documents have a resolution of 300 dots per inch (dpi). The result is typography and imagery that is extremely clear and sharp, as the actual dots are virtually invisible to the naked eye. Depending on the make and model of the monitor, screen resolution averages 72 to 96 dpi. This means that the 300 dpi print document translated to a screen results in a reduction of clarity and sharpness by more than two-thirds (Fig. 2).

Screen resolution is also referred to as *ppi*, standing for pixels per inch. A *pixel* is a tiny square that forms the smallest unit of space available for information on a screen display. Pixels are placed end to end to form rows and columns. The resulting grid is used to form type and imagery, and determines the monitor's display. For instance, a display with a resolution of 1,680 × 1,050 has 1,680 pixels along its horizontal axis and 1,050 pixels along its vertical axis. Because of this pixel grid, content can have a "block-like" appearance, also referred to as "pixelated." Serif typefaces tend to display a more pixelated appearance than Sans Serifs, due to the distortion of their finer details, such as brackets and serifs (Fig. 3).

Because individual pixels cannot be more than one color, a typeface detail element that divides a pixel unevenly will either be rendered as a complete pixel or be deleted. The key thing to remember is that pixels do not change size; therefore, the typeface details are reformatted to fit into the existing pixels when its size is reduced (Fig. 4). The degradation in quality occurs because the same typeface is now created with fewer pixels. This is why typeface choices and sizes must be carefully considered to assure maximum legibility and readability on device screens.

DEVICE SYSTEMS

When working on one's own computer, any font accessible in the computer is available for use in a design. This is considered a *closed system*. It is fine as long as the design is going to be used for printed pages or will be formatted as an image file (known as graphic text)

1 Today's society is plugged-in and turned on 24/7. Designers need to address this digital environment. 2 Side-by-side comparison of a 300 dpi letter for print versus a 72 dpi letter for screen. 3 Serif letterforms tend to break down when used in screen applications due to the pixel's inflexibility. 4 The letters need to refit to the pixel grid when they get smaller; this often causes parts of letters to shift or be eliminated.

for screen-based design. However, if the text needs to be searchable and editable, known as *live text*, then the font must be available to all systems that may access the content. This is called an *open system*. Taking a design from a closed system to an open system requires compromise on font choices. There is a selection of standard fonts found across device platforms that are guaranteed to be viewable in any screen-based design: Arial, Helvetica, Times New Roman and Courier (Fig. 5). Most devices can also display Georgia, Verdana and Trebuchet, though these fonts are not yet fully integrated into all devices' systems. There are also very generic fonts available, known as sans serif, serif, monospace and cursive. At a minimum, body copy should be set in an open-system–safe font to

5

Arial
Helvetica
Times New Roman
Courier
Georgia
Verdana
Trebuchet

6

It is also an honor, perhaps almost unique, for a private visitor to be introduced to an academic audience by the President of the United States. Amid his heavy burdens, duties, and responsibilities—unsought but not recoiled from—the President has traveled a thousand miles to dignify and magnify our meeting here today and to give me an opportunity of addressing this kindred nation, as well as my own countrymen across the ocean, and perhaps some other countries too.

7

It is also an honor, perhaps almost unique, for a private visitor to be introduced to an academic audience by the President of the United States. Amid his heavy burdens, duties, and responsibilities—unsought but not recoiled from—the President has traveled a thousand miles to dignify and magnify our meeting here today and to give me an opportunity of addressing this kindred nation, as well as my own countrymen across the ocean, and perhaps some other countries too.

8

Graphic Text

9

Live Text

10

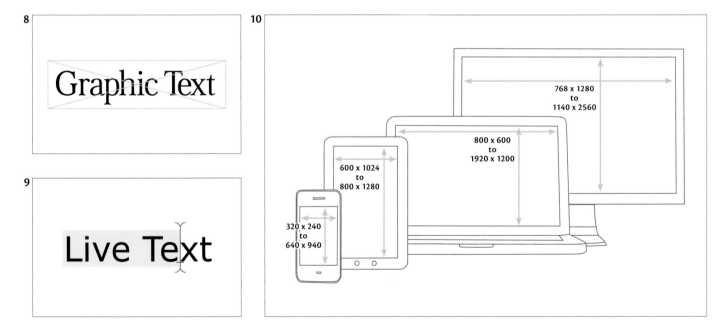

768 x 1280
to
1140 x 2560

800 x 600
to
1920 x 1200

600 x 1024
to
800 x 1280

320 x 240
to
640 x 940

5 Standard list of web-safe fonts guaranteed to be available on any system. **6, 7** Type samples depicting body copy set in Verdana, a sans serif, and Times, a serif, at 72 dpi. Note how much easier Verdana is to read at the low resolution. **8, 9** Graphic text is only good for instances when the necessary font is unavailable for use on the Web. Live text is ideal for the Web because it is searchable by search engine and selectable. **10** A drastic resolution size difference occurs from device to device and must be considered when designing for the screen.

assure that it can be read on any device. Sans serif is a safer choice, as it will not degrade at a smaller size (Figs. 6, 7).

The option exists to specify more than one font as well. A coding command can be written that gives the viewer's device the choice of several fonts to display. If the first font of choice is unavailable on the device's system, then subsequent choices will be searched in order; the first available option will load. While not ideal, this option still gives the designer some control over how fonts are viewed.

The urge to use custom fonts can be strong. Graphic text—text formatted to output as an image file—serves to quench that desire (Fig. 8). Limited to small amounts (headlines, subheads or navigation titles), graphic text is able to serve the creativity of a visual concept. It also helps maintain consistency when moving from an established print campaign to a digital design environment.

Font-hosting services are another solution for a custom typographic concept for those who desire all live text on the screen (Fig. 9). The possibilities for beautiful live typography in a screen-based design opens up dramatically with the use of font hosting. These custom screen fonts and coding language can also be used to reference a designer's own hosted TrueType or OpenType font with the @font-face CSS command, Embedded OpenType (EOT) or Web Open Font Format (WOFF). These methods work by hosting fonts on a server. Custom code is inserted into a page that refers back to the font on a server. The font is then accessed and made viewable on the page no matter what device called it up, eliminating the need for the specialty font to be available on the device's system.

The device in which the design will finally be viewed will also influence font choices. Tiny cell phone displays require simpler fonts, as the screen's resolution is lower than that of a computer monitor. Phone screen resolution ranges from 320 × 240 pixels to 940 × 640. Tablets typically have a display resolution of 1,024 × 768, whereas computer monitors can go as high as to 2,560 × 1,440 (Fig. 10). The better the resolution, the better the quality of the displayed imagery and content. A designer must consider all these different displays when translating a design into a screen-based format.

SHARING FONTS

You just designed the most awesome website ever using the coolest font you purchased from your favorite font house. You want live text, so @font-face was incorporated into the CSS coding. You tested and re-tested and the site is flawless. You are ready to upload and release its awesomeness to the world, right? Wrong.

In the world of sharing everything with everyone for free, sharing fonts is not included. The font license for the live text font must be read to check for Web usage. More likely than not, the license covers only use for a limited number of closed systems. @font-face and other forms of font hosting are technically considered distribution of a font since the viewer is accessing the font via your server. Traditional font licenses do not allow for distribution—it is akin to taking something you bought, making copies and giving it away for free.

Be sure to check with the font creator, retail font resource and original license to determine your legal options. Many resources offer the option to purchase the web license for a font in addition to the traditional license. Be aware, however, that not all font creators allow their font to be used on the Web as live text. If the particular font must absolutely be used and a web license is unavailable, the only solution is to create graphic text. To be safe, check the font license before setting any live text in your web design.

INTERACTIVITY

Pop-up books are wonderful examples of interactive print design; although, aside from some surface techniques and an occasional pop-up or two, print is quite limited in terms of interactivity. Designing for the screen, on the other hand, offers abundant opportunity for interactivity. This is what makes screen design so special and, let's face it, cool. Interactivity creates a multidimensional atmosphere, one that invites the viewer to become involved with the page on a deeper level. On a website about dogs, for example, a viewer can read about a dog, see a photo of a dog, follow links to other types of dogs, listen to a dog bark, watch a video of a dog running, watch live streaming video of dogs playing, use an app that allows a viewer to try different collars on a dog, play a game involving dogs, fill in a survey about favorite dogs, leave a comment responding to an article about a dog, post photos of the viewer's own dog and converse with other dog owners worldwide (Fig. 11). All of the aforementioned interactive techniques can occur on a single webpage. Other aesthetic interactions such as navigation rollovers, flash, HTML-based galleries and animations are also available. Interactivity creates a fun environment, one that encourages viewers to stay.

The interactivity must be appropriate, though. It is only natural for a beginning designer to want to add every possible bell and whistle on a page, but more is not always better. The best rule of thumb can be likened to women's fashion advice: Before heading out for the evening, take a look in the mirror and remove one accessory. Too many baubles and bling distract the eye and take away from the overall effect; less is more. The same principle applies to using interactive components in a web design. The viewer should be able to find the focal point of the page and view it in its designed hierarchy. Too many interactive elements distract the viewers, interfere with their ability to find important information and ultimately create an unsatisfactory viewing experience.

ELECTRONIC MEDIA

Advancing technology has greatly expanded the variety of electronic media that can be used to view webpages. Computers, phones, PDAs, tablet computers and other devices now allow the

user to view much more than unformatted text screens. This wide variety of systems makes it imperative to design flexible and readable layouts.

MAC VS. PC

The battle between Apple and makers of other PCs has been ongoing since the early 1990s, when computers became mass-market products. The programming languages of the computers are distinctly different. This is why designers of screen-based layouts must work to assure that their designs are viewable and operable cross-platform. Fortunately the code languages of the Internet are universal, so the structural aspects of layouts are mostly trouble-free. It is the aesthetic issues that fuel the Mac vs. PC battle, as it rages on in the hearts of designers.

The two biggest issues are fonts and color. Most monitors are capable of displaying about 16 million colors, although they do tend to display color slightly differently from each other. The way in which the monitor is manufactured, the system to which it is attached and the room lighting all affect the color displayed. Macs tend to display colors lighter than PCs and other third-party monitors. The color shift can sometimes be extreme: Purple on one monitor may look like pink on another and periwinkle on a third. More often than not, though, the color shift is subtler. A purple on one monitor may shift slightly to become a pinker purple or bluer purple on another monitor. This is not a problem if the exact color doesn't matter. However, if the color is supposed to reflect corporate branding or if an incorrectly displayed color conveys the wrong connotation, then color accuracy is imperative.

The solution is to choose from a set of 256 web-safe colors that all monitors, both Mac and PC, display consistently (Fig. 12). These colors also display correctly on phones, PDAs and tablets. Choosing from this list will guarantee the correct color, regardless of the device. Although this can be limiting, confining choices to this color set eases the frustration of trying to ensure the right color. Web-safe colors are coded by a series of six alphanumeric characters, preceded by a hash mark. For instance, #FF0033 is a bright red and #66FFCC is a pale aqua. Careful attention must still be paid to the combination of colors. Good contrast is a must.

11

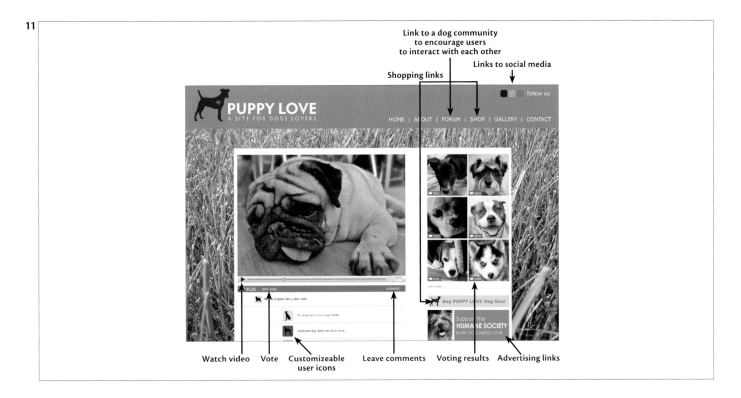

Link to a dog community
to encourage users
to interact with each other

Links to social media

Shopping links

Watch video   Vote   Customizeable   Leave comments   Voting results   Advertising links
                         user icons

12

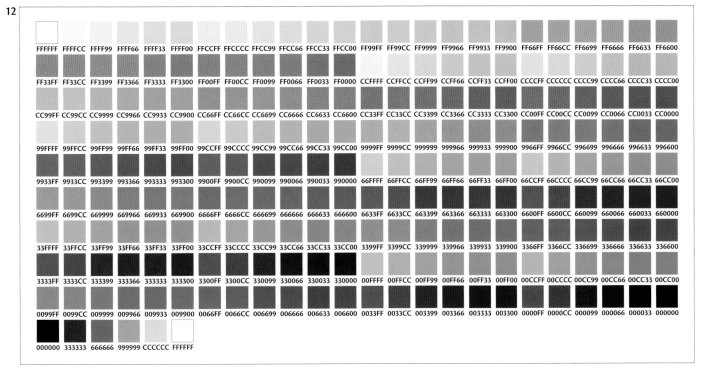

11 Interactivity sets screen design apart from print design. The more interactivity used, the more interesting the website and the longer a viewer is likely to stick around. Be careful not to use too much, however, or it will be hard for the viewer to concentrate. **12** Web-safe color chart.

BROWSERS

Most users prefer viewing the Internet with a specific browser—Internet Explorer, Safari, Opera, Firefox, Mosaic or Chrome, to name a few (Figs. 13, 14, 15). Browsers can be customized for preferences regarding page viewing, bookmarks, color skins and other small but handy tools. Browsers tend to have loyal followings. Because they compete with one another, manufacturers of browsers work with developers to continually update programming languages. This is a good thing, as it encourages new and experimental programming, giving web designers a greater outlet for creativity. The downside of this is that different browsers end up supporting different languages, making cross-browser web design a challenge at times. Testing is the key. Designing for the least sophisticated browser will help to ensure that a web design can be viewed in any browser.

OTHER DEVICES

We live in a world where devices for browsing the Internet and interacting with apps are held in the palm of our hands. It also means that designers must accommodate for this tiny new world. Screen design for non-computer devices takes careful planning. A stunning design on a 27-inch iMac will not appear the same on a 3.5-inch iPhone or 3.7-inch Droid screen (Fig. 16). These devices have the capability of displaying a webpage in its entirety on its full screen, but because the content is rendered so small, it hardly lends itself to effective browsing. Designing a secondary website specifically geared to non-computer devices is a great solution and one many web designers undertake.

The first thing to remember is that the screen is tiny. Dividing the page into chunks of information will help with the screen organization. Using only one column allows for faster browsing because a viewer needs to scroll in only one direction (Fig. 17). Tiny screens also mean small images. Small imagery effectively cuts down on the download time, which means a great deal to people browsing from their phone or other devices. Limiting imagery altogether also cuts down on download time. Fonts must be universal. Choosing from the list of standard cross-platform fonts will guarantee that a viewer can properly see the text display. Application design for phones follows the same rules as for web design. As always, the goal is optimal readability and communication.

Tablets are in between computers and phones in terms of using the Internet. They are large enough for a non-optimized webpage to display quite well, but they are small enough that problems can arise with extremely complex websites, such as those with multiple columns, abundant text links, tiny input boxes and overly detailed navigation. The average tablet size is 6.4 × 9.4 inches, far smaller than the average computer monitor screen. A multiple-column grid forces the tablet to scale the page down to fit the smaller screen. As a result, viewers must zoom in to read areas of interest. Abundant text links, especially if placed close together, often cause a viewer to mistakenly tap the wrong link. Tiny input boxes are also hard to tap and can become frustrating. Drop-down menus are often touchy and can disappear in the process of trying to make a selection, or fail to work altogether. Designing an alternative tablet website to make the visual concept optimal across all devices is a wise decision.

13, 14, 15 The same website viewed in Safari (Fig. 13) and Firefox (Fig. 14) on a Mac as well as in Internet Explorer (Fig. 15) on a PC. Note the differences in appearance.

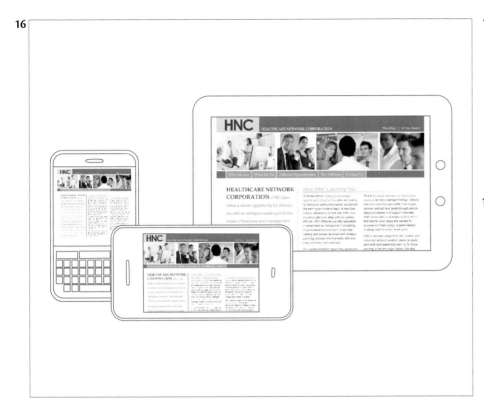

BETTER

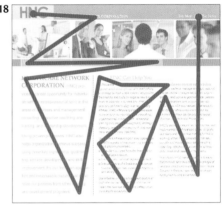

LAYOUT

A printed page is typically viewed from left to right and from top to bottom. Webpages are navigated differently. Readers jump around from section to section, rarely reading a page from top to bottom. A reader also will only visit the areas of the website that interest her. All forms of screen pages must be able to stand on their own, independent of the other pages before and after it. At the same time, the pages must maintain a consistent visual concept for them to form a cohesive website. Just because a design is viewed on screen instead of paper doesn't mean the rules and guidelines of design cease to apply. Headlines, subheads, body copy and imagery are all treated the same on screen as they are on paper. Gestalt and relationship principles are also the same. Type issues aren't off the hook either. Widows, orphans, jumping horizons, bad breaks and so forth all need to be addressed as well.

GRIDS FOR WEB

When a viewer first looks at a webpage, his eye begins in the upper left corner, moves across the top and then explores the rest of the page (Fig. 18). This means that the upper left corner serves as a focal point, although the rest of the page is pretty much fair game. The center is next in line for hierarchy, but the eye can bounce around from left to right and back again. The bottom, particularly the bottom right, is lowest in the hierarchy. Unlike in print design, the bottom right corner of the page does not automatically indicate that someone should "turn" the page. This is why a solid grid system must be in place to direct the viewer where to look.

A website has a complex system of elements that need organization and clear hierarchy. At a minimum, each page will have a logo, navigational system and content. The logo indicates to whom the website belongs. It should be prominent without being overbearing, as the website's purpose is to communicate more information

197

16 Designs for screen don't always translate well when reduced to fit on a phone. **17** Alter the programming to display a different design layout more compatible with smaller screens. **18** Typical eye-tracking for a website, though this can vary depending on the layout and designed hierarchy.

than just what the logo looks like. Navigation helps the viewer know where to go within the site, and it should be clear, simple and easy to find. If a viewer cannot easily figure out where to go, he will leave. Again, grid systems provide consistency. A viewer will become familiar with the placement of elements and be able to quickly seek them out on a new page. Text and imagery support the remainder of the website. This information must be easy to read, easy to find and engaging enough to maintain the viewer's interest.

A hierarchical grid system works best for web design because it allows for different sections of information and a hierarchy-within-a-hierarchy style of organization. Web grids need a header, a footer and a column system in between them. The header contains the logo and other important information, including whatever navigation must absolutely be seen. The footer appears below the columns and usually contains legal information and secondary navigation. The column system in between works like a print design column system, containing text or imagery. The number of columns is flexible, and compound columns can be created. Rows can also be added to create a modular grid system between the header and footer. Content will dictate what style of grid is needed after the header.

There is a school of thought that claims that six columns, also known as a 968 pixel grid, is the ideal amount for a web grid (Fig. 19). The far left and far right columns are dedicated to navigation and secondary information such as advertisements or lists. The middle four columns are then used for page-specific content. Navigation can also be placed in the header, allowing the far left column to revert back to more content. This grid system works quite well and is frequently found throughout the Internet. Of course, a six-column grid is just one way to approach a website. The more columns, the more flexible the page. With blog-style and news websites, eight to ten columns or more work better to communicate the plethora of information, dividing the content and developing the proper hierarchy (Figs. 20, 21).

With this complex a system, it often helps to add lines between areas of the grid to help give clear division between content elements and to set off the header and footer. In addition, columns can be programmed to have a fixed or flexible width. A fixed width means that if a browser window is enlarged or the site is viewed on a higher-resolution screen than it was intended, the columns will still remain the same size. In a flexible-width grid, the columns are

19

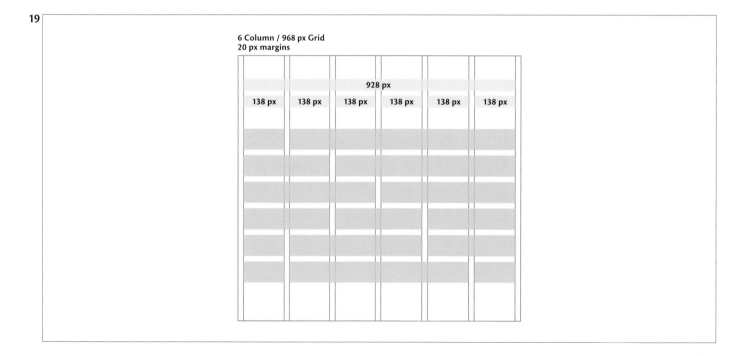

6 Column / 968 px Grid
20 px margins

928 px

| 138 px | 138 px | 138 px | 138 px | 138 px | 138 px |

19 Sample grid system for a 968 pixel grid. The gray areas indicate potential compound column arrangements to add more flexibility to the page layout.

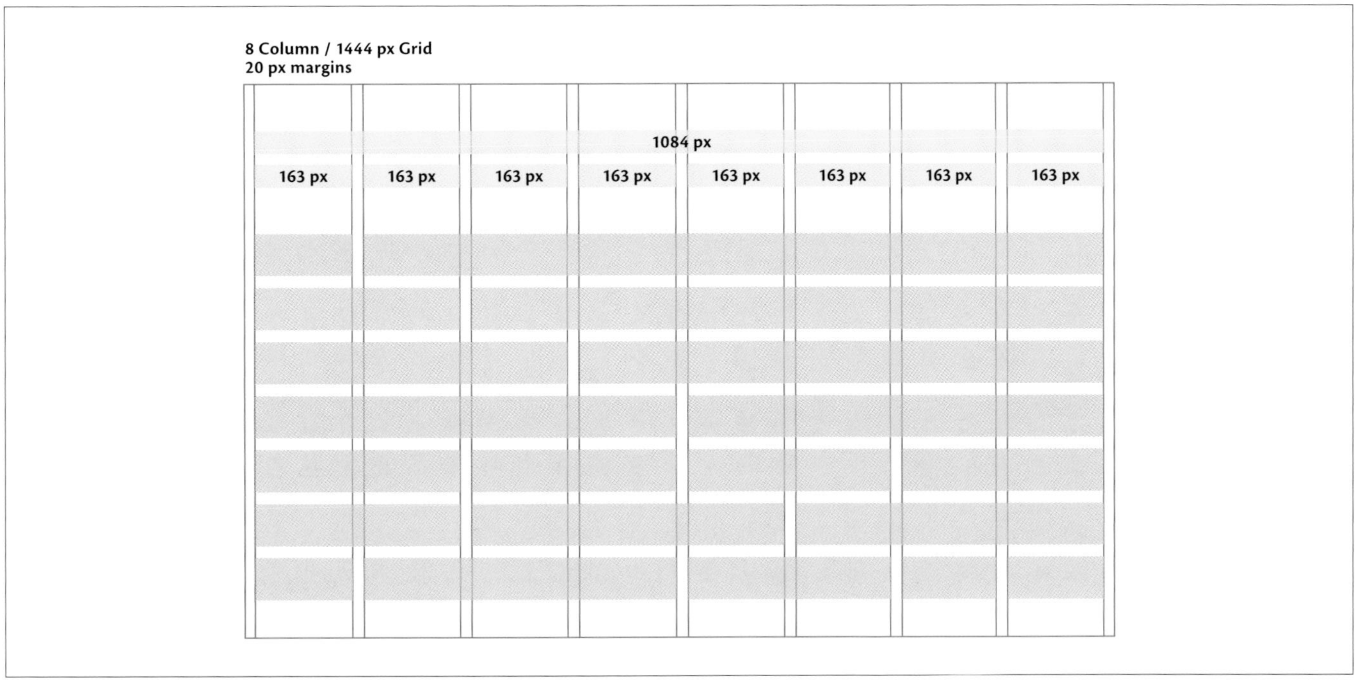

8 Column / 1444 px Grid
20 px margins

1084 px

| 163 px | 163 px | 163 px | 163 px | 163 px | 163 px | 163 px | 163 px |

10 Column / 1444 px Grid
20 px margins

1224 px

| 126 px | 126 px | 126 px | 126 px | 126 px | 126 px | 126 px | 126 px | 126 px | 126 px |

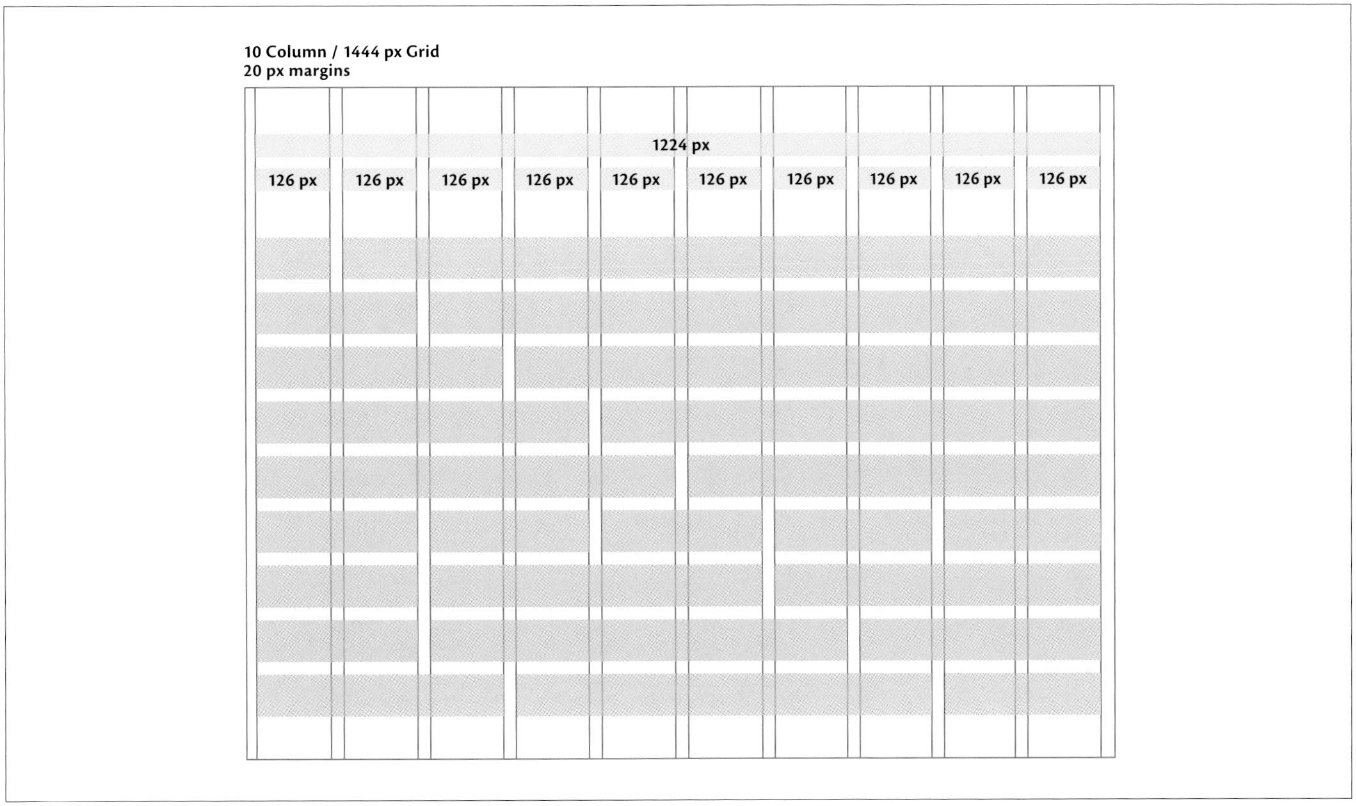

20, 21 Sample grid systems for a 1,444 pixel grid. The gray areas indicate potential compound column arrangements to add more flexibility to the page layout.

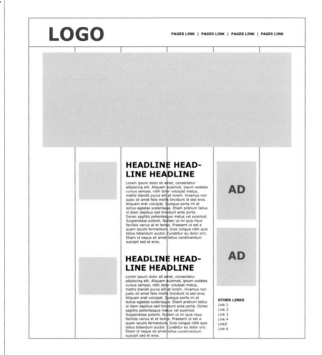

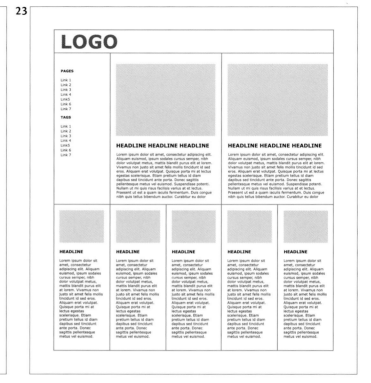

22 Sample six-column design layout.　**23** Sample five-column design layout.　**24** Sample seven-column design layout.

programmed to be a percentage of the total width and will resize based upon browser window width. In all cases, using a hierarchical grid means that a designer needs to approach each section of the grid independently. This may result in adjustments to the size, color, boldness or placement of elements once the page is assembled as a whole, which is fine as long as the visual concept is maintained (Figs. 22, 23, 24).

Now for the hard part: No matter what grid system is used, the appearance of the page will change from computer to computer and device to device. As previously discussed, different screens have different resolutions, which determine how a website is seen. An average computer screen is 1,024 × 768 pixels, though it can be as large as 2,560 × 1,440 or as small as 800 × 600. If flexible columns are used, then the column width will vary depending upon the monitor used to view it. This is why web grids should use left-aligned text. Center-aligned or justified text creates massive readability problems when the flexible column width grows or shrinks dramatically—center-aligned text because the left and right rag becomes more severe with larger widths, justified text because of dramatic rivers that reduce readability.

DIGITAL PUBLICATIONS

Screen design goes beyond websites. Digital publications are becoming more common as more digital devices emerge (Fig. 25). E-zines—digital magazines—as well as corporate brochures and newsletters have broken into the digital world. Grid systems for this style of publication bridge print and web. Navigation is often added, so a header or side column is needed to accommodate the navigation. Many designers incorporate dual flexible grid systems—the grid changes depending on which way the device is being held—for horizontal or vertical viewing of the publication. Unlike print design, a digital publication does not have to run horizontally. There is no need for pages to run in order from left to right or front to back. For example, an e-zine can be organized into a horizontal line for the first pages of articles, but then the viewer can scroll up or down through the pages to continue reading an individual article (Fig. 26). This design resembles a town's main street with small side streets extending from it, each revealing independent shops, even as the main street brings them all together.

Digital publications can also incorporate interactive content. In the early days of the electronic era, converting a magazine into a digital publication was accomplished merely by saving it as a PDF.

25

26

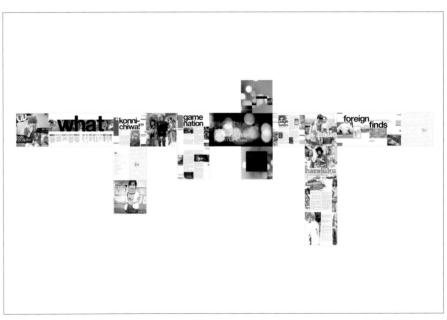

25 *LIV* magazine. **26** Digital publications have permission to run in several directions and not follow the left-to-right and front-to-back layout of traditional print magazines.

Nowadays, designers have embraced capabilities originally intended for the Web, incorporating them into digital publications. Static pictures become slideshows or videos. Hyperlinks can be added to the text, allowing a viewer to launch a website to obtain additional information. Adding a search dialogue box also enhances the user experience, as does giving access to archived content. Surveys, photo galleries, comment sections, games and other interactive content can also be included. The advantage of incorporating these elements into the digital publication instead of the main website is that they can change with every issue. Advertisers can also add interactive content, using clickable ads to generate a direct route to their own websites and products.

EFFECTIVE TYPOGRAPHY

Choosing the perfect typography for a print design is hard. Choosing the perfect typography for a screen design is even harder because screen resolution limits the typeface options. The perfect font for a print design may not display well on screens of various resolutions. Typography for the screen is all about readability and functionality. As mentioned, the theories of good typography and print design also apply to the Web. Complementary type pairs add variety and help with hierarchy. Remember that Serif typefaces do not read well as body copy due to poor pixel resolution, so save the serifs for larger text.

SIZES FOR SCREEN

Font size for screen body copy should be around 14 point, the somewhat larger size being necessary because of varying screen resolutions. Recognize that higher resolution will cause body copy to display somewhat smaller. Web text can also be set in such a way as to automatically resize to match the resolution and viewer's browser preferences. This is known as "inherent" setting. For example, body copy set to 90% and subheads or headlines set to 120% means that the type size is variable against the default size set in the individual's browser preferences. If the viewer has the body copy size preference set as 16 point, then the page's body copy will display as 14.4 point (90% of 16 point), while the subhead or headline will display as 19.2 point (120% of 16 point). This method of specifying size keeps a page flexible and adaptable (Figs. 27, 28).

27

Web Typography is fun

Lorem ipsum dolor sit amet, consectetur adipiscing elit. Mauris elementum, nunc sit amet porttitor pellentesque, libero mi molestie leo, id adipiscing lectus nunc at nibh. Sed enim metus, laoreet eget blandit a, iaculis id dolor. Lorem ipsum dolor sit amet, consectetur adipiscing elit. Donec scelerisque, eros vitae posuere tristique, risus dolor cursus lorem, id lobortis metus felis ut ipsum. Aenean et tempor nibh. Proin volutpat tempus tellus. Integer tempor rhoncus venenatis. Donec nec enim vitae dui vulputate bibendum nec imperdiet nisl.

28

Web Typography is fun

Lorem ipsum dolor sit amet, consectetur adipiscing elit. Mauris elementum, nunc sit amet porttitor pellentesque, libero mi molestie leo, id adipiscing lectus nunc at nibh. Sed enim metus, laoreet eget blandit a, iaculis id dolor. Lorem ipsum dolor sit amet, consectetur adipiscing elit. Donec scelerisque, eros vitae posuere tristique, risus dolor cursus lorem, id lobortis metus felis ut ipsum. Aenean et tempor nibh. Proin volutpat tempus tellus. Integer tempor rhoncus venenatis. Donec nec enim vitae dui vulputate bibendum nec imperdiet nisl.

27 Type set as headline at 120% and body at 90% of the default browser text setting of 16 point. **28** Type set as headline at 120% and body at 90% of the default browser text setting of 18 point.

Preset measurements are specified point or pixel sizes. This should be avoided if at all possible because of varying resolutions. For example, 14-point text on one machine can appear as small as 10 point on another, diminishing its readability.

Headlines and subheads are treated similarly to print design. Their size must be appropriate to the body copy, and they need to fall within the hierarchy. Using extra-large headlines to call attention to them is tempting, but use restraint. Large headlines push content lower down on the page. This is not an issue in print design, because the entire page is always visible. Content in screen design that falls below the lower edge of the browser window forces the viewer to scroll down to read the rest of it. Extra large headlines are also unnecessary with a well-executed grid, hierarchy and visual concept. Try to minimize unnecessary visual distractions.

For navigation text, text links that lead to other pages within the website, size falls in between headline and body copy. Navigation is extremely important to a page because it is the viewer's key to moving through the website. Because it is not part of the main content, however, it is lower in hierarchy. A good rule of thumb for navigation text is to set it either the same size or slightly larger than the body copy, but not as large as a headline. If the navigation needs to stand out more from the body copy or is not clear in its hierarchical rank, then color, boldness, caps or other stylistic modifications can be used.

A second reason to make an effort to achieve good typographic hierarchy is that search engines rely on the CSS coding attributed to typography to help with its ranking systems. CSS uses tags for headlines, subheads, body copy, captions, pull quotes, etc. These tags are used by search engines to determine the importance of each element on the page. A main headline is more important than a picture caption and, therefore, will have a higher ranking within the page and search engine results. Remember, a chaotic and hierarchy-deficient page is not only difficult for a viewer to read but results in poor search engine recognition as well.

LIVE AND GRAPHIC TEXT

Live text is text coded by HTML that can be copied and pasted into another webpage or computer program. Live text can also be read aloud by screen reading software, increasing accessibility to the visually impaired. Either web-safe or web-hosted fonts can be used for live text, as there is no guarantee that a chosen specialty font will be available to the end-user's system. Always remember that a designer's closed system doesn't necessarily reflect the content of other users' systems. Web-safe fonts are just that: safe to use for all systems, although as mentioned, the choices are extremely limited. The introduction of web-hosting services has dramatically increased the number of available fonts, although they are still limited by price and by the fact that not all fonts in print design have been converted to optimally legible screen versions. Neither web-safe fonts nor web-hosted fonts offer the designer the control of manual kerning or tracking, unless the designer is familiar with higher-level programming such as JavaScript.

Graphic text is the workaround. Created in an illustration or photo program and then imported as a picture onto the webpage, graphic text can be completely controlled. Perfect kerning, proper ligatures, good tracking and other fine-tuning can and should be applied. The advantage of graphic text is the ability to use specialty fonts to create a particular look or maintain corporate branding. Graphic text's major disadvantage is that it is not searchable by Internet search engines, nor can the text be selected for copying or editing without going back into the original software program. Graphic text should never be used for body copy, as search engines need live text to properly rank and categorize a webpage. The use of large amounts of graphic text will result in poor search results and longer download times, because imagery takes much longer to download than live text.

OTHER TYPE ELEMENTS

Pull quotes and initial caps are wonderful ways to add visual interest to a page. The rules of print design still apply. Pull quotes say something interesting, enticing the viewer to delve deeper into an article (Fig. 29). Because web viewers typically view a page for a shorter time than they do a printed page, anything that pulls the reader in is good. Initial caps, specifically drop caps, are a great way to generate interest. They create a focal point that leads a viewer into an article and creates hierarchy. As with print design, be careful about how many drop caps appear on a page. They should serve as enhancements, not distractions. Beware of inadvertently spelling out something inappropriate (Fig. 30). Ligatures and hanging punctuation can also be done for screen design with simple coding.

Lorem ipsum dolor sit amet, consectetur adipiscing elit. Vestibulum eu mauris arcu, et consectetur ante. Donec ut justo vitae justo sagittis sodales. Vivamus leo magna, euismod a sollicitudin quis, euismod at odio. Aliquam ut augue lacus, non scelerisque nulla. Mauris ac justo et mauris blandit accumsan a eu mi. Vestibulum rhoncus

"Pull quotes are a great way to draw interest and add a focal point on the page."

pharetra tortor, sed congue tortor pellentesque vitae. Pellentesque iaculis ultricies dolor, non molestie lorem convallis quis. Aenean sceleris-que nisi sed purus ullamcorper rhoncus id et magna. Vivamus pretium, neque eu laoreet posuere, erat risus posuere felis, gravida viverra felis ante sit amet velit. Suspendisse commodo, lectus vel imperdiet rhoncus,

Lorem ipsum dolor sit amet, consectetur adipiscing elit. Vestibulum eu mauris arcu, et consectetur ante. Donec ut justo vitae justo sagittis sodales. Vivamus leo magna, euismod a sollicitudin quis, euismod at odio. Aliquam ut augue lacus, non scelerisque nulla. Mauris ac justo et mauris blandit accumsan a eu mi. Vestibulum rhoncus pharetra tortor, sed congue tortor pellen-tesque vitae. Pellentesque iaculis ultricies dolor, non molestie lorem convallis quis. Aenean scelerisque nisi sed purus ullamcorper rhoncus id et

Aunc et quam at eros suscipit tempus eu sed tellus. Maecenas nisl felis, dapibus viverra convallis vitae, placerat at turpis. Proin tempus, orci nec faucibus porttitor, urna neque laoreet ligula, ac tristique erat metus nec metus. Sed vel ipsum ut lectus mattis venenatis sit amet ac tellus. Donec molestie mauris felis, sit amet porttitor tortor. Donec dui justo, laoreet et lacinia at, blandit sit amet nulla. Curabitur eu eros a metus lacinia imperdiet id et elit. Integer ultricies dictum quam, eget malesuada enim sagittis non. In consectetur lectus et lacus laoreet et

Murabitur placerat, sem in rutrum accumsan, dolor ipsum tincidunt mauris, varius interdum metus est sit amet sem. Aenean iaculis condimentum eros, nec rhoncus ipsum semper vel. Nulla sapien tellus, laoreet in sollicitudin at, lacinia eu dui. Nullam suscipit porttitor varius. In enim nisi, lobortis a malesuada eget, gravida vel sem. Integer ultrices lorem vitae velit pretium vitae lobortis urna elementum. In placerat urna eget metus vulputate rutrum. Curabitur sed nisi nulla, vel facilisis tortor. Nullam ultrices mi et orci blandit quis rutrum

THIS IS MORE DIFFICULT TO READ IN ALL UPPERCASE than in a Combination of Upper- and Lowercase.

29 Use pull quotes to grab attention. **30** Initial caps also draw attention but be careful that they don't inadvertently spell something. **31** Choose your text case carefully. All uppercase letters gives the impression of yelling the text.

There is very little that cannot be controlled with programming, so there is no excuse for poor typography. Underlining is a feature of live text that indicates the text is a hyperlink. Underlining should not be used elsewhere, or it will confuse a viewer and give the impression that the webpage is not working properly.

Avoid using all uppercase letters, as it has the connotation on the Internet that one is yelling. Uppercase is also more difficult to read, especially when set as body copy (Fig. 31). Special effects such as drop shadows, glows, blinking animation and other bells and whistles diminish readability and annoy the viewer. If there is a special effect that absolutely must be used, do so sparingly. Too many special effects on a page create problems with hierarchy and encourage the viewer to leave instead of delving deeper into the site.

DESIGNING FOR SCREEN

Web design holds many challenges for traditional print designers. The flexibility in layout, variable text size and the inclusion of interactive components are not found in print. Embrace the change. Throw your arms around the fact that a website will not look the same on every device. These nuances make for living designs that change constantly, just as the Internet is constantly changing. Interactive components bring another dimension to a page, encouraging viewers to involve themselves with a website. Let them be part of the visual concept. Some great websites use the viewer as a design tool, letting them create content and contribute to the overall site. If a visual concept is no longer working, change it. That is the beauty of the screen as opposed print: You're never stuck with five thousand expensive brochures that are now useless because the company president resigned. Change something on a webpage and it appears immediately. The Internet is an instantaneous medium at little to no cost to the designer.

WEBSITE DESIGN

Great websites have solid design and excellent content, embrace innovative technology and combine it with traditional typographic and layout principles. The most successful websites have strong hierarchy, complementary type pairs, a flexible grid system, good readability, well organized content and inviting colors. A website should be memorable and user-friendly. Its best friend is the repeat viewer who has bookmarked the site to explore the content often (Figs. 32, 33).

32 Insane play website. **33** JAS MD retail website.

DESIGNING WEBSITES

Content determines website design. Corporate branding and other company guidelines play a role, but it is the content that dictates the final structure and organization. First and foremost, the designer must know the audience, as everything from the overall grid system to the size of the body copy must meet their needs. A younger, more tech savvy audience gives the designer leeway to be more experimental with the site. An older, more computer phobic audience means that the designer must use simple, clean layouts that leave nothing to chance.

Begin by mapping out the entire website. The best method is literally to draw a map. Begin with a small box to represent the homepage, with lines extending out to other boxes representing each page to which it links. Label each one of the boxes with the name of the link. Draw lines extending from those boxes to represent links appearing on those pages. Continue in this manner for all pages of the website. This visual representation will help keep pages in order and keep the site on track.

Determining the grid system is the next step. The grid allows consistency and eases the design process. Experiment with different grids within a hierarchical system. Investigate different layouts using content from the homepage and one subsequent page. Try using a three- or four-column grid, as well as one with numerous columns and modules. Try at least three to five different grid systems before making a final determination. Each option will give a distinct look. Explore websites you like and examine the grid systems used. Blog design requires a grid with many columns to accommodate primary content, main and secondary navigation, secondary content, reader feedback and more. Choose the grid system that allows the most flexibility while still maintaining the desired visual concept.

Once a grid system has been chosen, focus on the header, as this is what people will see first. The logo should be prominent and the navigation must be clear. Make sure the navigation links are distinct, perhaps separating them with lines or bullets, or placing them in buttons. Rollovers help indicate to which navigation link a viewer is pointing. Be careful with drop-down menus that extend from navigation links, as these can be difficult to use on non-computer devices.

Placement of page content follows the same rules as print design. Complementary type pairs, color choice, text size and image selection

follow the same guidelines. The only difference is being aware of certain screen principles to optimize readability. Compound columns and modules increase visual interest and provide flexibility for placement of content. Make sure the text and background color are optimized for viewing on a screen. Black on white or white on black produces too much contrast for comfortable reading over long periods of time. Choose lower contrast color combinations like dark gray on white or white on dark gray. Subheads, pull quotes and graphic elements provide hierarchy, help with readability and add interest to a page. Lines are a device for dividing one section of content from another. If a page has a great deal of separate content, consider splitting it out onto more than one page.

Keep imagery small so that it loads quickly. Large imagery with long download times will cause a page to hang up, making it appear that the page has broken links. Assign alternate text to imagery to let the viewer know what the image should be in case the image fails to appear. Alternate text is also used for accessibility software. We live in a society of instant gratification, which means that viewers will get discouraged after a few seconds and leave the site instead of waiting for content to load. There are plenty of other websites out there, so it is incumbent on the designer to do everything possible to keep the viewer's interest.

Use live text as much as possible. Readership is driven by search engines, so the more accessible the site is to search engines, the better. Take advantage of font hosting to create a less generic look. Acknowledge that the text must be flexible within its layout to accommodate all devices that will be used to view the page. Avoid forced returns unless the text must be read in a precise way, or with exact breaks. Forced returns will cause the text to reflow with each different device's resolutions and column width variances, creating bad breaks. Remember to use underlining only for links. Use italics, bold, size or color variations for emphasis instead.

Test, test, test. It is imperative to test the site on all potential viewing devices and browsers, and on both the Mac and PC platforms. Call friends or relatives and ask them to view the design. Make note of any problems and address them as necessary. Double- and triple-check the typography to make sure the hierarchy, font and visual concept are being displayed as intended.

AN INTERVIEW WITH JASON SANTA MARIA

Jason Santa Maria is the founder and principal of Mighty, a Brooklyn-based design studio. He is creative director of Typekit; a faculty member in the MFA interaction design program at the School of Visual Arts; vice president of AIGA/NY; co-founder of the publisher A Book Apart; founder of Typedia, a shared encyclopedia of typefaces online; and creative director for *A List Apart*, a magazine for people who make websites. Discussion of design, film and sock monkeys can often be observed on his award-winning website (jasonsantamaria. com). His work has garnered him awards and pleasantries ranging from firm handshakes to forceful handshakes with a little hitting. Ever the design obsessive, Santa Maria is known to take drunken arguments to fisticuffs over such frivolities as kerning and white space.

© Jason Santa Maria

You have devoted much time to teaching others about the good use of typography. Why is this so important to you?

I think that it's the most basic building block of design. Everything that I do in my design work, and I know that everything I teach in my class, all comes out of typography. It's the mark of what separates a good designer from a bad designer—someone who has the level of attention that they can deal with typography. It's just such a detailed craft and such an important thing, and like anything else, when it's done well you don't even notice it, but when it's done poorly it really sticks out.

You are the founder of Typedia. You describe it as being a cross between Wikipedia and IMDB for type (Figs. 34, 35). What inspired you to create a community like this, and how does this site benefit a young designer?

The best ideas, I think, respond out of a personal need for something—not just that you see an opportunity to sell something but because you have the desire to use something yourself. Typedia came out of that a few years back. I was bothered by how impenetrable learning about type can really be. It's pretty easy to learn the basics of type, either through books or online, but I feel like after that to get a much more in-depth knowledge you have the option of either spending a lifetime working with typefaces or really delving into every single book you can find and cross-referencing it against everything else. I thought how easy would it be to harness what the Web already does and catalogue type based upon some sort of cross-reference system. There is tons of metadata associated with typefaces available—who designed

them, what year they were made in, what they were based upon, what different styles they might have or characteristics, and technical details—but none of these things are actually cross-referenced against other typefaces. It just made sense once I'd thought of it that way. This information is immediately comparable and it seemed very apparent that a tool like this could be really useful, mostly for me. If no one else even used it, I knew that maybe I could benefit from it, because it's too much information to store in your head. It made sense that if you could go onto a site and just cross-reference things based upon a designer or a time period or a style, you could learn a lot.

What characteristics do you look for when choosing fonts for a design? Headline vs. body text?

I tend to gravitate towards typefaces that kind of aren't ready-made typefaces. But I definitely tend to avoid typefaces that are trendy or have a certain visual effect, where it's almost as though the design is already injected. I see this all the time. For example, food packaging for burritos or salsa have those stylistic fonts that are trying to make something look tied to a certain culture or a certain time period. Beyond that I look for workhorse typefaces that can stand on their own, just be very pure letterforms, and don't need extra flare. I choose typefaces that have an evenness throughout all of the letterforms and throughout the different styles and extensions of the typeface. I really try to match the typeface with the usage. That's partially creative direction—what kind of typeface fits or doesn't fit with the material that's being designed.

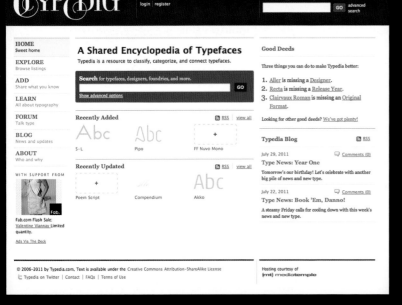

I also look at where it's going to appear, what size it's going to appear, how legible it needs to be at that size and if the typeface can fit those requirements. There's definitely a technical overlay that is relevant that determines how well the typeface is going to serve its purpose, especially when we're talking about the Web. That can be a tough thing for students to get. They think typography is either an art or a talent, and it's neither of those things. I keep telling them that it's a craft of intent. I feel like that sums it up really well, because it's something you have to learn, you have to nurture and keep building upon for an entire career. You're never going to be an expert. I feel like if you strive toward it, there's always intention behind it. There's always some sort of remark or mood that you're trying to convey, and that's where it gets fun.

Speaking of fun, who or what are your inspirations from a design standpoint?

Maybe it's because I started out in print, but a lot of my inspiration comes from print design. It's all the typical, usual suspects, but they're usual suspects for a reason, because they were just that good. They had that mind-set of how to imbue a design with emotion. Paul Rand and Alvin Lustig and people like Ladislav Sutnar are people who really had an understanding of what design can do. In particular, all those people have an undercurrent of the design of information—vast amounts of information, or ways to design and describe information visually—which is very interesting to me. I'm working on the Web and the vast amount of information that goes with it is what led me to the Web. In print, those are the kinds of designs that appeal to me as well, so definitely the postmodern look has always done it for me.

Being trained in print design, did you have any difficulty transitioning to web design?

At the time, I didn't think so. When I really got into the Web, I was just getting out of school. So I had absurd amounts of time to devote to learning a new thing. The Web is a community that really rewards that sort of thirst for knowledge. It's not a closed-off community, and there are so many resources available to learn and to get your feet wet. Because it's such a malleable medium and an immediate medium you can keep trying new things. You don't have to send away to get stuff printed and bound or anything like that. It's all immediate, so you can basically see a lot really quickly, and that's really handy. That was a good thing. If I had any push back, it was from what I felt was possible from a design perspective and what I had just learned from school. I didn't always figure out a way to bring it all into the web work that I was doing at the time.

What advice do you have for young web designers for creating websites that are not only aesthetically dynamic but effective for the end-user as well?

I think the thing I struggled with for a number of years, and finally gave up, is the idea that I have control. It's a seemingly very small thing but its impact is gigantic. What I mean by control is a user can do whatever they want to my design, and that isn't the case with a book or anything that has permanency. A web design can be completely remade for different devices or different screen sizes or different browsers. Once you're able to let go of that, you find that there are all these things you can

actually embrace. Despite all of the controls that you are giving up, you're opening the door to lots and lots of new opportunities to have information available across a variety of different forms and devices and still be legible. For instance, a lot of people struggled with that when they moved from print design to web design because they were working primarily with Flash, which is a very fixed tool. Or they were trying to control the display of everything by using lots of images for text. That happened a lot more in the earlier days of the Web than it does today. People are starting to really get hip to the way that things should be done now. I guess it's a small detail, but one of the things that I know that I fought against was what I perceived to be ugly elements—things like form elements, buttons and form fields. I would go through so many different ways to try to hide them or downplay them. I felt that they were so clunky in the design. But that's kind of the nature of just what the Web is and there's power in those elements being identifiable immediately.

36

37

36, 37 A List Apart website.

What do you do to deliver a fresh creative look for a client and what influence does typography play in that creation?

I gear towards clarity more than anything. I try to really produce things to their simplest, let the information in the design speak for itself, and not let those things get in the way of people understanding what the message is. Typography plays the biggest role in that. It's the means for that visual communication to have voice. You can say a lot with imagery, but when it comes down to it, people need to take in the information as well.

Of all the web designs that you've created, what's currently your favorite, and why?

I still love the design I did for *A List Apart* (Figs. 36, 37). It was designed in 2005 and at the time it really made a big splash. I liked it because it made people think differently about what they could do with their type online. Right now when you look at it, it probably doesn't look like anything special, but at the time there was definitely something to that—just very simple, stark layouts, and very considered typography. Something else that was considered odd—it was a wider site designed for screens that were 1,024 pixels in width during a time when people were thinking maybe they needed to stick with 800 pixels wide. It got a lot of people upset,

but it was the good kind of upset because it provoked discussion, not outrage. I feel like it still holds up pretty well to this day.

You are the creative director for Typekit, a website that hosts "real fonts so that they can be viewed universally on the Web" (Figs. 38, 39). How will this impact type use for the Web and other digital devices?

I feel like it's the next big thing. Just the ability to use a much wider palette of fonts on a webpage. Only, using default web fonts has been the biggest obstacle affecting designs online since the Web started. Hosting fonts has opened so many new doors. I feel these are the basic building blocks, like the atomic elements of design. They can have a really huge impact, and not only that, we're talking about no text-as-images anymore. All of this text is readable by search engines, it's selectable, it's copyable, it's completely malleable like any other text online, but now we have new letterforms.

How do you think this will influence or has influenced type designers, or do you think it is just business as usual for them?

I definitely don't think it's business as usual for them. This has brought a lot of discussions to the forefront. Type designers can be sort of wary of new technologies, because for the longest time the Internet has been where people steal their work. People share

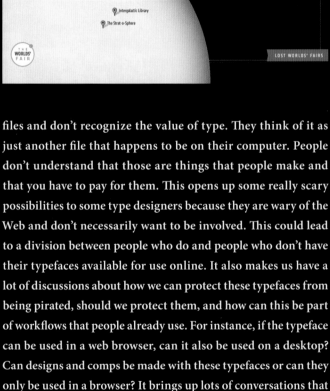

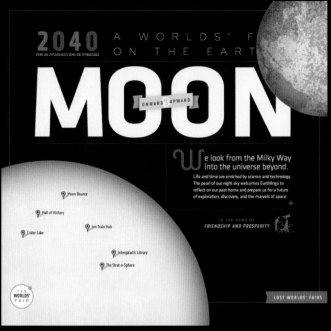 40

41

42

files and don't recognize the value of type. They think of it as just another file that happens to be on their computer. People don't understand that those are things that people make and that you have to pay for them. This opens up some really scary possibilities to some type designers because they are wary of the Web and don't necessarily want to be involved. This could lead to a division between people who do and people who don't have their typefaces available for use online. It also makes us have a lot of discussions about how we can protect these typefaces from being pirated, should we protect them, and how can this be part of workflows that people already use. For instance, if the typeface can be used in a web browser, can it also be used on a desktop? Can designs and comps be made with these typefaces or can they only be used in a browser? It brings up lots of conversations that we haven't had to have before, because the ability wasn't there.

And in the same terms, how do you think it's affected the type design itself?

That's a really interesting question. Are typefaces supposed to be designed specifically for screen rendering? Can you have typefaces that work on-screen and off-screen? I'm undecided on this. Some of my most favorite typefaces are designed specifically for screen. Matthew Carter did an immense amount of good and an immense amount of work with that. Verdana and Georgia are fantastic typefaces, but they don't look that great in print. And by the same regard, how valid is it for a classic book type to be on a webpage? Yes, you can use Caslon on your webpage, but does it actually make sense from a technical perspective and from a historic, aesthetic perspective? Those are really interesting questions to me. I'm curious where designers will take this. I know some type designers are specifically designing new types for screen or attempting to augment their old ones for better screen rendering. We might end up with more like a forked font, where you have a version that renders well on-screen and a version you would primarily use in print.

Do you think the introduction of PDAs and tablets has affected professionally designed fonts?

I feel that all of this came to a head at the same time. By the time that you had things like the iPhone and the iPad, people were doing much more high-fidelity work with how they would render a

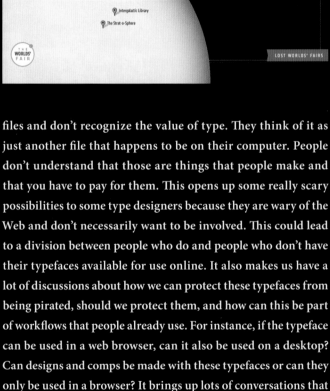

40, 41, 42 More samples of Jason Santa Maria's work.

webpage. All of the technologies for screen are pushing it forward at the moment. The way that the Web is now, there's the mobile Web, there's the Web on my desktop, the Web that you can access anywhere, and you want to have tailored experiences on all those devices and all those locations.

With the emergence of so many digital technologies, what trends do you see for type in the future?

Something that I really love is that people who are part of the community that I identify with are not necessarily coming from design backgrounds. I kind of love that these people are learning typography now, because it makes their work possible and distinctive. I love that typography has really become part of the conversation for design online, and people are really understanding and appreciating good typography. That makes me very happy. It was not the case before because it didn't need to be.

What myth or myths would you like to bust about print vs. digital typography?

It gets my blood boiling when I talk to traditional graphic designers who outright disregard web design. I feel to disregard

outright admit that you don't know what the Web is all about. What I mean by that is that the Web cannot be judged and cannot be critiqued on the same criteria used for traditional print graphic design. The modes are different, the medium is different and the goals of the design are different, and the interactions around that design are vastly different. To judge it at face value only on the aesthetics really disregards the entire process of what web design is all about.

What is one of your biggest digital design pet peeves?

It's putting the aesthetic of a design before the function of a design. Those two things need to be in balance. Something can look beautiful and read beautifully but those two things need to be in balance. If a design is in the way of the actual communication, it's ten times worse. There are so many places that a person could be other than your website and you're only giving them so many more reasons to leave. It's a mortal design crime to me. Many people don't understand. The Internet is primarily about transference of information and transference of connections, and you're putting up walls between the people that you want to talk to and the information by putting your own agenda first.

TYPE TIDBITS

Serif or Sans Serif?
Serif, um yes, I think.

Favorite letter?
J.

Guilty pleasure font?
Rosewood.

Arial or Verdana?
Verdana.

Favorite complementary font pair?
Titling Gothic and Chaparral.

Pen and paper or Wacom tablet?
Pen and paper.

Mac or PC?
Mac.

Uppercase or lowercase?
Lowercase.

Design: Lifestyle or just a way to earn a living?
Lifestyle.

Play darts or create design?
Create design.

Sock monkeys or G.I. Joe?
Sock monkeys.

SCREEN
GALLERY

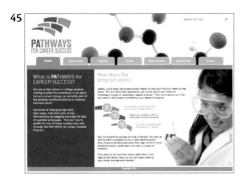

43 AIGA Get Inspired Video Screenshots. **44** Jeep Troller website. **45** Pathways for Career Success website. **46** Video still from The Nature of Space. **47** LYPInsider e-mail. **48** TYPOGRAFFIT.™ **49** Social Urban.

50

THE SOCIETY OF DESIGN IS
ADVERTISING, ARCHITECTURE,
ART, FASHION, FILM, GRAPHICS,
ILLUSTRATION, INDUSTRIAL,
INTERACTIVE, INTERIORS, MUSIC,
PHOTOGRAPHY, READING, WRITING,
& MANY OTHER GOOD THINGS

51

THE SOCIETY OF DESIGN IS
ADVERTISING, ARCHITECTURE,
ART, FASHION, FILM, GRAPHICS,
ILLUSTRATION, INDUSTRIAL,
THROUGH 1024 INTERACTIVE, INTERIORS, MUSI
PHOTOGRAPHY,
GOOD 50x70 & MANY OTHER

52

THE SOCIETY OF DESIGN IS
LOCAL ADVERTISING, ARCHITECTURE,
ART, FASHION, FILM, GRAPHICS
PROJECTS ILLUSTRATION, INDUSTRIAL,
INTERACTIVE, INTERIORS, MUSIC,
2NITE PHOTOGRAPHY, READING, WRITING,
& MANY OTHER GOOD THINGS

53

THE SOCIETY OF DESIGN IS
ADVERTISING, ARCHITECTURE,
ART, FASHION, FILM, GRAPHICS,
ILLUSTRATION, INDUSTRIAL,
2x4 INTERACTIVE, INTERIORS, MUSIC,
PHOTOGRAPHY, READING, WRITING,
1118 & MANY OTHER GOOD THINGS

54

NYC THE SOCIETY OF DESIGN IS
ADVERTISING, ARCHITECTURE,
TRIP ART, FASHION, FILM, GRAPHICS,
1203 ILLUSTRATION, INDUSTRIAL,
INTERACTIVE, INTERIORS, MUSIC,
PHOTOGRAPHY, READING, WRITING,
& MANY OTHER GOOD THINGS

55

THE SOCIETY OF DESIGN IS
ADVERTISING, ARCHITECTURE,
STEVEN ART, FASHION, FILM, GRAPHICS,
HELLER ILLUSTRATION, INDUSTRIAL,
INTERACTIVE, INTERIORS, M
D217 PHOTOGRAPHY, READING, WRITING,
& MANY OTHER GOOD THINGS

56

ARMIN THE SOCIETY OF DESIGN IS
ADVERTISING, ARCHITECTURE,
VIT ART, FASHION, FILM, GRAPHICS,
ILLUSTRATION, INDUSTRIAL,
INTERACTIVE, INTERIORS, MUSIC,
PHOTOGRAPHY, READING, WRITING,
0324 & MANY OTHER GOOD THINGS

50, 51, 52, 53, 54, 55, 56 Introduction video. 57 Sundance History of Hairstyles homepage. 58 Séura website.

59  **60**  **61**

62  **63**

64  **65**  **66**

67  **68**  **69**

59, 60, 61 Projekt, Inc. website. **62** Birch Tree Catering website. **63** West Philadelphia Orchestra website. **64, 65, 66** Cult-shirt website. **67, 68, 69** Pond & Company website.

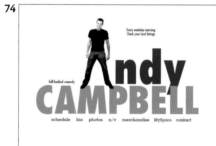

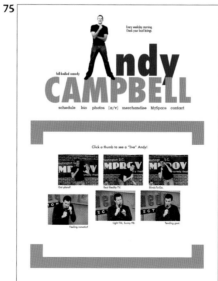

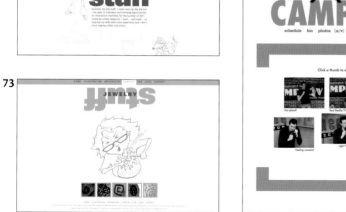

70, 71 Ship Shape Health & Fitness website. **72, 73** ilike2makestuff website. **74, 75** Andy Campbell website. **76** Tom's River Nursery and Kindergarten website and logo.

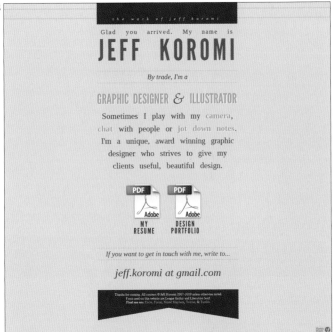

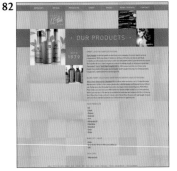

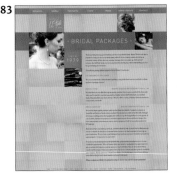

77 Zulugraffi website. **78** The Work of Jeff Koromi. **79, 80** Cheryl Agulnick website. **81, 82, 83** Salon l'Etoile & Spa website.

84, 85, 86 Middletown Lumber website.   **87** Fadhli Stencil cutout spray-painting style frames.   **88** Conceptual weather website.   **89, 90** Katherine's Boutique website.

ABOUT THE IMAGES IN THIS CHAPTER

Figs. 25, 26
TITLE: *LIV* magazine
UNIVERSITY: Kutztown University
PROFESSOR: Denise Bosler
DESIGNER: Josh Seibert
FONTS USED: Helvetica Neue,
    Trade Gothic

Fig. 32
TITLE: Insane play website
UNIVERSITY: Kutztown University
PROFESSOR: Denise Bosler
DESIGNER: Justin Herb
FONTS USED: Hand lettering, Helvetica

Fig. 33
TITLE: JAS MD retail website
DESIGN FIRM: Denise Bosler LLC
DESIGNER: Denise Bosler
FONTS USED: Halvorsen, Verdana

Figs. 34, 35, 36, 37, 38, 39, 40, 41, 42
© Jason Santa Maria

Fig. 43
TITLE: AIGA Get Inspired
    Video Screenshots
DESIGN FIRM: TV Land In-House
    Brand Creative
ART DIRECTOR: Marc Nahas
    & Alanna Siviero
DESIGNERS: Marc Nahas,
    Alanna Siviero
TYPE DESIGNER: Marc Nahas
    & Alanna Siviero
FONTS USED: Custom hand-drawn type,
    Avant Garde, Lubalin Graph, various
    "You Work For Them" fonts
CLIENT: AIGA (National)

Fig. 44
TITLE: Jeep Troller website
DESIGN FIRM: Buzz Comunicação
    and Renata Figueiredo design
ART DIRECTOR: Ligia Kempfer
DESIGNERS: Renata Figueiredo
    and Fernando Alexandrino
FONTS USED: Trade Gothic,
    Rusted Plastic and Verdana
CLIENT: Troller

Fig. 45
TITLE: Pathways for Career
    Success website
DESIGN FIRM: PPO&S
DESIGNER: Tracy L. Kretz
FONT USED: Great Escape
CLIENT: Pathways for Career
    Success Website

Fig. 46
TITLE: Video still from
    The Nature of Space
DESIGN FIRM: Nanyang
    Polytechnic
DESIGNER: Mathan Raj
FONTS USED: Avant Garde,
    TypoGraph Pro

Fig. 47
TITLE: LYPInsider e-mail
DESIGN FIRM: Quantum Dynamix
FONT USED: Helvetica Neue
CLIENT: Lancaster Young
    Professionals

Fig. 48
TITLE: TYPOGRAFFIT™
DESIGN FIRM: Grafit, LLC
ART DIRECTOR: Acci Baba
DESIGNERS: Main API Development:
    Masato Yamaguchi
MOBILE APPLICATION DEVELOPMENT:
    Kirk Herlitz
PROTOTYPE DEVELOPMENT:
    Joachim Michaelis
DATA AND WEBSITE MANAGEMENT:
    Kaede
FRONT-END CODING: Yuki Eno
TYPE DESIGNER: Internal developer
    and all of the TYPOGRAFFIT
    contributors around the world

Fig. 49
TITLE: Social Urban
DESIGN FIRM: Xosé Tiega Studio
DESIGNERS: Xosé Tiega
FONT USED: Helvetica
CLIENT: Social Urban

Figs. 50, 51, 52, 53, 54, 55, 56
TITLE: Introduction video
DESIGN FIRM: Go Welsh
DESIGNER: Scott Marz
FONT USED: Trade Gothic
    Condensed Bold
CLIENT: Society of Design

Fig. 57
TITLE: Sundance History
    of Hairstyles homepage
UNIVERSITY: Tyler School of Art
PROFESSOR: Keith Somers
DESIGNER: Justin Morris
FONTS USED: Gil Sans, Benguait
CLIENT: Sundance

Fig. 58
TITLE: Séura website
DESIGN FIRM: 23K Studios

DIRECTOR: Aaron Shupp
CLIENT: Séura

Figs. 59, 60, 61
TITLE: Projekt, Inc. website
DESIGN FIRM: Projekt, Inc.
ART DIRECTOR/DESIGNER: Sean Costik
FONTS USED: Typekit fonts:
    Adobe Garamond Pro,
    Atrament Web, Nudista Web,
    Proxima Nova

Fig. 62
TITLE: Birch Tree Catering website
DESIGN FIRM: Kathy Mueller
    Graphic Design & Art Direction
DESIGNER: Kathy Mueller
FONTS USED: Neutraface, Headline
    Helpers, Mesquite, Trade Gothic,
    Rosewood, Futura Extra, Mrs. Eaves,
    Blackoak, Sign Painter, Poplar,
    New Century Schoolbook, Isadora
CLIENT: Birchtree Catering

Fig. 63
TITLE: West Philadelphia
    Orchestra website
UNIVERSITY: Moore College
    of Art & Design
PROFESSOR: Rosemary Murphy
DESIGNER: Kate Ricci
FONTS USED: Folk, Trade Gothic

Figs. 64, 65, 66
TITLE: Cult-shirt website
DESIGN FIRM: Renata
    Figueiredo Design
DESIGNER: Renata Figueiredo
FONT USED: Plantagenet Cherokee
CLIENT: Cult-shirt

Figs. 67, 68, 69
TITLE: Pond & Company website
DESIGN FIRM: Projekt, Inc.
ART DIRECTOR/DESIGNER: Sean Costik
FONTS USED: Helvetica Neue +
    browser-driven font: Helvetica
CLIENT: Pond & Company

Figs. 70, 71
TITLE: Ship Shape Health
    & Fitness website
DESIGN FIRM: Projekt, Inc.
ART DIRECTOR & DESIGNER: Sean Costik
FONTS USED: Neutraface,
    Univers + browser-driven fonts:
    Trebuchet, Georgia
CLIENT: Ship Shape Health & Fitness

Fig. 72, 73
TITLE: ilike2makestuff website
DESIGNER: Elaine Cunfer
FONT USED: Trebuchet; Univers Ultra
    Thin, Extra Black, Extra Black
    Extended, Bold Condensed;
    Garamond Pro

Figs. 74, 75
TITLE: Andy Campbell website
DESIGNER: Todd McFeely
CLIENT: Andy Campbell

Fig. 76
TITLE: Tom's River Nursery and
    Kindergarten website and logo
DESIGN FIRM: Quantum Dynamix
FONTS USED: Bully Narrow, Georgia,
    Trebuchet MS, Helvetica
CLIENT: Tom's River Nursery
    and Kindergarten

Fig. 77
TITLE: Zulugraffi website
DESIGN FIRM: Chaiti Mehta Design
ART DIRECTOR: Chaiti Mehta
FONTS USED: Vitesses (Thin, Bold)
CLIENT: Zulugraffi

Fig. 78
TITLE: The Work of Jeff Koromi
DESIGNER: Jeff Koromi
FONTS USED: Liberation Serif,
    League Gothic

Figs. 79, 80
TITLE: Cheryl Agulnick website
DESIGNER: Todd McFeely
CLIENT: Cheryl Agulnick

Figs. 81, 82, 83
TITLE: Salon l'Etoile & Spa website
DESIGN FIRM: Projekt, Inc.
ART DIRECTOR/DESIGNER: Sean Costik
FONTS USED: Avenir, DIN +
    browser-driven fonts:
    Trebuchet, Times
CLIENT: Salon l'Etoile & Spa

Figs. 84, 85, 86
TITLE: Middletown Lumber website
DESIGN FIRM: Projekt, Inc.
ART DIRECTOR/DESIGNER: Sean Costik
FONTS USED: Ashwood, Bullion,
    Bullion Extra Condensed, Gatlin
    Bold, Madrone, Ophir, Shelley,
    Thousandsticks, Trade Gothic +
    browser-driven font: Georgia
CLIENT: Middletown Lumber

Fig. 87
TITLE: Fadhli Stencil cutout
  spray-painting style frames
DESIGN FIRM: Nanyang Polytechnic
ART DIRECTOR: Charles Lee
DESIGNER: Mohamad Fadhli Bin
  Mohamad Hata

Fig. 88
TITLE: Conceptual weather website
UNIVERSITY: University of Zagreb,
  School of Design
ART DIRECTOR: Ian Borčić
DESIGNER: Mihovil Vargoivć
FONT USED: Auto 1

Figs. 89, 90
TITLE: Katherine's Boutique website
DESIGN FIRM: Quantum Dynamix
FONTS USED: Freestyle Script,
  Times New Roman
CLIENT: Katherine's Boutique

{ APPENDIX }

by Aaron Shupp

THE EVOLUTION OF TYPE HIERARCHY IN INTERACTIVE DESIGN'S TRANSFORMATION TO TRADITIONAL MEDIA

There was a time when the Internet existed to serve a single purpose: to connect researchers and knowledge together in a distraction-free, no-form-all-function collection of black text on white background pages. This was fine and good for years, until people realized they could easily create personal pages about their cats. And thus, the Internet as we know it was born.

As the network grew ad infinitum, the need for a web presence to be different and uniquely engaging became a top priority for business-es and persons looking to get noticed. Until the mid '90s, webpages were still primarily text based, differentiated only by which of the six cross-platform web-safe fonts was used. Creative design consisted of horribly dithered animated GIFs and low-resolution graphics.

Headlines, subheads, navigation objects and callouts are the most important elements in which a user needs to interact, and designers began to realize that the poorly kerned, boring web stan-dard fonts weren't turning any heads. So breaking the laws of the web-safe standards became an art form in itself that grew more elaborate as designers developed richer techniques for making their sites different.

Many of these tricks are still used all across the Internet. And while they do—in a loose definition—succeed in enhancing design, these tricks often cause more harm than good. A new dimension of style was created with graphic text for all the text on the page. The result was an exceedingly time-consuming process where making revisions on the fly was difficult.

Programmers started thinking dynamically. Flash is able to embed typefaces, so the next step was to create blank .swf template headlines that could accept and render text on the fly. Scalable Inman Flash Replacement (sIFR) grew from these roots. This tech-nique made using custom type treatments much faster, but the fact is the type in the layout still was not actual text. If a user had a slow system, didn't have the plug-in or wanted to select the copy, then they were out of luck.

Any designer worth their salt knows the purpose of typograph-ic hierarchy is to give their content an order of importance that can be easily understood by the reader. But on the Web, humans aren't the only ones reading your content. Search engine indexing bots, spiders and link crawlers utilize headings and similar ordering ele-ments to understand what the page is about and assign relevancy and value to the content.

An amazing thing has happened over the last few years. The Web has transitioned from a passive indulgence into an active

1 PURPOSE: To position a new brand of super high-end HDTVs and home technology equipment, and showcase what makes its display technology the best in the world. FONT REPLACEMENT NOTES: It was a necessity that the product website exude the super-refined essence of the product itself. This was achieved with immersive rich media and a dynamic font hierarchy that carried the same aesthetic of highly designed print pieces. **2** PURPOSE: The transformation of a high-end, monthly home technology lifestyle magazine into a daily source of articles, product reviews and news written by the industry experts and manufacturers themselves. FONT REPLACEMENT NOTES: Typeface selection is a key decision in setting the tone of any design. By leveraging a contemporary, strong Sans Serif, the pages of this online magazine convey maturity and the confidence of industry expertise.

extension of almost every part of our lives. Providing a unique experience for your audience is no longer the icing on the cake, it's 90 percent of the recipe. If the website isn't a perfectly refined, aesthetically pleasing, fully branded adventure, the visitor isn't going to stick around for more than a few seconds.

The need for impressive design has rocketed layout techniques into a new era of possibility, breaking free from the chains of Arial and Verdana, exporting folders full of graphic headlines, and ending reliance on proprietary plug-ins.

Two extremely effective techniques have emerged allowing true font replacement. The first, @font-face, emerged in CSS2 coding but is empowered greatly by CSS3. The @font-face function allows remote fonts to be downloaded to the user's cache, temporarily activated and displayed on the website. In that sense, the real typeface is used in your webpage, allowing true usage of heading tags. But it's not without some major disadvantages. To work across platforms, the same font needs to be made available in three formats at once—SVG (scalable vector graphics), TrueType or OpenType and WOFF (Web Open Font Format). Rendering is often buggy on older computers since quick download is needed.

In addition, commercial font houses aren't particularly pleased that their actual typefaces can be freely (and often carelessly) made available by any website that isn't concerned with licensing. All a user needs to do is fish the files out of their cache for a "free" copy to use as their own.

The second technique is more flexible and has a very promising future—the dynamic rendering of a typeface in real time for the user using the jQuery JavaScript library and a powerful script engine named Cufón. Just as with @font-face, actual text exists on the page and inside your tags, allowing it to be read by people and search engines. But instead of it being restyled with a typeface's real font file, the typeface is broken down into a matrix of points that are assembled, in real time, into the font.

The benefits here are vast. The typeface cannot be stolen by an end-user; the downloads are much faster to render; kerning, leading and pairing can be tightly controlled; the technique works in every major browser; and additional JavaScript, CSS and WebKit effects, such as gradients and inner-shadows, can be applied to the render. For the first time, live headlines, body copy, links, navigation and text can display all the properties of a graphic headline—but still be selectable and readable.

As interactive development moves toward overtaking traditional print media, more pressure will be put on designers and programmers to make the process an enjoyable one, especially now that tablets are threatening to replace the printed page. The time to consider interactive and print design as two separate entities is over.

Aaron Shupp is the director of interactive marketing at 23K Studios, a full-service ad agency. He specializes in state-of-the-art interactive design techniques and creating unique, engaging online user experiences.

ABOUT THE IMAGES IN THIS APPENDIX

Fig. 1
TITLE: Elite Experience
DESIGN FIRM: 23K Studios
CREATIVE PRINCIPAL: Tom King
DIRECTORS: Aaron Shupp, Tom King
DEVELOPERS: Aaron Shupp,
 Julie Mitchell
DESIGNERS: Mike DiLuigi, Ryan Lynn
CLIENT: Sharp USA

Fig. 2
TITLE: *HD Living* magazine
AGENCY: 23K Studios
CREATIVE PRINCIPAL: Tom King
DIRECTOR: Aaron Shupp
DEVELOPERS: Aaron Shupp,
 Julie Mitchell
CLIENT: Home Technology Specialists
 of America

{ GLOSSARY }

alley: small vertical space separating columns

apex: the top point of a letterform where two angled strokes meet

arm: a secondary stroke that extends horizontally or diagonally from a stroke at the top and does not connect to another stroke

ascender: the part of a lowercase letter that extends above the x-height

asymmetrical: balance with unequal visual weight

bad break: multiple line headlines that do not break to flow with natural pauses in speech

barb: the terminal for a curved capital serif letter

baseline: the horizon on which letters sit

beak: the terminal for a straight capital serif letter found on the horizontal strokes

body copy: the text that makes up a paragraph—it reads best when set between 8 and 11 points in size

bowl: a curved stroke that connects to either a vertical stroke or to itself

bracket: a piece that connects a stroke to a serif

buried subhead: a subhead that stands alone as an orphan or has only a few sentences after it before the paragraph splits into the next column

caption: small text that appears next to an image for artist credit, description or clarification

closure: the principle that states the eye will complete a path of an object

column: vertical space that runs top to bottom in between the margins

compound column: text that spans more than one column

compound modules: formed by combining modules horizontally, vertically or both

connotation: the idea or feeling the typography invokes in a person

continuity: once the eye begins to follow something it will continue traveling in that direction until it encounters another object

contrast: differences in objects through size, color, texture, type, alignment and other properties

counter: any enclosed space in a letterform. If the space is completely enclosed, it is referred to as a closed counter. An open counter occurs when a curved, straight or angled stroke does not connect to another stroke but still creates an enclosed space.

cross bar: a stroke that horizontally connects two strokes

cross stroke: a stroke that crosses over another stroke but doesn't connect on either side

crotch: inside of a vertex

CSS: cascading style sheets; coding for webpages that defines text and page formatting

denotation: the literal meaning of a word

descender: the part of a lowercase letter that extends below the baseline

drop cap: a larger letter at the beginning of a paragraph that drops down into the lines of text below it

ear: the small extension that protrudes up and out from the top of a stroke or bowl and is often teardrop-shaped or rounded

em dash: a long dash that indicates either a change of thought or emphasis

en dash: a medium-length dash indicating a range of items or the passage of time

eye: the closed counter of a lowercase *e*

e-zines: digital magazines

font family: all the variations in weight, width and angle of a typeface

Gestalt theory: the whole is greater than the sum of its parts

graphic text: text formatted to output as an image file

grid: a matrix of vertical and horizontal lines that come together to create a two-dimensional structure

gutter: interior margins where a left and right page meet

hanging cap: a letter at the beginning of a paragraph that literally hangs outside the edge of the paragraph

headline: line of text that stands out from the rest of the page and sets the tone for the document, generally set at 18–24 points or larger in size

hierarchy: content composed of different types of information of varying degrees of importance

hyphen: a short dash used for words that break at the end of a sentence and for compound words

hyphenation: the splitting of a word at the end of a line and continuing onto the next line

ideograms: symbols or combination of symbols that represent a concept

illuminated manuscript: books that were handwritten and included illustrations, often adorned with gold and silver leaf, which depicted scenes from the stories being told

indent: a small space before the first word of a paragraph equal to an em space, the space occupied by a capital *M*

inherent web text: text programmed to automatically resize to match the resolution and viewer's browser preferences

italic: angled version of letterforms that are redrawn, but the letters remain consistent with the essence of the overall look

jumping horizon: poor alignment of side-by-side paragraphs' baselines

kerning: a manual adjustment of the space between two letters

leading: horizontal white space between lines of text

leg: a secondary stroke that extends horizontally or diagonally from the bottom of a letter

legibility: the ability to discern all parts of a character and all the styles within a font family

letter: a character or symbol that represents sound used in speech

ligature: two or more letters that touch

lining numbers: numbers that line up along the cap height

link: the small piece which connects the upper bowl with the lower loop of a traditionally shaped lowercase *g*, also known as two-story *g*

live text: searchable and editable text

loop: the lower bowl of a traditionally shaped lowercase *g*, also known as two-story *g*

margin: the space around the edge of a page

module: space created when a column and row cross

monogram: a design that contains overlapping letters, usually the first, middle and last initials of a person's name

negative space: space on a page not occupied by a design element

oblique: angling letterforms with little or no change to the letterfoms

old style numbers: numbers that have varying heights with ascenders and descenders when set along the baseline

optical alignment: aligning letters that are curved or pointed above the cap height, below the baseline or outside vertical alignment to allow them to align optically

orphan: one or two lines of a paragraph at the end of a column separated onto the top of the next column of type, or the opening line of a paragraph stuck at the end of a column while the remainder of the paragraph is in the next column

phonograms: images that represent sounds

pictographs: images that represent their literal meanings

pixel: smallest unit of space available for information on a screen display

point: measuring system used for type size—there are 72 points in an inch

prime marks: symbols that denote inch and feet, also known as dumb quotes

proximity: objects that are placed close together and are perceived as a group

pull quote: text that has literally been pulled from the body copy and set separately to grab attention

readability: the level of a word's comprehension based upon font choice, size, style, kerning, tracking, case and location on the page

repetition: strategically placed repeating design elements that create a visual connection for the eye to follow

resolution: quality of print or screen display

rhythm: a pattern that creates the flow through a page

river: white space that runs vertically through the text

row: run horizontally across columns

Rule of Halves: columns may be divided into half and text may flow from half column to half column, or half column to full column

sans serif: typeface with no extra structural extensions coming from the horizontal and vertical strokes. *Sans* is a French word meaning "without"—hence the phrase *sans serif* means "without serif"

serif: small structural extensions that are at the end of a letter's horizontal and vertical strokes. Serifs come in a variety of shapes and sizes. Serif also refers to the category name of a font that has serif extensions.

shoulder: a short rounded stroke that connects two vertical strokes or a vertical stroke and a terminal

similarity: shared visual characteristics

sink: a row set a specific distance down from the top of a page

smart quotes: quotation marks that curl or angle toward the text, also called curly quotes

space after: a small, adjustable space between paragraphs

spine: the curved stroke through the middle of an *s*

spur: a small pointed extension typically coming off the top or bottom of a vertical stroke that connects to a rounded stroke—oftentimes on a serif lowercase letter

standup cap: a letter at the beginning of a paragraph that is several times larger than that of the surrounding text but shares the same baseline as the body copy

stress: the axis created by the thick and thin stroke contrast of a letter

stroke: a straight or curved line that creates the principal part of a letter

subhead: brief line of text that divides the body copy into sections between headlines and body copy

swash: the extra flourish that accompanies many script and blackletter style typefaces

symmetrical: balance that has a central axis, with both halves having the same visual weight

tail: the stroke that crosses the lower half of an uppercase *Q*

terminal: a stroke ending without a serif

tombstoning: subheads that align on similar baselines across the page or pages

tracking: the spacing between all of the letters in a word or sentence

underlining: the non-designer's way of highlighting text—italicize or bold the text instead

unity: similar aesthetic qualities such as color, shape, texture and line quality forge relationships between the common or similar elements

vertex: the bottom point of a letterform where two angled strokes meet

visual concept: a game plan for a design—it consists of type, images, Gestalt principles, design relationship principles, and grid

visual tone: the combination of words, tracking and leading that is perceived as color

web-safe colors: colors that will display as the correct color, regardless of the device

weight: varying degrees of thickness built into a font with a standard range being light, roman (also called book), medium, bold, heavy and black

whispering headline: a headline that fails to attract the attention of the viewer because it is too small, blends in with the text to which it is assigned or is of insufficient boldness or color contrast

widow: a line at the end of a paragraph that is one-third or less of the length of the other lines in the paragraph

x-height: the center area of the baseline and cap height, measured against the height of the lowercase *x*

BIOGRAPHY

Photograph: Chris Demeo Photography

Denise Bosler is a graphic designer, illustrator and professor of communication design at Kutztown University in Pennsylvania. She earned a B.F.A. from Kutztown University and an M.F.A. from Marywood University in Scranton, Pennsylvania. Denise has focused her design work on print collateral, product packaging and identity development in both print and digital projects. She is dedicated to creating custom typography, which she brings to the work she creates for her clients. She has produced numerous award-winning logo and packaging designs featuring hand-rendered and custom type. For the past eight years, Denise has taught typography and upper level graphic design classes, allowing her to share her professionally applied and tested knowledge. As a professor, she is known for her obsession with the proper treatment of type and is frequently heard admonishing her students when they fail to kern accurately with, "You could drive a truck through there!"

Denise lives in Pennsylvania with her husband, daughter and two large dogs.

ACKNOWLEDGMENTS

This book could not have been completed without the kind help and support of many people. My deepest sincere thanks to Dr. Lucy Hornstein, who went above and beyond with her investment of time and wonderful advice, and who helped me say exactly what I wanted to say.

I extend my warmest thanks to Ken Barber, Holly Tienken, Jessica Hische, Amanda Geisinger, Steven Brower and Jason Santa Maria for agreeing to be a part of this project.

I am grateful to Beth Shirell and Aaron Shupp for their gracious addition of text and imagery that helps make the content livelier.

Special thanks to Tracy, Elaine, Vicki, Kyle, Troy, Erin D., Roman, Roger, Matt and Erin G. for their encouragement and contributions to the content and imagery.

I extended my deepest gratitude to the faculty and staff of the Kutztown University Communication Design Department for their guidance over the years. To my former and current students—you are my inspiration.

Thank you to Megan Patrick for her belief in both me and this book, Amy Owen for being my fabulous editor, and Grace Ring for helping to visualize my idea.

And last but not least, I can never express enough appreciation to my parents, John and Doris, and my husband, Rob, for their generous offer of time, assistance and support so I could see this typographic vision through to completion.

{ INDEX }

Check out these other great products and offers from HOW Books!

TYPE IDEA INDEX

With whole conferences and blogs devoted to type, the subject continues to capture the attention of designers. Now there is a book that does the same. *Type Idea Index* eschews the ponderous style found in other books in favor of a fresh, accessible approach. You'll find an in-depth examination of the creative and practical issues involved in all the important areas, such as font anatomy, headlines and body text. This is just the type of book you've been waiting for!

CREATIVE WORKSHOP

Have you ever struggled to complete a design project on time? Or felt that having a tight deadline stifled your capacity for maximum creativity? If so, then this book is for you. It contains 80 creative challenges that will help you achieve a breadth of stronger design solutions, in various media, within any set time period. Exercises range from creating a typeface in an hour to designing a paper robot in an afternoon to designing webpages and other interactive experiences. Each exercise includes compelling visual solutions from other designers and background stories to help you increase your capacity to innovate.

WRITTEN ON THE CITY

Written on the City is a glimpse into a vast conversation happening illegally and in public. All over the world, people are writing messages on the walls and sidewalks of the cities in which we live. They are staying up late, breaking the law and taking risks to say something to you. Some of it is funny. Some of it is beautiful. Lots of it is upsetting, crazy and brilliant at the same time. And all of it is important. The images contained in this book serve as a global survey of urban typography as they reveal the fears, questions and visions of their creators.

Find these books and many others at MyDesignShop.com or your local bookstore.

SPECIAL OFFER FROM HOW BOOKS!

You can get 15% off your entire order at MyDesignShop.com! All you have to do is go to www.howdesign.com/howbooks-offer and sign up for our free e-newsletter on graphic design. You'll also get a free digital download of *HOW* magazine.

 For more news, tips and articles, follow us at Twitter.com/HOWbrand

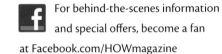 For behind-the-scenes information and special offers, become a fan at Facebook.com/HOWmagazine

 For visual inspiration, follow us at Pinterest.com/HOWbrand